Father of the Comic Strip

RODOLPHE TÖPFFER

Father of the Comic Strip

RODOLPHE TÖPFFER

GREAT COMICS ARTISTS

M. Thomas Inge, General Editor

DAVID KUNZLE

University Press of Mississippi / Jackson

Publication is made possible in part from a
grant from Pro Helvetia, Zürich, Switzerland

prohelvetia

with special thanks to Pierre Schaer

www.upress.state.ms.us

Designed by Todd Lape

The University Press of Mississippi is a member of the
Association of American University Presses.

First edition 2007

∞

Father of the comic strip : Rodolphe Topffer / David Kunzle.
    p. cm. — (Great comics artists)
Includes bibliographical references and index.
ISBN-13: 978-1-57806-947-7 (cloth : alk. paper)
ISBN-10: 1-57806-947-5 (cloth : alk. paper)
ISBN-13: 978-1-57806-948-4 (pbk. : alk. paper)
ISBN-10: 1-57806-948-3 (pbk. : alk. paper) 1. Töpffer, Rodolphe,
1799–1846—Criticism and interpretation. I. Title. II. Title: Father of the
comic strip.
PN6790.S93T65 2007
741.5'092—dc22
[B]
                                        2006028494

British Library Cataloging-in-Publication Data available

To Marjoyrie, founding and
sustaining member of the Silly Party

Contents

Preface   [ix]

Introduction   [3]

CHAPTER 1. Töpffer the Satirist: Contexts for Themes   [9]

CHAPTER 2. Goethe, Töpffer, and a New Kind of Caricature   [49]

CHAPTER 3. *Jabot, Crépin, Vieux Bois*   [57]

CHAPTER 4. Töpffer Launched, Comic Strip Defended, Literary Fame, *Festus*   [74]

CHAPTER 5. Politics and Absurdity: *Pencil* and *Trictrac*   [83]

CHAPTER 6. The Last Years: *Cryptogame*, *Albert*, Aesthetics and Physiognomics   [95]

CHAPTER 7. Töpffer the Professional Dilettante   [120]

CHAPTER 8. *Voyages en Zigzag*: Humor of the Unexpected   [128]

CHAPTER 9. The Legacy   [143]

Envoi   [183]

Appendix A. Histoire de Sébastien Brodbec   [185]

Appendix B. Töpffer's Comic Picture-Novels by Professor Fr. Vischer   [187]

Notes   [191]

Bibliography   [197]

Index   [201]

Preface

Scholars and academics take nothing so seriously as the comic. They should fear nothing more than grinding it into scholarly dust. I hope this book does not love Töpffer to death, while it aligns itself with the tradition that sees in a comic masterpiece matters of life and death. Freud established wit and humor as essential psychological components for expression and survival. Shakespeare, Rabelais, Molière, Dickens, Sterne (to cite just a few names treasured by Töpffer), and a host of other writers, but (curiously) fewer artists, understood the need for laughter. Without getting at all theoretical about this (theory exists in excess) let us just say that humor resists the oppression of the daily social and political grind; like music it relieves heartache of the mind and body; it is medicine to the soul. We see no problem in greeting the humorous and serious as two sides of the same coin, or as fused into one. I now see, and take seriously, the serious underlay to Töpffer's "little follies," and I do so on the understanding that the century-long interlude between Hogarth and Töpffer represents a struggle between caricature tightening its grip on personal and social real life, and then loosening it in order to embrace the fanciful, imaginative, impossible, and even nonsensical.

This book and its companion, the facsimile edition *Rodolphe Töpffer: The Complete Comic Strips*, seem like a lifelong dream come true. I remember well the moment in 1960 when I first toyed with the idea of tracing the development of the picture story (following a suggestion of E. H. Gombrich in *Art and Illusion*, just published) from William Hogarth to Töpffer as a PhD thesis. Before it transpired that I would have to stop short of Töpffer, so great was the material before and between, I began to read heavenly funny comic strips by the Swiss under the celestially blue dome of the (then) British Museum Library. I was mesmerized, unable to contain my laughter in a place where you are not allowed to laugh out loud—subject to what Töpffer called *le fou rire*.

I could take that laughter home with me, but not the texts. There was nowhere else to find the elusive Swiss, in no other library, and certainly not on the market. No one had heard of him anyway. It is astonishing, in retrospect, to record that outside that bottomless national library you could not find reproductions of many Hogarth engravings either, until Paulson's compendium appeared in 1965. Finally there came in 1975 the much-desired Horay edition of Töpffer's comic strips, which is not complete but served me very well while I prepared the substantial chapter on Töpffer in my *History of the Comic Strip* vol. 2: *The Nineteenth Century* (1990). Now we have also the two oblong volumes from Seuil 1996, with its fine introduction by Thierry Groensteen (also coauthor of the excellent *Töpffer, inventeur de la bande dessinée*), but limited to six, fewer stories than Horay's seven. The bilingual German edition from Herbig (n.d., 1967-68?) with six stories is also incomplete. There are numerous editions of single stories and facsimiles of some of the manuscripts, of which latter the Italian Garzanti boxed-set edition is the most complete as well the most rare. (I hereby thank again the Musée d'art et d'histoire in Geneva for giving me a copy when I needed it most.)

The complete correspondence of Töpffer, an indefatigable letter-writer, is under way thanks to the indefatigable Jacques Droin. This has proven a great boon, and I thank the editor deeply for his kindness in putting at my disposal advance print-outs of his work, of which the third of five volumes is due in 2007. The last years of the correspondence became available to me while this book was in press. To him, who answered many questions, and to the great expertise of Philippe Kaenel, I owe much. Marianne Gourary in New York enthusiastically and wholeheartedly opened to me her incomparable collection of Töpfferiana; to her I dedicate my Töpffer facsimile book. Her sweet encouragement of my Töpffer studies has, over the years, meant a lot to me.

I am also indebted to Helène Meyer of the Musée d'art et d'histoire in Geneva, for giving me access to manuscripts of the sketchbooks, and to Michael Twyman, who explained lithographic processes to me, which were kindly demonstrated in practice by Cynthia Osborne. A thank you, too, to Wilhelm Busch editor Hans Ries for encouragement and advice.

Töpffer became his own publisher; we scholars cannot. We owe publishers a lot: their encouragement, their faith, their energy and attention to details that slip through the fine veil of authorial consciousness. The University Press of Mississippi, under the direction of Seetha Srinivasan and her staff, has been exemplary in these respects, and I thank especially Will Rigby and Anne Stascavage for careful and discreet copy editing, and Todd Lape for intelligent design.

I have inevitably drawn on my presentation of Töpffer as master and virtual (re)inventor of the comic strip in my big *Nineteenth Century History* of 1990. I have reworked many of the ideas and information from that volume, but most of the material here is entirely new, and I have incorporated the considerable new research available over the last twenty-five years. I have tried to further the idea

of Töpffer, with his world-conquering invention, as essentially a *Genevan*, to localize him in the great, small, and very cosmopolitan town in which he lived all his truncated life, and of which he was so proud, as well as to introduce on occasion the European perspective. This is no more than the way he was seen at the time.

Criticism of the Töpffer literary oeuvre as a whole, and a sense of the centrality of the comic strips, has not been lacking. The Société des Études Töpffériennes, Genevans, and others have kept the bibliography rolling and the spirit of Töpffer aflame. The major recent contributions are signaled in the bibliography. Recognition that an "obscure" Genevan could be truly the father of the comic strip, way back in Europe of the 1830s, was delayed in Anglophone countries by a chauvinistic insistence in the U.S.A. that this arch-American phenomenon was invented there in 1896, with the advent of the newspaper supplements. Europeans knew better of course. Official Swiss philatelic recognition came late, only in 1999, for the bicentennial of Töpffer's birth, setting aside a Pro Juventute stamp of 1946 (centenary of his death) with a portrait of the man as writer. The 1999 issue used, quite properly, scenes from the comic strips. Yet the Swiss postal system had already celebrated Wilhelm Busch (in 1984), and all Europe and the U.S. had been celebrating Tintin.[1] The Rue Rodolphe Töpffer (actually and wrongly, Toepffer) in Geneva recognizes the current order of things by listing him as caricaturist first, and writer second. The plinth of the bust (1879, p. 6) nearby gives equal prominence to five of the comic albums on one side, and five of his best-known writings on the other—a prescient (but at the time not the general) view accorded the picture stories relative to the rest of the oeuvre.

The publication of the enormous Töpffer correspondence makes it possible and necessary, for the first time, to write a new critical biography of Töpffer, the last full-dress ones (of Auguste Blondel and Abbé Pierre-Maxime Relave) being now a full 120 years old. I deal with biography here only insofar as it affects the life of the picture stories; but I do give some Genevan and European sociopolitical and cultural context, of the kind one would expect in a book someone (else) should write in the future under such a title as *Rodolphe Töpffer: His Life, Art, and Times*. Such an enterprise would take more account of the prose fiction, landscape drawing, art, and social theory of this singularly versatile man than I can manage here. This might also be the place to plead for English translation of the best of Töpffer in these domains; and a new critical edition of the *Complete Works*, Pléiade-style, which is overdue.

I am reminded by Philippe Kaenel, who kindly read the whole manuscript, that even for the full understanding of the comic strips, let alone the purely literary oeuvre, more is needed than I can offer here on the role of literary antecedents—Rabelais, Sterne, Cervantes (for *Festus*), Molière—and on the relationship with Töpffer's theatrical farces, unpublished as they were at the time.

The concurrent facsimile edition I have prepared of *Rodolphe Töpffer: The Complete Comic Strips*, with English translation, includes a critical apparatus giving minutiae of the Töpffer versions (manuscript, printed), their dating and plagiary, annotations of captions, and other such matters deemed to be of scholarly interest. I also include there all significant manuscript fragments of picture stories cut from the printed versions, some fragmentary sketches of stories aborted, and a scenario for one never sketched. Here (in the *Voyages* chapter), on the other hand, it is appropriate to assess a literary aspect of Töpffer, as a *verbal* inventor and fantast, in a way that runs parallel to his graphic invention, and to compare him with the immortals in this domain, Edward Lear and Lewis Carroll. For this reason I have also included in the appendix a little-known, aborted story (*Sébastien Brodbec*) that seems to me to anticipate Carroll, even as it looks back to E. T. A. Hoffmann or Grimm. The *Voyages* demanded consideration for their enactment in real life of Alpine excursions with his schoolboys, of comic situations and moral attitudes embedded in the picture stories. The inclusion in an appendix

of a translation of considerable segments from F. T. Vischer's essay on Töpffer from the first collected edition of the picture stories (1846) is justified by the inherent merit of this, the first sustained analysis of the originality of the new genre, and by its general neglect by critics since.

In the Legacy chapter, which limits itself to the generation succeeding Töpffer's, I have seized the opportunity not only to recapitulate in brief the immediate effect of Töpffer on some European (mainly French, but also German and English) disciples whom I deal with more thoroughly in my *Nineteenth Century History*, but to add some new discoveries, notably Thackeray and Lear, whose essays in the Töpfferian genre are little known. Thackeray is a good example of a might-have-been for whom the audience was simply lacking.

A word on terminology: Töpffer called his invention by all kinds of disparaging terms, and more formally, as *histoire en estampes* (story in prints, picture story). I use the terms picture story and comic strip indifferently; I usually refrain from the tempting new coinage *graphic novel*, which has now overtaken *comic book*, although that is exactly what Töpffer's are. What distinguishes the new graphic novel from the old comic book is length, unity of theme, and a real moral focus; so too, Töpffer is distinguished from most of his followers in the 19th century, who typically ran their strips over a single page, double pages, or at most a few installments of a magazine.

Töpffer's "graphic novels" were always a sideline, a hobby in a very busy literary and academic career. Yet they comprise a total of eight stories (one not quite complete) and 1523 drawings. His total output of other drawings, not counting those (about equal in number) of the sketched versions of the comic strips but including about 1164 drawings for the *Voyages*, has been estimated at 3,000–5,000. Some of his prose works never went out of print, as did his picture stories; perhaps the time has come to give the man his literary due, as well. But that is another book. One thing is clear: even if his literary importance (as opposed to commercial viability) remains shadowy, the international effect of his picture stories is easily provable.

In rendering into English the captions to the illustrations I have sometimes translated as accurately as possible, but at other times paraphrased and compressed (mainly with non-Töpffer pictures) in the interests of brevity.

Another thing: it is too late now, but I do wish I had been sent to the Pension Töpffer in Geneva as a youngster. My grandparents were all Swiss, my mother too, and should have known. I drool at the thought: a real *vie de famille* presided over by Mrs. Töpffer, Mr. Töpffer acting as the "witness and friend of their games as of their work," no exams, few rules, no physical punishments, no punishments at all (virtually), a fun principal who took me on hikes in the Alps and wrote plays for me to act in, and drew silly stories for me . . .

Father of the Comic Strip

RODOLPHE TÖPFFER

Introduction

Go, little book, and choose your world . . .

Rodolphe Töpffer was born in 1799 at an intellectual crossroads of Europe: Geneva. Apart from a nine-month stay in Paris as a student, he scarcely ever moved from his native town and its immediate environs. When he did so, for a few weeks every summer, it was to hike with the boys of the boarding school he had started, in the nearby Alps. He turned the chronicle of these hikes into a galaxy of little adventures, full of funny incidents and surprises, which he wrote up imaginatively and eventually printed and illustrated. He visualized the funny little worlds around him as easily in pictures as in words, and wanted to be a painter like his father. Fortunately he was afflicted with poor eyesight at an early age, which led him to evolve a manner of sketching as quick as thought and quick with ideas, so that he mutated almost unconsciously into pictorial storytelling: the narrative comic strip. On his own, new recipe combining the visual and the verbal, he cooked up and seasoned with assorted satirical spices a new comic medium. He did this as a relief from the humdrum life of the schoolmaster and, later, university lecturer.

The schoolmaster liked to complain that his pedagogic duties prevented him from writing and socializing. Yet he socialized (much, to be sure, in an epistolary way) and wrote prodigiously. In terms of sheer literary output, he, the self-proclaimed literary-artistic amateur, resembled the most prolific of professionals: essays on art practice and theory,

short sentimental novels growing on occasion to full length, annual accounts of Alpine excursions, reviews of books and exhibitions, little dramatic farces, literary squibs of various kinds—and eight longish (serio-) comic strip stories. Towards the end of his truncated life (he died in 1846) he wasted himself (it is said) on polemical, political journalism to combat the incipient Genevan revolution.

Deeply conservative in his social philosophy, fearful of the budding economic and cultural industrialization and of social change generally, Töpffer the anti-democrat created the most democratic of art forms. Made originally for an educated elite, his picture stories were copied, popularized, and plagiarized in various languages. They straddled generations, from the older child to the adult, and social classes. Out of the austere, Calvinist, scientific Geneva came imaginative fireworks fizzling with the impossible, the absurd, the surreal, illumined with flashes of serious satire.

His domestic life, with long-lived parents, a wife, and four children was, by his own account, idyllic. Grandson of a German immigrant tailor, he wrote a pure French tinged with archaisms that charmed the Parisian elites. He learned quickly to fit into the tight little Genevan ruling oligarchy that finally succumbed to the radicals—happily for Töpffer, only after his death. He died as one of the most famous of all Genevans. Letters were addressed to him "M. Töpffer, à Genève." He was famous, of course, for more than the comic strips, but his quasi-accidental invention of the genre did

Self-portrait of Rodolphe Töpffer (Coll. Emanuel de Geer, Geneva, from Maschietto, 1962).

not pass unappreciated, and there were those in his circle and farther afield who enjoyed them above all his other works, as we do today. But no one, least of all the author, could have predicted that he had sired a progeny that would come to populate the wider world.

Töpffer the innocent, Töpffer and Geneva

The long biographical obituary published in *L'Illustration*, the popular French magazine to which Töpffer had been closely bonded, lauds the "honest and tender heart, delicate and sprightly wit, naïve yet refined talent. . . . A pure and simple life, peacefully full of sweet affections and gratifying attentions, divided between serious and modest duties and innocent pleasures, a life spent entirely in the bosom of the family."[1] "Thoroughly pure, moral and lacking in French galanterie" (i.e. adultery, sex), is the judgment on the picture stories of a German critic in another obituary;[2] "the sweet and healthy flavour" of his work as a whole is what makes him unique, in the view of his best French critic, Charles-Augustin Sainte-Beuve.

The *Illustration*'s portrait of the man and his art living in perfect harmony as they seldom do in reality, idealized ("false as an epitaph," Töpffer would have called it) as befits an obituary, and forefronts what was and would remain a critical reflex: the virtuous innocence of the man and his writing. We shall be contesting this prevalent idea. Töpffer and his innocence (or naïveté) were always viewed as the quintessence of Geneva, especially when he was placed within the larger context of European culture in the legacy of Genevan Jean-Jacques Rousseau. His "innocence" was his individuality, as well as his Genevanness, what separated him from the French. It was deemed to infuse his oeuvre as a whole, including his picture stories. Professor Friedrich Vischer in 1846, the first to look deeply into the picture stories as a genre unique to the Swiss (see Appendix B), saw him straddling a German kind of humorous amiability (*Gutmütigkeit der Komik*) and French theatricality; he transcended the "prosaic and moralistic" Hogarth, and was closer perhaps to George Cruikshank, but *more naïve* (my stress). Töpffer himself recognized only one model, William Hogarth, but the favored question was whether he was more French than German. The best French historian of caricature in the 19th century, John Grand-Carteret, thought he was more German; the German Vischer could only compare and contrast him to the French. Maybe he was just Genevan, Swiss?

Théophile Gautier, the premier French art critic before Baudelaire, sees Töpffer as a caricaturist who is simply different from everyone else: "He has neither the elegant subtlety of Gavarni, nor the brutal power of Daumier, nor the comic exaggeration of Cham, nor the sad burlesque of Traviès. His manner is more like that of Cruikshank; but with the Genevese there is less wit and more naïveté."[3] When it comes to the picture stories, one can hardly speak of Töpffer having less wit than anyone. Further comparison tended to break down on an intuition, not always made explicit, that a completely new genre was at stake here. The usual criti-

INTRODUCTION

cal criteria were simply lacking: "Criticism would be ill-advised to get up on its high horse and look severely down on [such an invention], which would only make it look pedantic."[4]

Vischer, who was particularly attracted to the erotic ambiguities of Gavarni lithographs, made an extensive comparison between the two artists.[5] Töpffer is immediately distanced from Gavarni by his ability to string together incidents into narrative. Gavarni gives you sharply heightened moral moments, with a malice mitigated by elegance of form; this is not so much comic as *comédie humaine*, in the Balzacian sense. Töpffer gives you many moments through which a character and an idea develop, the narrative of a destiny. We enter here the realm of pure comedy, says Vischer, an autonomous, absolute world of humor where the laws of physics are suspended, chance and accident rule in epic fashion. Notably absent from Töpffer, notes the German approvingly, is the typically French obsession with adulterous sex ("French frivolity"); this too sets Töpffer apart.

But this Töpfferian world is mad, a madhouse. The next step, taken by another German professor of aesthetics, Karl Rosenkranz, in his *Aesthetic of the Ugly* (1853, but in preparation since 1839), is to view this fictive mad world as reflecting one made so in reality by industrialization, poverty, immiseration, and class hostility. This is the "modernized" and "progressive" world in the waking nightmare of Töpffer's later years; he had transmuted it into benign-seeming dreams in his comic strips, which, like all escapist phenomena, bore the marks of what they were escaping from. Society, says Rosenkranz, has become self-caricaturing; socialism is a caricature of social and ethical world-laws.[6] Without having set eyes on the Cruikshankian grotesques (*Fratzen*) of the London proletariat to which Rosenkranz points so distastefully here, Töpffer would have agreed.

The author liked to insist on the *grain de sérieux* in his comic albums; his seriousness was more than a pinch, it was a bite, barbed and not socially innocent. This was sensed by his intimate friend the illustrious Auguste de la Rive, a leading Genevan scientist, professor, and intellectual, writing just after Töpffer's death of those albums "in which the most excursive imagination is everywhere mingled with the severest morality and the most practical good sense."[7] The persistent idea of an essential innocence in the Swiss had much to do with his avoidance of the French fictional staple of sexual passion and adultery, which allowed the "Albums Töpffer" in the Garnier edition of 1860 to be marketed as "suitable to all drawing rooms, without shocking anyone, amusing all ages and constituting a suitable gift for ladies, girls, adolescents and even children."[8]

Geneva, "the world in a nutshell"

There are five continents, and Geneva
—TALLEYRAND, 1815

The question went: Was Geneva "the smallest of the great towns," or the "greatest of the small towns"? (We may likewise ask: Is Töpffer the smallest of the great artists, or the greatest of the small ones?) No one denied the town a distinction out of proportion to its size, about 20,000 inhabitants. Everywhere Töpffer was regarded as very Genevan, only Geneva could have produced such a figure, he was the local literary as well as (less respectably) caricatural hero. In a Geneva otherwise devoted to science, banking, watchmaking, and tourism, Töpffer was the bright literary star, easily outshining the lesser lights not only in Geneva but also in French-speaking Switzerland (Suisse romande) as a whole. Geneva had no poets;[9] how could it, lacking imagination, it was said; it was the enemy of genius; culturally it was even boring.

But this "boring" town was the crossroads of European science and travel. A galaxy of literary and artistic talent passed through, some on extended stays: Wordsworth, Byron, Shelley, Hugo, Balzac,

Sand, Sue, Turner, Dickens, Ruskin, Eliot. . . . "All that is thought and written in Europe passes through our magic lantern. Geneva, it's the world in a nutshell." "Our little Geneva is a target the great take a potshot at as they pass by."[10]

Little Geneva was cosmopolitan, a synthesis of European national characteristics: "English phlegm, German bonhomie, French frivolity, Italian brio," "ground up together by the irresistible power of the republican spirit."[11] Geneva was Romantic. Its vast mountain recesses inspired *Frankenstein* and sublime thoughts. Ironically, the Genevan cultural elite itself resisted romanticism, at least in its literary form. The politically conservative academic criticism of which Töpffer was a pillar stood its ground for "old values" against the French neophiliacs: Hugo, Balzac, Sand, and Sue, who were "detestable and harmful," be it for their social utopianism or their taste for unreal, monstrous extremes, or be it for their philosophical (unchristian) pessimism, immorality, and materialism. Victor Hugo, disparaged in Töpffer's *Albert* and elsewhere, was more generous to the Swiss,[12] sending him a copy of one of his books, flatteringly dedicated to "the author of the Presbytère." Balzac, who consummated his relationship with Madame de Hanska in Geneva, told her that Dubochet, Töpffer's publisher, had given him a copy of a Töpffer piece in prose.[13]

Can we call Töpffer himself a Romantic? He would have chafed at the label. He feared all that the Romantics stood for politically: the social engineering, the anarchism, egalitarianism, and revolutionism. But he was himself (in *Vieux Bois*) a parodist of the romantic attitudes not unlike the Romantics themselves, not unlike Byron, the romantic ironist par excellence. His short story *Le Grand St Bernard* contains an amusing parody of the affected, turgid (and false) romantic literary style, on which he himself often fringes. His short story *La Peur* (Fear), with its ghost in a cemetery, its phantom beast and decomposing horse, is an exercise in Radcliffian Gothic.

Much of the Genevan's fiction is sentimentally romantic, fringing on passion but never get-

Monument to Rodolphe Töpffer, Place Rodolphe Töpffer, Geneva. Bronze bust by his son Charles, 1879 (photo by author).

ting there, as if frustrated by his own very Genevese (sexual) inhibitions. Töpffer's first translator Heinrich Zschokke even found himself adding a kiss here and there. It is that of a youth who both desires and fears love. It is morally conformist and avoids emotional extremes. But it is not all of a kind. It speaks in many voices. His little-prized last novel *Rosa et Gertrude* has a dark undercurrent of Gothic, and sexual, terror seething through the narration of a virtuous but narrow-minded Genevan pastor. Töpffer's aborted continuation of the story of Jules, "Jules Marié," was about to deal with the adultery of a virtuous hero. His *Sébastien Brodbec*, also aborted, features what is evidently a nasty attempted rape. Here is passion breaking social boundaries, so beloved of the Romantics. Töpffer has Albert's philistine father kick romanticism (his son) in the butt, as something both anti-social and impractical. But the Swiss author reputed for the "propriety" of his novels was more attracted to the "depravity" of the Romantic school than he could publicly admit. He spoke in many voices, graphic and verbal, but there is no doubt that it was his comic strips above all that served as an amused critique of antisocial passions, monomanias of many kinds, including the inordinate quest for knowledge, and indeed the very concept of genius so dear to the Romantic heart.

Geneva City of Art

By his example in drawing landscape, as well as through his art-critical and -theoretical writings, Töpffer helped launch Geneva as a school of landscape art. Genevese artists no longer needed to settle in Paris in order to win medals, fame, and European patronage. Two Genevan landscape artists stand forth today, although their work is scarcely visible outside the city museum: Alexandre Calame and François Diday. Calame has a wall in the Musée d'art et d'histoire in Geneva filled with his Four Seasons, which also present the Times of Day, a manifesto of art's capacity for the most subtle tonal differentiation in a very localized place. His effects here are bolder and broader than those of Diday, his master, whom Töpffer, having championed Calame, unfairly scants. Both made visible the upper reaches of the Alps that travelers admired and

sometimes scaled, and that Töpffer imbued in his own writings with a patriotic moral mysticism: the higher, wilder, and more remote was the more pure, innocent, sanctified. Töpffer the Genevan patriot was telling artists to look not to Italy but closer to home, at what is around them. *Soyons de chez nous!* he cried, before the French realist painters and Baudelaire. His promotion of the sublime and his anti-classicism that preferred Géricault to David or Girodet, Shakespeare to Corneille, and Schiller to Racine make him very much the Romantic in art. He literally raised the sights of the art-going public and elevated their taste in landscape. In 1844 he could marvel that the Genevese "school" of painting had imposed itself on Europe.[14]

Töpffer, having in his early essays complained about the philistinism of his fellow citizens who claimed to know and love art but would not actually pay for it, helped organize public subscriptions to buy noteworthy paintings for the "nation," to be housed in the Musée Rath, which was (from 1826) Europe's first public museum of contemporary art, holding regular exhibitions. With several good private collections (including one owned by Rodolphe's brother-in-law François Duval-Töpffer), free state-subsidized art instruction, and an active Société des Arts, Geneva was, as it were, preparing for Ferdinand Hodler. Did Töpffer "invent" a Genevan school of landscape painting, as he did the picture story?

Chapter One

TÖPFFER THE SATIRIST: CONTEXTS FOR THEMES

Töpffer, once lauded as the "innocent" and "naïve" humorist, on closer view of the picture stories takes on a more aggressive, polemical, and satirical edge. He who prided himself on never attacking individuals, targets currently cherished ideas and causes, and on occasion individuals too. He cuts a wide swath of sociopolitical issues that he largely avoids in his prose works and that crop up in his picture stories alone: war and militarism, absolutism, bureaucracy, law, cholera, frontiers, religion, the peasantry, and science. We here offer local and European contexts for all of these, deferring the two major topics of education and revolution, dealt with under the stories of *Crépin* and *Albert*, respectively, which are dedicated primarily to those burning issues. That Töpffer's critique takes place in a world of dream and farce should not deceive us into thinking that he was not sublimating serious concerns such as exercised his liberal-minded and critical contemporaries. We must also remember that his picture stories were for the most part conceived in his liberal period, before he became a political reactionary.

Soldiers, foreign and Swiss

Popular graphics, as a medium of middle class and commercial interests, had for centuries been hostile to the military. Witness the popularity of the biblical theme of Massacre of the Innocents,[1] and the lurid view of military crime and punishment by Jacques Callot in his famous series of etchings *Misères et Malheurs de la Guerre* of 1633. English caricature of the Golden Age around 1800, then French caricature after 1830, made fun, sometimes bitterly, of the militarism of their governments.

We shall start with the militarist repression and warmongering engendered by the Restoration fears of democracy and revolution. In *Monsieur Pencil* Töpffer takes up a favorite theme of the lithographs of Daumier and company in Paris, the national guardsmen who constituted a more or less voluntary, armed auxiliary police force under the new king (from 1830) Louis-Philippe. They were especially active during the cholera scare of 1832, and were recruited mainly from the middle classes, typically at the lower end, such as tradesmen. The bespectacled, portly "grocer" then became the stereotype of ridiculous paramilitary vanity, pompously parading himself in uniform. The regular army was active too, especially in putting down strikes.

Töpffer's handling of mindless policemen (*force armée*), as in *Festus* and *Trictrac*, is surely tinged by the view from Paris, and no less surely partakes of the traditional bourgeois hostility to the regular, professional soldier excoriated in *Monsieur Pencil*. In that story, the "20th Light Cavalry" are obviously coded as a numerous regular army unit, whereas the couple of human automata attending the Mayor in *Festus* evoke the kind of minimal, possibly volunteer, badly or untrained police force serving the mayor of a small commune, and imagined surely like the 20th Light, as foreign rather than Swiss. Yet they may be in some measure modeled on local

1-1. Wolfgang-Adam Töpffer, *The Conscripts*, etching, c. 1814 (from Boissonnas).

rural guards, used by the Genevan government to modernize and control the newly acquired, backward bits of the canton. Both kinds of armed force, regular and auxiliary, share a mechanical mindlessness and stupidity with which the comic strip in the nineteenth century generally invests the police, who haunt the genre like an evil incubus.

What was Töpffer's own experience of Genevan soldiery? Was he always thinking of repression abroad? What were the older influences on him in caricature? With respect to the latter, the first and most immediate influence was surely caricature by his father, Wolfgang-Adam Töpffer. The elder Töpffer proved himself something of a rebel from the start when he quarreled with his teachers and sponsors in the Société des Arts of Geneva, who sent him on a scholarship to study in Paris in 1791. There he found himself sympathetic to the Revolution (pre-Terror), but back in Geneva, now under French occupation, he soon became anti-French. His large, highly finished, privately circulated watercolor *Café Public* of 1798 shows an assembly featuring a number of ugly, arrogant French officers, in an ensemble which has

been seen as an allegory of occupied Geneva under the Terror.[2] His critique of the French Revolutionary abuses turned, after the French were expelled in 1814, to that of the counterrevolutionary and counterreform Genevan constitution of 1814.

Wolfgang-Adam passed on to his son a hatred of extremism of all kinds, and was a Swiss patriot. He detested the French imperial military tyranny, for all that he was favored in Paris under Napoleon—giving drawing lessons to the empress Josephine and being represented in the Salon of 1812 with five paintings that won a medal. His etching of c. 1814 *Les Conscrits* (fig. 1-1), done presumably after the first exile of the emperor, ridicules the Genevan or Swiss "volunteers" for the French army as a bunch of fatuous, ill-assorted, strangely accoutred, and bewildered nincompoops. He seems not to pity them, although pity could not have been absent from the realization that, of those unfortunate enough to be press-ganged into the half-a-million-strong polyglot French army that marched into Russia in 1812, only a small fraction, perhaps not 300 out of the original Swiss contingent of 12,000, returned.

This etching, which quâ etching must have circulated more widely than the (more numerous) watercolor caricatures, has been called a "vibrant indictment of the forced conscription which then struck so hard against the Department of Léman" [i.e., Geneva]. The appeal for conscripts (3 August 1799) was thus menacingly worded, in the year of Rodolphe's birth: "As for the cowards who have renounced the glory of defending their country . . . if they continue to persevere in their revolt, they must realize they have no more fatherland, that they are excluded from the rights and society of citizens."[3]

There survive several sketches in oil and pencil, one of them dating back to 1805, for this etching and relating to conscription. The artist's alarm must have echoed with the many anti-French, anti-militarist Genevese. Wolfgang-Adam was also motivated by a grievous personal circumstance: his own brother-in-law Jean Francois Bautte had sent his promising

1-2. Wolfgang-Adam Töpffer, *Village Fair* (detail), 1815 (private collection; from Boissonnas).

nephew, Adam Counis-Bautte, Rodolphe's cousin, to sacrifice his eighteen-year-old life to the Napoleonic megalomania. A (probable) portrait of him called *The Young Conscript* shows "fatalist resignation and unconscious suffering."[4] Even the Austrian "liberators" of 1813 and 1814 proved unpopular for the damage they caused to private property.

The return of Napoleon in 1815, and the carnage of Waterloo, revived the artist's anti-militarism in a painting benignly called *Foire de Village*, dated 1815 and exhibited with great success at the London Royal Academy the following year (fig. 1-2). This detains us for two reasons, the first anecdotal and trivial but significant in the light of Rodolphe's own, partially suppressed, impulse towards "schoolboy humor" of the bodily functions. Reporting the success of the picture to his wife (25 May 1816), Wolf-

gang-Adam tells how the Royal Academy authorities feared the man urinating far left (not visible here) to be potentially offensive and covered him with a number label, which the public would peel off, so that it had to be stuck on afresh each day.[5]

The painting also includes prominent, fancily uniformed recruiters standing on a dais, one with a trumpet, the other with huge, banner-sized documents—an authority to recruit duly sealed, and another, larger one, a lengthy account perhaps of some Napoleonic victory, which the girls, at least, bend over to peruse. Heavier persuasions are transpiring nearby, in the foreground: a trio of recruiters are violently seizing men, while women and girls look on anxiously, and infants hide and bawl; one resisting woman has her head yanked back by the hair, while another loudly laments—a typical contrasting pair known from Netherlandish seventeenth-century painting of military abuses. These (three) are the main incidents in a subject that should, from its title, have been about peasant jollities. The picture was bought by Wolfgang-Adam's principal patron in England, the rich banker Edward Divett, and it must have struck a chord in an England also bereaved of so many young men, and not to be consoled by patriotic works like the famous *Chelsea Pensioners Reading the News of Waterloo* (1816–1822), by Wolfgang-Adam's friend David Wilkie.

Meanwhile, in Berne, after the French had departed the soon-to-be federal capital, the artist was called upon to portray Swiss military types and uniforms and to do a "caricature" of the artillery officers and soldiers, their cannon, etc., "which embarrasses our man a bit," the artist "not much liking the military, and often satirizing them." Whether embarrassed or not by the commission, Wolfgang-Adam did a number of fine, detailed drawings of portrait heads and figures in uniforms, which were not in the least caricatural, any more than the very large watercolor called *Caricature des troupes d'artillerie suisse* (1804).[6] The human interest is heightened by some emphatic physiognomic characterization, all of this being a lesson to the son, who played, in his own very different, shorthand manner, on a scale between character and caricature.

The fate of his cousin Adam Counis-Bautte might have befallen Rodolphe had the empire lasted a few years longer. Under French law, applied in Geneva since 1799, the young Rodolphe Töpffer might have been conscripted in 1817. In 1813 his future bête noire, the revolutionary James Fazy, had to pay the huge sum of 6,000 francs for a substitute. Not even his poor eyesight would have saved Rodolphe from military duty then, as it did when he was called up in liberated Geneva in 1822 and again in 1823. Exemptions were limited to those with severe handicaps such as the loss of an eye, a limp, or (very Swiss) "voluminous goitre." His relatively slight visual handicap would have relegated him to the reserve had not his profession of schoolmaster gained him exemption altogether.[7] Rodolphe approved of the Swiss soldiery. Three of the many sons of Mr. Crépin become military officers. But one can guess that the busy young schoolteacher was happy not to have to rise for drills from six to nine on Sunday mornings.

War and the absolutist state

So Töpfferian critique of the military was directed not at home, but at foreign powers, at the threat of absolutism re-engulfing Europe. Töpffer summarizes the characteristics of the absolutist state in his prose version of *Dr Festus*:

> "The kingdom of Vireloup enjoys a paternal government. The king there is the father of his subjects, whom he treats as children; watching solicitously over their reading, their conversations, their eating, their clothing, and desirous that they take everything from him. That is why he prohibits books, ideas, merchandise, goods from outside, and why he has those who talk under surveillance; punishing them by throwing them into the royal jails if they say bad things, or if they don't say good things, or if they persist in not talking at all. As the king of Vireloup likes to go fox-hunting, and because he would not have the time to follow all his children all day long, he has himself aided by ministers who have themselves aided by the armed forces, customs officials, and priests; so that I would willingly compare him to a tender father who surrounds himself with faithful domestic servants and esteemed tutors. . . . The king, always good and indulgent, imprisons them in the royal jails; but if they chatter about this, or write about it to their friends, he is pitiless, and finds means to make them disappear one knows not how. So that I would compare him to a truly tender, prudent father who feels severity to be sometimes a duty."[8]

Cependant la Commission chargée d'examiner les pièces saisies étudie les chiffres de la blanchisseuse, trouve la clé de cette correspondance secrète, et découvre une vaste conspiration ramifiée.

Informé des dangers qu'a couru le Trône, le Roi de Vireloup prend mal, et la Reine aussi. Après quoi il ordonne, par un édit que la chose publique n'ait à souffrir aucun détriment dans sa personne.

44

1-3. The committee finds the laundry list to be the key to a vast conspiracy. The King of Vireloup falls ill at the news (*Festus* 44).

This king's problem was that he had a province called Balabran on the frontier with Ginvernais (which is partly Geneva or Switzerland), which province was much given to smuggling and apt to be infected by the neighboring political system, where the government was constitutional with a social contract and a king reduced to being the child of his very emancipated subjects—the exact opposite of Vireloup. The English Milord, whose politics in the *Festus* comic strip are limited to wrathful, xenophobic bouts of boxing, in the prose version is mistaken for Pierre Lantara, whose costume he has donned, and who is a Balabran exiled for having said of the Vireloup government, in a pub, that it smelled fishy (*sentait le mic-mac*). This is sufficient evidence of a conspiracy, which causes the king to sicken and demonstrate the pacifism of his intentions toward the neighboring state by sending

50,000 of his best soldiers to the frontier ready to invade and meanwhile fire upon anyone trying to get into his country. He sets up special tribunals to dispatch suspects without trial. For good measure, Töpffer adds a parody of servile, humiliating court customs.

All this is summarized in the comic strip without reference to a Balabran-Geneva. Milord, Milady, and the Mayor are accused generically of plotting, with Milady's laundry list the main evidence against them, while the prose version parodies the more baroque kind of official paranoia, with "immense, decisive, frightening revelations, fit to strike terror into the hearts of all good citizens," involving twenty-eight barrel-organ players whose constant noise acts as a narcotic on the palace guard. The civil authorities would be seized and wrapped up in bales of cotton, sent to the customs

113 *114* *115.*

Le lieutenant ayant recouvré en grâce, le président de la Cour porte la supplique au Roi qui admire la gentillesse de son petit fils, jeune prince d'une haute espérance.

Le jeune prince ayant pris la supplique en fait un joli petit bateau.

24 heures s'étant écoulées sans message du Roi, le lieutenant est pendu d'une cour intérieure. Heureusement l'émollient amollit la pression de la corde et il conserve quelque espoir.

1-4. The Lieutenant's petition for mercy is handed to the King, but used by the young prince to make a paper boat. The Lieutenant is saved from hanging by his emollient (*Trictrac* 113–15).

who, bribed in advance, would beat them up, throw petards into the citizens' pockets, put up posters, open the country to the Ginvernais, proclaim a provisional government, seize the king and offer him a constitution or death. All this, and much more, would have made, to our eye, for excellent comic graphic lazzi.

In 1840 Töpffer added to the picture story a scene of a bewigged commission examining the laundry list, followed by the king and queen of Vireloup collapsing sick with fear (fig. 1-3). This was considered by later editors of Töpffer's comic albums (from 1846) as potentially offensive to reigning monarchs, and cut. Relations with Savoy (and France) were never easy: in 1826 a patriotic, anti-Savoy play by James Fazy called *Les Lévriers* was suppressed in Geneva, no reason given. The riot-

ous behavior of his (mayorless) commune, and his appearing in shirtsleeves, are sufficient to condemn the poor Mayor. A few years later, with *Albert* in 1845, Töpffer would treat conspiracy rather more seriously.

This satire on monarchical tyranny is very Swiss. In the unanimous view of the Genevan intellectual elite, a view shared by foreign visitors, Geneva was a civilized little republic governed by civilized men who had no need to resort to the kind of repression characteristic of other, monarchical regimes. The Töpffers, father and son, respected the local system of law and order. Unlike some of their colleagues in France, Germany, or England, neither father nor son suffered harassment for their caricature, or at the hands of authority in general, except of that trivial kind universal at frontier customs posts when they passed through them on Alpine excursions. The one moment when Rodolphe had direct experience of military tyranny was during his nine-month sojourn as a youth in Paris, where he saw an army shoot down unarmed civilians and barely escaped being hurt himself. This never happened in republican Geneva of the Restoration; such things were foreign, and faithful to this view, the armed force in *Festus* reports to a king, the king of Vireloup, who is either French or, more likely, Savoyard, although the name exists for a hamlet in the canton Geneva on the French border which had its own customs post. (The word Vireloup evokes "virulent" or virer = chase off and loup = wolf). In *Trictrac* (113–14) a petition to the king from the Police Lieutenant, unjustly condemned to be hanged because of a mistaken identity, is casually found by the little prince and turned into a paper boat (fig. 1-4). A similar incident is taken up in the prose *Festus* (80); the Police Lieutenant is hanged and only saved by the accident of emollient plaster round his neck. Such is the judicial frivolity under absolutist regimes.

War and the symbols of war were abhorrent to Töpffer. On an Alpine excursion, passing through Vintimiglia in Savoy (today's Vintimille in France) he encounters the construction of a citadel "so sad in a smiling countryside," with "hateful gun slots [*meurtrières*; the word also means murderous], dreadful embrasures, long walls, so many sinister objects against which the most charming impressions collide and flatten. Yes, war, massacre, whatever their origin, are always infamous, everything that is the sign or instrument of it is hateful, and the pleasure of having frontiers, a name on the map, a prince on the throne, has never been worth the blood it has cost."[10] On one of the rare occasions when he refers to military history of any kind (the staple of guidebooks), he picks up a bit of local lore in order to disdain the pride attached to it: on the Tyrolean border between Austria and Italy there is "An excellent bit of country, as is known, for mutual

destruction with cannon-balls. . . ." All battle-fields, he continues with heavy irony, "carry glorious memories of carnage. Unfortunately, we are not tacticians, so that the hideousness of war does not disappear for us behind the elegance of manoeuvres or the cunning beauty of operations."[10]

The revolutionary turmoil in Geneva at the end of Töpffer's life made him realize that Geneva was not, after all, exempt from the common lot of so many European cities; and, although such disturbances were altogether deplorable, it is characteristic of his unfailing respect for law enforcers in his hometown that he does not condemn them for their inability or unwillingness to contain the rebels, as he had never condemned them (as far as we know) for defections in earlier threats to the public order. In a Geneva where he saw the authorities as virtually disarmed, he himself, weak with a fatal illness as he was, joined the 600–700 volunteers at the Hôtel de Ville in their armed confrontation with the radicals.[11]

There were few disturbances in Geneva before the revolution began in 1841. The "potato riots" in 1817 were minor and easily quieted, with some arrests and eight jailed. From that moment all was overtly peaceful until 1834 (that is, through the period of composition of the comic albums), the year of the Affaire des Polonais, a minor affair that merely ruffled the "happy period" which lasted until 1841. The Affaire des Polonais was caused by the attempt of some hundreds of Polish and Italian refugees inspired by Mazzini (the name surfaces in *Albert* as Mangini) to use Geneva as a staging post for the invasion of Savoy and an insurrection against the ruling house there. It fizzled out when the Genevan authorities were able to peacefully disarm and disperse the revolutionaries. The incident, which pitted the neutralizing policy of the Genevan government against the sympathies of the crowd hostile to it, involved the defection of some of the militia, who found themselves disciplined, but not, it seems, seriously.

In 1836 there was a considerable mobilization of Genevan and Swiss forces at the borders with France. The French rattled their sabres to demand the expulsion of Louis-Napoleon, the future French emperor, who had been living in Thurgau as a Swiss citizen. Töpffer joined actively and patriotically in the popular enthusiasm for armed resistance. The danger ended when Louis-Napoleon left voluntarily. The Affair of the Aargau convents also involved both Federal and Genevan troops, who found themselves blocked by crowds of citizens and undermined by defections in their own ranks: James Fazy (not a neutral observer, to be sure) put the defections as high as two thirds.[12] This was a prelude to the revolution of November 1841, which brought universal male suffrage to Geneva. (Other cantons had long enjoyed this.) When the militia were called out, and subsequently in the street battles of the failed coup on 13–14 February 1843, they were found to be unreliable; and their unwillingness to shoot at fellow citizens (many simply refused to accept cartridges), as well as a reluctance on the part of the commanders to inflict too much damage to the city in clearing barricades, meant that the Genevan revolution, consummated in 1846 shortly after Töpffer's death, was relatively bloodless and caused relatively few fatalities and little material damage. The many European-wide revolutions of 1848 were certainly much more bloody and destructive.

Töpffer had academic friends and colleagues in the military. Adolphe Pictet (1799–1875), professor of aesthetics and modern history and literature, and a well-known scholar of Celtic and Sanskrit, was a colonel of artillery, and Töpffer was wont to address letters to him by his military title. One wonders if the artist was quite aware that Pictet's military expertise included the invention of percussion shells and rockets, to which he sold the secret most lucratively to the Austrian army.[13] At the regular military reviews, complete with the thundering of cannon and the crackling of rifles, Töpffer was there to applaud and vent his civic patriotism: "There

was the fatherland, all of it, united, happy, modest, with no fancy bigwigs, with no miserable populace, deriving its only lustre from the happiness and concord of its children. There was the army, small but made up of citizens, our own, composed of fathers, the husbands of those women who circulated in the crowd. Our banner . . . [and all the banners visible on neighboring mountaintops and valleys], represented for me the fatherland we shared, great in trophies, in happiness and liberty."[14] There were always up to 15,000 Swiss troops on the western frontier, a third of them volunteers or militia.

Such starry-eyed patriotism may have grown brighter over the years, but the Genevan author's sentiments cannot have been much different eight or ten years earlier when he was composing his picture stories. So we can confidently assert that his satires on the military, as well as being traditional to caricature, were clearly directed at the neighboring autocracies, in Savoy, France, Germany, Spain, and Russia, with their ever-active armies suppressing democracy and revolutions at home and abroad.

In the picture stories the military make a very sorry showing. *Festus* (6) features a rural guard, a Force Armée, composed of two persons, George Blême (called La Mèche) and Joseph Rouget (called L'Amorce). The nicknames "The Wick" and "The Bait" suggest criminal antecedents, although a comparable nickname was also given to a blameless peasant, George Luçon (in *Pencil*), called—more innocently—Le Trèfle ("The Clover"). This Force Armée is totally incompetent, more likely (happily!) to stick a bayonet through a tree than their human target. They are automata, moronic robots with a perpetual inane smile on their faces, mechanically following the uniform of their commander, the Mayor, whoever may be occupying it at the moment, or even when unoccupied and hanging fluttering on the branch of a tree. They react mechanically to simulacra of orders, as when the sleeve of the disembodied uniform is shaken by the wind into the appearance

TÖPFFER THE SATIRIST: CONTEXTS FOR THEMES

1-5. The Armed Force stands guard by the Mayor's uniform, discarded by Milord while he bathes. A breath of wind raises the right sleeve, the Armed Force does a left turn at the double (*Festus* 11).

of a command (fig. 1-5). When the wind shakes loose the hat, they collapse in terror and demand quarter (this embellishment added 1840) until the uniform is found and donned by Milady, whom the Armed Force follow obediently and likewise Festus when the uniform is adopted by that gentleman (12–15). After finding their dual bayonets are no match for the club of a herculean English Milord that literally sends them flying, and having no longer a uniform to follow, they lose all discipline, trample the crops, and suffer a rain of carrots from angry peasants—mild treatment, considering what angry peasants could do to errant soldiers! Ignoring the Mayor (out of his uniform, wearing Milady's dress), they march roughly over his recumbent form. Thus is authority stripped of its symbols, flouted; but worse is to come when the World Turns Upside Down, and the Mayor

himself, in his shirtsleeves, is arrested as a thief in a reversal typical of Töpffer's comic method.

Later the mere leeward proximity of the uniform (*sous le vent de l'habit*), now worn by Festus hiding in a windmill, restores to the comic duo a touch of discipline, reinforced by visual contact, which impels them to join their supposed commander on the arms of the windmill, whence they are, once more, flung into the air so as to land twenty-six scenes later, most fortuitously upside down, bayonet plunged right through the chest of the two soldiers taking Milord, Milady, and Mayor to the galleys, and thus allowing them to escape. The Force Armée extracts its bayonets and "go off most playfully, but unfortunately without discipline."

In *Monsieur Pencil*, by contrast, Töpffer stages a regular professional army unit that behaves in the

En poursuivant les voleurs le Vingtième Léger gâte beaucoup de blés.

35

1-6. The 20th Light destroys the crops, opens the locks, burns the woods, and takes refreshment (*Pencil* 36–37).

Le Vingtième Léger ouvre les écluses pour inonder les lieux bas à cause des voleurs.

Le Vingtième Léger brûle un bois pour incendier les lieux hauts, à cause des voleurs.

37

après quoi, le Vingtième Léger ayant chaud se fait rafraîchir par le Maire

Comme il passe devant le jardin du Maire, George Luçon se voit arrêté par le Vingtième Léger et traîné devant le Conseil de guerre.

Ouïs les témoins, et le flagrant délit constaté George Luçon est condamné à être fusillé. 39.

1-7. George Luçon is arrested by the 20th Light, found guilty by a council of war, and condemned to be shot (*Pencil* 39).

traditional way toward the peasantry who, as tradition demanded, then and since, are treated as an enemy. The army destroys the crops, causes flood and fire in the countryside, seizes peasant carts and horses, and sets about executing an innocent peasant (figs. 1-6, 1-7). Their task is to find robbers, but with their raised swords and angry faces they look as if they trying to slaughter Mother Nature herself. They even seize a scraggy mule—always for Töpffer the symbol of patient service—to the pathetic distress of the owner (36), and arrest a decent young farmer, who was only trying to help by rescuing some abandoned mounts and who is condemned out of hand by a war council shown in solemn assembly (fig. 1-7). This farmer, George Luçon, is saved from being shot only by the drunkenness and incapacity of the firing squad, who kill their captain instead, thereby unwittingly rendering a true military "justice."

Further justice, and revenge for the age-old suffering of peasants at the hands of the military, is offered by this peasant, who bears the enlightened name of George Clare (or Light—Luçon) and who, having adroitly donned the uniform of the Captain Ricard shot in his stead, orders the Ricard company to dress by the right, and double-quick march into the Batracian lake. They do this in blind obedience to the sartorial symbol of authority, and presumably drown (48).

Pencil gives us a wider, indeed European context for the perils of militarism, for the political crux of the story is the manner in which accidents of telegraphic transmission, caused by a little dog making the arm of a telegraph waggle at random, are capable of bringing the nations of Europe to the brink of war. The seasoned military and diplomatic figure Xavier de Maistre, a great enthusiast for Töpffer's

88.

89.

Le père apès avoir fait des excuses au médecin, dépêche des gens à la recherche de son fils, leur disant qu'ils le reconnoîtront à l'émollient. qu'ils amènent toute personne ayant un émollient ou cataplasme.

Cependant la Réserve, en tourbillonnant, cause d'affreux désordres le 16. Courant.

1-8. The father excuses himself before the doctor, and sends his people off to find his son, recognizable by his emollient or cataplasm. The Reserve meanwhile causes terrible chaos on the 16th of the month (*Trictrac* 88–89).

work, particularly liked this episode: "the idea of European diplomacy thrown into disarray [*bouleversée*] by a little dog is very happy one."[15] In Alexandre Dumas's *Count of Monte Cristo* (1844–46, ch. 41), Dumas shows the telegraph as a sinister-looking agent of social chaos and economic disruption: "black, accommodating arms shining in the sun like so many spiders' legs . . . strange signs cleaving the air with such precision." The count is greatly moved by it and imagines it governed by occult powers, genii, sylphs, gnomes, rather than by some ill-paid wretch reacting to similar apparatus many leagues away. Vindictively, the count has the telegraph manipulated so as to send false reports causing stocks to soar and fall to his advantage, and has the error blamed on fog. Real history offers some examples of war

by telegraphic error, such as the Ems telegram that might have started the Franco-Prussian war.

The moronic, mechanical Force Armée reappears in *Monsieur Trictrac*, this time under the name of The Reserve. In a foretaste of classic early cinema farce, it gets stuck in a ladder, causing chaos in the streets (60), and later again, causing more chaos (fig. 1-8). *Trictrac* involves marvelously imbricated reversals of identity that may be taken as an extended metaphor for the arbitrariness of order and authority, and the propensity for social hierarchies to slip into reverse and upside down. Apart from the riotously clumsy Reserve, there is a small police force sent against them by the Thief disguised as a Lieutenant of Police, who also gets stuck. The People, exasperated at his inability to keep order (106),

1-9. Cholera Morbus (*La Caricature*, 1831).

actually have the thief-as-top-cop arrested. In jail he meets the real Police Lieutenant who makes him sign an affidavit attesting to his true identity, which the thief is happy to do, so that the real Police Lieutenant is convicted of corrupting the police and causing social disorder, and nearly hanged (110).

Another type of law-enforcement officer appears briefly, and very secondarily, in Töpffer's comic albums: the rural guard, or *garde champêtre*, a type who appears in French caricature as the bane of the city clerk hunting or stealing fruit in the countryside. But his brief appearances in Töpffer show him in a positive light: in *Crépin* (15, 39–40) he does his job, chasing a criminal, all the more meritoriously for his being hampered by a wooden leg (is he a veteran of the Napoleonic wars?). In *Albert* (10) the eponymous hero is rightly upbraided by a garde champêtre for hunting without a permit. It may be added that, in this stridently antirevolutionary album, we see a mob attacking what should be a military post

(called *le poste*), a multi-storey building from which figures in civilian hats (and one wig) shoot back—is this then real civil war, civilian against civilian, that Albert has helped unleash?

Cholera: Morbus Diabolus

The telegraph in *Pencil* accidentally causes a war and cholera panic; it was in reality used to transmit news of war, and of the advancing cholera. Mr. Jolibois, escaping from his crate after being fumigated against the cholera, is taken for the cholera in person (64f). The episodes relating to the cholera, which occupy no less than twenty scenes in both the 1831 and 1840 versions, represent an exceptional prescience on the part of the author, for the *Pencil* album, first sketched as we know in the summer of 1831, demonstrates the effects of fear of the cholera advancing from the east, and some of the precau-

Cependant Mr. Pencil et Mr. Jolibois arrivant au même lieu, la même invitation leur est faite. Mr. Pencil répond qu'il s'est purgé en route; et Mr. Jolibois qu'elle ne se purge jamais. Ce qui fait rire l'officier sanitaire, homme de beaucoup d'esprit.

Les effets du Docteur sont fumigés. Mr. Jolibois (car hélas la passion aveugle) y voit la continuation du complot tramé par sa femme et les deux vils séducteurs, et il suffoque de jalousie.

Les ais de la caisse ayant cédé, les deux valets de Santé n'ont que le temps de crier : au Choléra ! … au Choléra ! ! ! 64

1-10. Invited to purge themselves, Mr. Pencil says he did so en route, Madame Jolibois that she never purges herself. The Professor's effects are fumigated; Mr. Jolibois suffocates with jealousy. The crate gives way, and the health officers cry . . . Cholera! (*Pencil* 64).

tions taken against it after it struck western European cities from the summer of 1832. The epidemic lingered for a few years but the next serious outbreak came only in 1853–54, so that by the time *Pencil* was published, in 1840, it relied on recent memory and aftermath of a very terrible affliction.

From India, and the east generally, the cholera had reached Moscow by August 1830. The *Journal de Genève* carried news of the advance into Europe in autumn 1830. By the spring of the following year it was all over eastern and central Europe; in May and June it was in Budapest and St. Petersburg, by August (after *Pencil* was completed) in Vienna, by early 1832 in England. It was officially announced in Paris on 29 March of that year, and by April had claimed 13,000 victims, by September 18,000, in France as a whole 100,000. The capital was in the

grip of terror. Paintings, cartoons (fig. 1-9), and a flood of articles all over the press represented its horrors. Death, though generally swift, caused horrible disfigurement and acute suffering. In vain did governments strain every reserve of medical and sanitary measure to counteract it and discover its means of transmission. It was immediately apparent that cholera settled in the poorest urban districts, nourishing itself on poverty and squalid, overcrowded living conditions. But it also dispatched some of the elite, killing in a short space of time French prime minister Casimir Périer, naturalist Georges Cuvier, and Egyptologist Champollion, "in a single stroke, politics, science and the arts."[16] To which list may be added the military, in the person of the popular General Lamarque, whose funeral caused a popular riot. Civilization itself was threatened.

But Geneva, and Switzerland generally, which was not afflicted with really bad slums like most industrializing European cities, was spared now and in the future. Not even trade was markedly interrupted, although the artist had to fear fumigation of the albums he had sent Goethe, on their return from Weimar in 1832. Before setting off with his boys for Milan in 1833 he enquired whether it was cholera-free. In *Pencil* Töpffer is reacting to fears of invasion and preventive preparations. Insofar as the story shows as the supposed effect of cholera, the death by asphyxiation of scientists gathered to examine samples of a new gaseous "subterranean wind" (composed actually of odorous latrine particles sent to them by the Professor), Töpffer ridicules the very real and often self-confessed ignorance of medical scientists confronted with a disease which left them completely at a loss. Some believed that lethal underground gasses were indeed escaping.[17] The causes and means of transmission of the disease would not in fact be discovered until Robert Koch isolated the bacillus or vibrio in 1883, which finally ended the epidemics in Europe. While Töpffer spoofs the (reasonable) sanitary precautions of quarantine, fumigation, and purging which added to the usual hassle of frontier checks, he also seems to ridicule a superstitious fear of the disease, as if he, as many, could not bring himself to share the belief that the cholera would really strike as close as France, not to speak of Switzerland. Fear of cholera was supposed to induce the cholera. It was like fear of the devil; cholera was (the work of) the devil, and could be personified, as Töpffer shows it, when Jolibois is taken for the cholera in person (fig. 1-10).

The medical profession, with their learned pretensions and unproven remedies that smelt of quackery and folk tradition, was always fair game for the satirists: in this case the bleeding, the special "punches," the heating machines, the felt fabrics, peculiar diets, the chlorine, the camphor used in vain against the "impenetrable mystery" of cholera.[18]

A major symptom of the cholera was extreme and rapid dehydration caused by diarrhea and vomiting. Some supposed this to be the means by which the body could rid itself of the disease, and the "purging" to which the protagonists in *Pencil* are invited by the sanitary officials at the frontier replicates the symptom-cum-remedy. The "pharmacists rubbing their hands" in glee (59) is no exaggeration: there was gross profiteering on the supposed remedies, especially camphor.

But there was an intuition of a higher reality that Töpffer cannot have consciously foreseen, for it expressed itself only after the cholera had struck in France: that the physical and social epidemic, even revolution itself would be twinned in the public imagination and the minds of writers, artists, scholars, and publicists. In *Pencil* the randomly waggling telegraph is understood to announce the imminence of both war and the cholera (56). Both threats cause social chaos, both were believed to be "caused" by popular agitation, in the aftermath of the July 1830 Revolution. To be sure, *La Caricature* had already in 1831 pronounced the cholera to be a bearer of a new barbarism,[19] but it was only after the epidemic had taken hold in Paris in the spring the following year that the myth was created which twinned "Cholera and Socialism [as] the two scourges of the 19th century" (in the title of a painting after Horace Vernet).[20] Töpffer himself called the Cholera and (social) Progress the twin plagues of the age.[21] A theater critic saw "insurrection and cholera embracing one another like brother and sister." Chateaubriand compared it to the Terror of 1793. The cholera was the consequence of the Revolution of July 1830 (as the Archbishop of Paris declared), it was transmitted by a kind of "revolutionary infection," and it incarnated the cult of violence and death embodied in all revolutionaries.[22] In England, a Seymour caricature of December 1831 showed how "John Bull raves Cholera and Reform"[23]—the struggle of the radicals around the Reform Bill of 1832 was at its height.

The cholera was the *maladie populaire* par excellence, and the sanitary measures taken against it also served to control and repress the "dangerous classes," reborn as the "contagious classes." Radicals on the continent also blamed, rightly, the armies used to repress nationalist uprisings for spreading the disease. The war on cholera was in some respects conducted like real war, with increased militarization of the frontiers. The lower classes, seeing that the cholera singled them out and already resentful in the aftermath of a revolution that had betrayed them, rose up and rioted, even accusing the government doctors and hospitals of deliberately poisoning them. In St. Petersburg in July 1831 a howling mob stormed the hospital and destroyed it, "rescuing" the patients.[24] In France, Italy, and Germany the "lower orders" accused governments of poisoning them. Töpffer, by contrast, shows the health officers, and nurses male and female of a hospital or "bureau de secours" themselves fleeing the supposed epidemic en masse (65). The "people" had already fled Jolibois in his crate when they took him for the Beast of Gévaudan.

It is ironic, then, that in *Pencil* it should be a member of the "popular classes," the Servante who, when all about her panic, defies the supposed cholera and bravely seizes Jolibois, its supposed incarnation, and who roughs up the health officer who tries to make her purge herself. She does this in the same spirit of simple-minded skepticism, ironized by Töpffer as ignorance, vis-à-vis the crazy scientific theories of her master the Professor. Superstition, supposedly a malady of the ignorant and lower classes, is mocked by a member of those classes, the Maid, representing as it were the Enlightenment and the author himself.

Bureaucracy

We all experience the pain of bureaucratic procedures that seem designed to frustrate, humiliate, and prevent things from getting done quickly or at all. The great social and economic changes of the age required great bureaucracies to further their growth and institutionalize them, but the procedures adopted, by civil servants who might be idle and more interested in feathering their own nests than the public weal, often appeared to the public as obstreperous or even downright tyrannical. Politically, bureaucracy was often seen as just another form of social control, like police. New and ever more petty regulations seemed the only way to keep order in the crowded cities. In Germany in mid-century there was even created a continuing comic character, almost the first of his kind, called the *Staatshämorrhoidarius* (for whom see chapter 9), devoted to the processing of paperwork for its own sake. In Germany bureaucracy was sacrosanct and protected a social order that might otherwise come tumbling down like dominoes. Töpffer like any other citizen was alert to the absurdities of the bureaucratic mindset.

The Mayor in *Festus* is a bureaucrat whose ideals of perfect order, themselves rendered in grotesque metaphor, are torn to shreds. His entrée shows him spending five hours taking down the evidence of the theft of Milady's trunk, which sets the ball of crazy adventures rolling. Having fallen asleep in a hay-barn, he has his "great normal dream" in four scenes (added 1840, 21–22) set in a model commune where, from a throne of twenty-six volumes of archives, he registers civic improvements (enumerated), and sees an eight-foot-high legal report dancing the horn-pipe with the goddess Thémis; 300 bailiffs then appear to him, singing the five codes (of law), and finally 3,504 hitherto unknown legal texts cooking in a huge parchment pot, the overflowing pulpy sides of which are licked by 62 clerks.

Freed of the constraints of Mayor and Armed Force, the commune runs riot, burning the communal woods and turning the town hall into a cabaret (36). An individual called Louis Frelay goes hunting in the rye fields without a license; another,

Sur quoi les Frelay et les Roset étant accourus, ils maltrai-
tent le garde champêtre, disant avoir le droit de dé=
fendre leurs parens.

Les autres de la commune ayant pris parti les uns
pour les Roset, les autres pour les Frelay, il s'en suit
une roulée universelle au grand détriment du seigle.

Au plus beau moment on aperçoit l'Habit et la force
armée cheminant au haut des airs d'orient en
Occident. Toute la commune s'écrie: C'est le
Maire! et elle court à sa suite, sans le perdre
des yeux.

38.

1-11. The Frelays and the Rosets beat up the rural guard. The whole commune joins in the fray. The Mayor's uniform and the Armed Force are seen in the sky (*Festus* 38).

called Claude Roset, cutting his rye, also cuts the calf of Frelay, at which both are arrested by the garde champêtre, who gets beaten up by the Frelay and Roset clans, at which the whole commune engages in a free-for-all on one side or the other, and only desist when they recognize the Mayor's uniform and the figures of the Force Armée in the sky (fig. 1-11). They ignore the Mayor in person when he escapes from jail (39) and rush into and drown in the grand canal.

Still searching for his commune by the wayside, the mayoral bureaucrat buys stamped paper on credit, interrogates possible (absent) witnesses, draws up fictive reports, and becomes suicidal (56). The absence of the proper civic authority after "all policing [is] suspended" leads to complete social breakdown also in *Monsieur Trictrac* (63–68). This

happens as the result of progressive petty infractions of petty rules, most of them surprisingly real. They range from the commonsensical, such as an apothecary needing a license to practice, to the picayune, such as children not being allowed to walk on certain grassed areas; from the reasonable, such as not wearing a sword-stick in town, to the unreasonable, such as not being allowed to raise nasturtiums in a windowbox, and to the plain silly, like a pig deciding to avoid the tollbooth by walking independently straight to the butcher's. All these ordinances, except perhaps the last, correspond to actual police regulations in Geneva at the time. The sequence climaxes seriously with the captain of the fire brigade failing to arrive in time from his country seat, and consequently the sapper-firemen failing to assemble in time, which allows the people to take the law, and a fundamental civic function, into their own hands: they put out the fire themselves. This moment replicates a passage in Töpffer's novelette *L'Héritage*, clearly set in Geneva, with the significant difference that the authorized firefighters are also present, to whom the people act as auxiliaries. In the novelette Töpffer is more circumspect. In all of this, "the good old boys regret the good old days."

There follows a hilarious parody of government emergency measures coupled with a statistical survey of the kind that was beginning to haunt the age, and put real bureaucratic meat on the table. A free distribution of emollients on the production of a certificate of good conduct is the occasion of a statistical survey on the comparative morality of various quarters of the town. Trictrac *père* is trying to track down his son, who supposedly wears an emollient. His terms of exclusion and inclusion cancel each other out in another amusing parody of bureaucratic logic.

Crime

Trictrac pullulates with ideas of crime, punishment, mistaken arrest, farcical trials, and social anarchy. These infiltrate other Töpffer picture stories, and inform the nineteenth-century comic strip as a whole. Some of these crimes, notably that of the Police Lieutenant in *Trictrac*, are treated as capital offenses when they clearly should not be. Was Töpffer mocking the harsh and arbitrary punishments of absolutist states; was he an opponent of the death penalty? His view of the latter was probably divided or uncertain, and we may take seriously the incident in *Monsieur Crépin*, a relatively serious story, when a smuggler who commits murder gets off scot-free owing to the specious and dangerous phrenological arguments of his lawyer. Töpffer, rejecting phrenology, rejects the judgment and agrees with the prosecutor that "the victim and soci-

ety should be avenged." The author does not specify that this vengeance should take the form of death, the standard punishment in Europe for any kind of murder and a penalty appealing, in Töpffer's picture novels, all too readily to the constituted powers for much lesser crimes. Geneva had long since virtually abandoned the death penalty, as it had, altogether, judicial mutilation of bodies, under the influence of Cesare Beccaria's famous, humane *Crimes and Punishments* (1st ed. 1764).

There are other, lesser crimes in *Crépin* that are met with what seems excessive severity: Fadet goes to jail for allowing his charges to run amok in the streets (42). School principal Töpffer had occasionally to deal with the police about a window broken by one of his boys, or a stone that accidentally hit a passerby, and tried mildly to discourage casual filching the odd fruit on the highway by hungry and thirsty boys on their excursions. Systematic trespass with intent to rob fruit is another matter (*Crépin* 36–37), followed by urbane insult of the rural guard, and is justly reprimanded. But it is patently absurd and unjust to throw into jail the respectable, if wildly passionate, Vieux Bois for *tapage nocturne* (nocturnal disturbance of the peace) caused by his jumping for joy at his marital prospects, and for his *tapage diurne* (daylight disturbance), that is, playing ghost (41). Tutor Fadet escapes, and it is fortunate that one can escape from a Töpffer jail as easily in fact as one can get into it—and more easily than from the real Genevan jails; much attention was paid to the security and design of prisons, and the building of new ones on the improved, English model. Töpffer's classic novelette, *La Bibliothèque de mon Oncle*, has a touching episode testifying to the boy's (misplaced) sympathy for an eloquent and persuasive prisoner in jail, whom he helps escape.

Caricature and cartoon were never kind to the law. Töpffer and the nineteenth-century comic strip abound in trials, prisons, executions, and suicides (often faked) involving innocent people, preposterous accusations, and idiot law courts. M. Vieux Bois,

1-12. Mr. Vieux Bois gets heated in his peroration (*Vieux Bois* 42).

Une péroraison à la Démosthène

1-13. Daumier: A peroration, Demosthenes-style ("Gens de Justice," *Le Charivari*, 1 November 1847).

accused of disturbing the peace, in his self-defense merely imitates the oratorical theatrics of a Daumier lawyer—and suffers for it (figs. 1-12 and 1-13). The age was obsessed with crime and punishment, as French and English novels reveal. For Ainsworth, Dickens, Victor Hugo, Stendhal, and Balzac, and of the course the popular press at large—even a satirical journal like *Le Charivari*—crime and criminal offered dramatic material galore. We may cite Balzac's Vautrin in *Le Père Goriot* (1834), based on real-life ex-criminal Vidocq who became chief of police and employed ex-cons like himself, in a switch of identities used by Töpffer systematically and hilariously in *Trictrac*, where a thief steals not only the identity of a police chief, but also the very limelight from the hero.

Frontiers of absurdity

For Töpffer and the boys he led on excursions in the Alps, frontiers were the bane of pedestrian existence. They no longer functioned to deter brigandage, a vanishing danger; the brigands were now the customs officers.[25] In 1837 Töpffer could confiscate (or buy back) from a boy who bought a knife with an eighteen-inch blade "admirable to disembowel brigands," with the joke that he undertook to do all the necessary disemboweling of such people. Confiscation was the caprice of the customs, who on the Savoy frontier on one occasion and in one particularly benighted place proved interested not in passports, sugar, or tobacco, but only novels, which were forbidden.[26] The customs and passport "bureau" was a "bourreau" (hangman), and a "bandit."

The twin plagues of nationalism and political repression were exacerbated by Napoleonic conquests, Restoration policies, and the realignments of national states. With the fear of mobile, international conspiracy, and particularly of the Carbonari in France and Italy, frontiers became militarized as never before, making travel more expensive and potentially embarrassing and even painful. Quite apart from having to get passports in advance from the respective foreign consulates in Geneva, and pay fees which, likely as not, went straight into the pockets of the officials issuing them, Töpffer and his troop of boys on their annual tours were hardly out of Geneva but they were faced with the customs and passport formalities, which varied a great deal in rigor from time to time and place to place, but were usually resented. Being closely confined within a few miles, and on three of four sides by the neighboring, not always friendly states of France and Savoy, the Töpffer *pension* found itself reminded almost immediately how Geneva, of all Swiss towns, was vulnerable to the caprices of the frontier.

The Swiss had generally lower tariffs on imports than the French, especially with regard to the Swiss speciality of luxury goods. This enlarged the advantages of smuggling, and the need for customs officers, who became a huge paramilitary corps: In 1845 France one state functionary in five (or eight) was a customs official.[27] In *Crépin* (79) we see the tutor Bonichon, relegated to customs duty, chasing a dog loaded with watches and jewelry. This was no fantasy: dogs were much used for smuggling, could carry up to five or six kilos of goods, and for a three-franc bonus could be killed—but in Töpffer it is Bonichon the customs officer who is killed. Watches were hidden inside disemboweled chickens and even in apples, as well as in specially made smuggling waistcoats. A standard guidebook of 1841 puts the number of watches smuggled into France annually at 100,000.

The problem was such that the comte de Saint-Cricq, Director General of Customs in France, decided to make a personal investigation in Geneva, a prime accomplice. He bought from Bautte, the most fashionable jeweler in town (the Bauttes were relatives of the Töpffers), 30,000 francs worth of jewels, paid a 5 percent surcharge to guarantee (illegal) tariff-free shipment, hastily exited Geneva and,

TÖPFFER THE SATIRIST: CONTEXTS FOR THEMES

passing by the frontier, lectured the douaniers on better vigilance. The jewels were awaiting Saint-Cricq on arrival in Paris, shipped in clandestinely by Bautte's agents. Thus "Monsieur le Directeur des Douanes était le premier contrebandier du royaume," notes Alexandre Dumas drily, who tells the story in full[28]—a truly Töpfferian role reversal.

The *Voyages en Zigzag* are full of complaints against the "abominable ingredient of passports."[29] Is Théophile Gautier thinking of Töpffer's tribulations when he writes that in exchange for a passport he was given a "whimsical form beginning like the M. Crépin and M. Jabot albums, by Töpffer, the witty caricaturist, with this funny instruction: 'See below'"?[30] The natural honesty of the schoolmaster jibbed at the enforced hypocrisy of kowtowing before this petty authority. In a patriotic spasm he describes his relief at entering Swiss soil, where he could set down this heavy burden and where one could travel around the twenty-two cantons without showing a passport or paying a fee, where "all is air and light," compared with the "servile mercenaries, the shifty henchmen, shady commissaires," "behind me, gloomy dens, stifling lairs!"[31] Worst of all was to undergo a body search, to be "palpated" in some "filthy hut," which was "humiliating, ignoble, intolerable." He minded paying much less than having "filthy hands of the scum of customs officials running all over one."[32] "Where do you ever see a customs post or customs official, that is not dusty, filthy, and annoying in the worst way?"[33] This outburst, at the Austrian frontier out of Como, causes the otherwise antirevolutionary schoolmaster to "rise in revolt against Austria," to conspire in his innermost heart against that paranoid authority, and wish that Tessin, in Switzerland, were not so lax by contrast, which made the Austrians worse. How he would have reviled current airport security!

The interflow of time and of space in Töpffer is a denial of frontiers, which seem to raise their ugly heads out of nowhere. These frontiers had, to be sure, been much rationalized after the Congress

1-14. Daumier: Customs post. The traveler is visited, searched, stripped, and robbed. His clothes do not pass because the like are made in China [i.e., France]; his wig, because the like are not made there; his boots, because leather is prohibited; his clyso-pump because it is a mechanical object of suspicious use . . . everything is seized and he has to pay duty on the rest, after which he is as free as the air . . . (*Le Charivari*, 19 January 1844).

of Vienna, since the time when fragments of Genevan territory were enclaved (that is, as islands with no corridor) within France and Savoy, in order to align the canton of Geneva better with the Swiss Confederation, which it joined in 1814. But France and Savoy were two powerful monarchies that saw no reason to spare tiny Geneva, or little Switzerland for that matter, the imposition of unfavorable tariffs, anti-smuggling measures, and the triage of persons suspected of being undesirable. Certain communes, traditionally tied to Geneva, were still claimed by France, notably the pays de Gex, through which

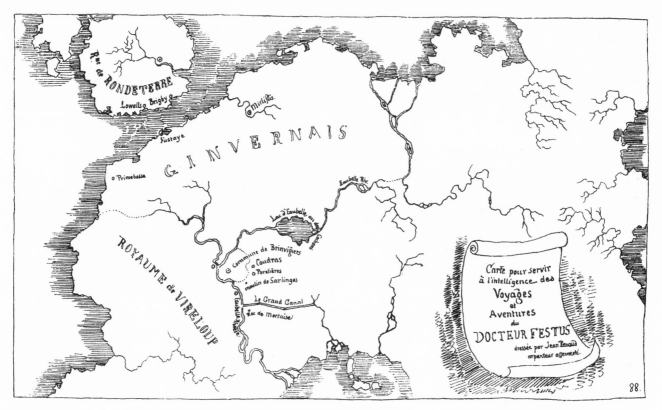

1-15. Map of Ginvernais, Vireloup and Rondeterre (illustration to *Festus*).

the Genevese had right of way on the roads but no more. Ferney-Voltaire, straddling the border with France, was claimed by both sides; the French, force majeure, won.

Frontiers became, justifiably, supersensitive when the cholera struck as it did in 1832. In *Pencil* (1831, then 1840), the stringent measures imposed at the frontier are theoretically justified by the cholera and just those, as we have seen, to which Töpffer's own albums might have been subjected on their return from Weimar. They are an exercise in humiliation in normal (non-cholera) conditions that Töpffer otherwise denounces in his *Voyages en Zigzag*. Ironically, in *Pencil* the fumigation at the border actually releases what is believed to be the cholera "in person" (i.e., Monsieur Jolibois escaping from his crate). In this episode there are also sinister references to mandatory "purging" or else quarantine, which takes on the air of the alternative of jail

and a virtual sexual assault in the form of a close body search, such as aroused Töpffer's indignation in the passage above. Pencil and Mrs. Jolibois (64) escape purging by lying. It is only the Maid who reacts in what one feels is the honorable way: outraged at the demands of the sanitary inspector, she tells him roughly to "go purge yourself, you old demon," and obstructs him with physical force.

Töpffer and his school traveled with human guides rather than the paper kind, or maps. A complete cartographic survey (1:100,000) of Switzerland was not undertaken until 1834, continuing to 1864, under direction of the illustrious Genevese general G.-H. Dufour, who installed the Federal Topographic Bureau in his hometown. Adequate maps of Alpine passes were generally not available, and it was left to the local guides to determine the best paths for the occasion, familiar and well-trodden as they usually were. Danger lurked, especially

TÖPFFER THE SATIRIST: CONTEXTS FOR THEMES

in unpredictable weather, and one can intuit a sense of lurking danger as Töpffer's characters flit back and forth, to and fro, never knowing when they might hit a frontier, or be hit by a sudden storm or an avalanche. Politics and nature, ever rival jokers, like to strew accidents and obstacles in our path.

In *Festus*, the Mayor and Milady are both arrested at the Vireloup frontier for lack of papers. According to the highly distorted and schematic map placed at the end of the album (itself a cartographic parody, fig. 1-15), the kingdom of Vireloup lies to the west of Ginvernais, which basically occupies the position of France, adjacent to what might be, if the map were real, Genevan territory with its conspicuous lake, here called Lac d'Eaubelle ou des Cochons, featured large in its center. Ginvernais has some features of Geneva beyond a certain assonance of name, a Geneva that stretched scientifically (and astronomically) as far as England, reaching the channel dividing it from "Rondeterre," which is obviously Angleterre in this map. As we have seen, Vireloup is ruled by an authoritarian king, while the rival Ginvernais is ruled by a constitutional but Bourbon (that is, French) king, to judge by the cry "Vive les Bourbons" used by Töpffer at first (1829) before he changed it to "Vive le roi" in 1840. Vireloup-Savoy (the name actually appears in the 1829 manuscript: *à la douane de Savoie*), has tyrannical frontiers; we remember how (in the 1840 version) Milady is arrested and convicted as a Carbonarist spy on the basis of a laundry list found on her. She was merely trying to find her husband and get back to England.

Religion: Vicious monks and white devils

Geographical frontiers were also religious frontiers, for Geneva, the "Protestant Rome," the fortress of Calvinism, was surrounded by Catholic countries and in its canton incorporated many Catholic communes, some of them recently acquired in the post-1814 readjustment of frontiers. No one has accused Töpffer of religious bigotry, and he is in many places at pains to validate moderate Catholicism, if only because he soon realizes that his public will be Catholic French people as well as French-speaking Swiss. But he retains contempt for surviving Catholic superstition, monastic idleness, and a fear of their intolerance of hell-bent "heretics." Rodolphe's religion is ethical, not doctrinal; he is a liberal who believes that religious instruction should content itself with inculcating the simple virtues of hope, humility, and charity. In a letter he describes religion as a kind of bureaucracy attempting to regulate souls left better off self-regulated.[34] He must have picked up his father's hostility to rigidity, sectarianism, and theological disputation, which only encourage civil schism. Wolfgang-Adam's watercolor entitled *The happy Reformation against the Catholic faith* of c. 1817 is an allegory of the historic enmity between Calvin and the Dominican-Jesuit propagandists, both parties riding monsters who face off angrily, heedless of their flocks (literally sheep) who are hooked down to hell by demons.[35] His *Machine à hacher les écritures* of the same period indicts the logic-chopping of newer enemies to social tranquility and religious unity, the puritanical Methodism in the persons of (named on the print) Robert Haldane and Henry Drummond, whose presence in Geneva had made inroads on the dogmatic, excessively rationalist, official Genevan Calvinism. Religious fanatics, called in Geneva *mômiers* (extreme puritans) or *englués* (reactionaries), could be lethally dangerous, as Monsieur Vieux Bois discovers, and as is hinted in a cartoon by Rodolphe's father showing bearded heads in snail shells, praying with a crucifix in hand but a dagger in the belt.[36]

Calvinism was the state religion in Geneva as much as Catholicism was in Savoy or France, but the Catholic curés who ministered in the Catholic communes of Geneva were paid for out of Genevan state funds, which gave the state some right of control. There was concern over the growth of Catholicism in the canton: among the peasantry from 39 percent in 1822 to 44.5 percent in 1843 (by 1860 it would be 51 percent). In the town, 21 percent in 1834 would rise to 26 percent in 1843.[37] There were accusations of discrimination against Catholics in the job market and public charity. Protestant fear of demographic domination by Catholics was exacerbated by a Catholic hierarchy that came up with petty provocations of their own, such as a refusal to bury an Italian suicide in a Catholic cemetery.[38] Some of these provocations were instigated by the curé of Geneva and Catholic leader abbé Vuarin, who made no secret of his vision to re-Catholicize the whole republic. When Vuarin, the thorn in the flesh of conciliators, died in 1843, his successor Marilley was expelled. Catholics also resented the official Jubilee celebration in 1835 of the Reformation (1535). But this was also the time (1834–35) when education was taken out of the hands of the Protestant clergy, and the Academy was legally separated from the Venerable Company of Pastors, which was no longer allowed to vote in Academy elections or run the state schools.

Ironically, the Calvinist government, the Conseil d'État, found itself siding, for political reasons, with Catholic forces in Geneva, and with the Catholic Swiss cantons, when disputes arose, as they did in the affair of the Aargau convents (1841). This controversy mobilized public opinion, generally on the side of intervention, against the government that tried to stay neutral, and similarly in 1844–45, with the affair of the Jesuits in Lucerne. Nonetheless, Geneva should be regarded as an island of tolerance and neutrality caught in a continental sea of Catholic reaction. In France, Savoy, and Austrian Italy, the Restoration sought aggressively to restore the primacy of Catholicism as well as monarchy. Secularization was fought tooth and nail, especially in vulnerable rural districts; the Savoyard peasantry were deliberately kept by the clergy, it was thought, in a state of benighted ignorance and poverty.

In *Mr. Vieux Bois* Töpffer taps into a tradition of the Gothic novel, with its chambers of Catholic/monastic horrors. The Gothic, anti-monastic novel par excellence, *The Monk* (1796) by Matthew ("Monk") Lewis, was quickly translated into French and was read by Töpffer in Paris in 1820. Lewis had been at the Villa Diodati near Geneva, trading ghost stories with Byron and Shelley. *The Monk* established the stereotype of the vicious, evil, lecherous monk in hair-curling fashion. Töpffer may also have used news of the restoration of the Inquisition in Spain in 1814, and its resurrection again after the failure of the Spanish revolution of 1820–23. These were the years of Goya's drawings of Inquisition victims, and of the Pinturas Negras (Black Paintings) executed in his house, called that of the Deaf Man. In Goya's *Pilgrimage to San Isidro* from that series we see cretinous monks and satanic clerics; passing from the sublime to the ridiculous, one can imagine it a monastic procession to celebrate the capture of Monsieur Vieux Bois and his Beloved Object, and their prospective burning at the stake. The terror campaign in Spain, although it no longer burned heretics at the stake in the way still implied as late as Goya's *Caprichos* (1796–99), seemed to confirm the worst prejudices of the Gothic novel, especially in England. Religious repression was less terrible but still could be savage in France, and was as bad in its way in Russia. The religious reaction as a whole has been deemed the underlay of Goya's *Saturn Devouring His Son*: Saturn, fearing the prophecy that he will be dethroned by his own children, devours them as they come into the world, as the Catholic governments of the "Holy Alliance" devoured the rebels who threatened them.[39] As late as 1826, the year before the first draft of *Mr. Vieux Bois*, a poor schoolmaster of blameless character named Cayetano Ripoll was executed (garotted) at Valencia on a charge of professing Deism. This was reported to an astounded Europe as a burning alive, with monks leading an assembled multitude in hymns to drown out the despairing shrieks. The inquisition in Spain was not formally abolished until 1834.[40]

1-16. Mr. Vieux Bois cuts the beard off a monk, and escapes a legion of vengeful monks (*Vieux Bois* 49).

1-17. Mr. Vieux Bois and the Beloved Object are condemned to the stake (*Vieux Bois* 78).

Monastic terror is threaded throughout *Vieux Bois*, Töpffer's first essay in his new medium. In the final (second published) edition of 1839, the nefarious monks occupy no less than twenty-seven scenes, including four panoramic ones, in ten separate appearances. Romantically, innocently, and to escape from brigands, Vieux Bois in his amorous despair takes to the life of a hermit and finds himself drifting willy-nilly into a monastery. Quitting that life, and that institution, is not so easy; he has to escape by stealth, only to be caught later by the monks and thrown into jail, together with the Beloved Object. Our hero has learned to know his enemy, and when he meanwhile happens on one of the monks in his peregrinations, he casually drowns him; but the monks pursue him to the end. They are ridiculous, of course, but they are also vicious: greedy for gold, merciless, senseless, and cruel. Having recruited lovelorn Vieux Bois, so to speak, they treat his attempt to escape as that of a military deserter. Reading between the lines, one may guess that the monks' hostility is fueled by their finding the new acquisition sexually disgraced, for he is captured in the company of his ladylove and jailed with (or rather separately from) her. Later, after he blithely cuts the beard off another stray monk, he causes a veritable stampede of "vengeful monks" from the monastery (figs. 1-16 and 1-17).

The monks in their monastery represent not just a barbaric hostile religion but an enemy country, the *Terre des Moines* (capital letters original, 75), with its own irrational hatred of foreigners or interlopers, an army (a "legion" of monks, some armed), a fortress in which they live (these aspects were heightened between 1827 and 1839), hostile agents, and frontiers with "toll rights" (*droits de péage*) of perilous passage. Above all, these monks, like any tyrannical government, are apt to condemn suspects to death without trial. They do so, moreover, in the manner notorious of the Spanish Inquisition, where the church—hypocritically denying itself the pleasure of shedding blood directly—would hand over the victim, duly condemned, to the secular arm for execution of the

death sentence. This is a Töpffer touch easy to miss: we see (fig. 1-17) a regular soldier standing by with a burning torch at the ready. Vieux Bois's only ally in his battle with the monks is his mule, nature itself as it were, kicking a monk into the air (added in 1839). Having narrowly escaped being burned alive, Vieux Bois gets a commensurate revenge, although in the end he generously commutes it: he buries two greedy monks alive, a stellar occasion, for it is the only moment when the Beloved Object relaxes her habitually mournful expression, and actually smiles (added 1839). Töpffer also in 1839 embellishes the scene with the anguished heads of the monks projecting above ground level, and infested by birds of prey (86).

The nefarious spiritual influence of the monastery shows up in the superstitious villagers who pursue Vieux Bois, dressed perforce only in his burial shroud, as a ghost, a guise which serves to frighten out of their wits his apparently equally superstitious family, the "heirs" gathered, it seems, to celebrate his demise. A similar incident in *Pencil* has Jolibois escaped from his crate, taken for the Beast of Gévaudan, an already mythic wild creature, in reality a wolf or perhaps hyena escaped from a zoo that killed many people in the 1760s near the southern French Gévaudan and was heavily exploited by the clergy as a warning from God and punishment for sin. The clerically induced superstition rife in the countryside is a theme in *Festus*, where the villagers of Coudraz and Porelières (names invented, but similar to local ones of the canton of Geneva), armed with pitchforks and headed by the local curé in his black soutane and hat, run away in droves at the mere sight of a screaming farmer who is white from the lime into which he has fallen (fig. 1-18). In later editions, the curé's clerical dress was secularized. The curé rushes fearfully up to exorcise a supposed speaking tree, which is taken for the White Devil. The peasants who bring Dr. Festus, wrapped up in a corn-sack, laden on an ass to the mill, are so frightened when it (the sack) begins to walk off with one of them on its back, that while one runs for help, the other whimpers an Ave Maria from

Le Docteur Festus trouve prudent de Sortir de l'arbre, mais il trouve Suspecte la figure du Sieur Taillandier qui est blanchi de chaux maigre

Au trente deuxième coup la Scie mord l'orteil du Docteur qui pousse un énorme cri en vingt deux langues. A ce cri, le Sieur Taillandier tombe dans un baquet de chaux maigre, et les Scieurs de long s'en vont porter la nouvelle d'un arbre parlant dans les hameaux de Porelières et de Coudraz.

26

Ensorte qu'il s'enfuit au plus tôt.

D'autre part ceux de Coudraz et de Porelières accourent, le Curé en tête, pour exorciser

27

Mais à la vue du Sieur Taillandier qui hurle tout-blanchi de chaux maigre, ils le prennent pour le Diable blanc, et rebroussent au plus tôt, le curé en queue.

1-18. The saw bites into Dr. Festus's toe, he screams and the Sieur Taillandier falls into the chalk, while the sawyers spread the news of a talking tree. Dr. Festus exits the tree, but finds the chalk-covered figure of Taillandier suspect. While Dr. Festus escapes, the villagers run up, headed by their priest, but seeing the screaming, chalk-covered Sieur Taillandier, they flee, taking him for the White Devil (*Festus* 26–27).

1-19. Capucin monks ("Voyage aux Alpes et en Italie," 1837, *Voyages en Zigzag*, 1844, p. 77).

behind a winnowing basket (added 1840, 30). Meanwhile the whole village has arrived at the rumor of a devil incarnate, using pitchforks to threaten the poor peasants, Claude and Gamaliel, whom they upbraid as cowards, taking sacks for demons and corn grains for the coals of hell.

In the prose version of *Festus* (49) the peasant George Luçon adds courage to his honesty by daring to mount a ladder in order to confront the devil (i.e., Dr. Festus, hidden in Samuel Porret's barn), but only after being duly confessed and absolved by the curé, and performing other necessary last social rites. But it is the recidivist criminal Jean Baune, having taken Festus' place in the barn roof, who shoots at Luçon, is taken for the devil, and escapes, while the villagers, seeing the devil in person again, seek to exorcise him by setting the cornfields on fire and conducting processions in the streets; in Croix-Blanche the village is surrounded with string and blessed at great expense, which worked a treat, for the devil never bothered people there.

Later in the *Festus* album (73) a peasant called Jaques André sees a washed-up giant telescope, which, with its gaping mouth, he takes for a malabar cachalot whale and gallops off in terror. It even

faces a firing squad before, circumnavigated from behind, it is recognized as a belltower, a miracle. The curé comes to take possession of it in the name of the church, and a procession is held in honor of St. Clochard (the word means tramp, but connotes *cloche*, meaning bell), author of the miracle. The prose *Festus* (113) specifies a further ridiculous miracle: the vibration of the bells, placed inside the telescope/belltower, shakes out all the ratkiller powder (*mort-aux-rats*), which causes those sitting in the choir to sneeze, a wonder that the envious bishop of Faribole could not buy for his diocese even for 20,000 Patagonian écus.

The Abbé in *Cryptogame* has to be secularized for mass Catholic consumption in *L'Illustration*, lest he be taken as a typical Catholic priest. For the Abbé is fat, torpid, and gormless. His inability to free himself from the beam on his leg as the Europeans escape from Algiers may be no more than the kind of happenstance farce we know from the movies: in Charles Chaplin's *A King in New York* the king's inability to free himself from a firehose is not intended to show him as stupid, only accident-prone. But it is the Abbé, not Cryptogame, who becomes thus encumbered (and thereby starts a forest fire); I wonder if the beam does not function in some way as a blinder, an obstacle to understanding, on one in a constant state of bewilderment as to what is happening to him.

Monks, it seems, were fair game. And while Töpffer was warned not to alienate Catholics with any criticism of their curés, few seem to have objected to his view of monks in *Vieux Bois*, or for that matter in the relatively documentary *Voyages en Zigzag*, published for the French public at large. Of the fat, idle Capucins monks whose only existence is to batten on the tourists: "pouah! Ignoble, stupid, dirty, self-seeking."[41] They are "Jabots."[42] They resemble "really scary brigands." Their disgusting fatness contrasts with the pathetic boniness of the peasants (fig. 1-19). Priests likewise living off the tourists could be as bad, frivolous, and degraded;

to say that they scrounge out a living like rats in a mansion is a slander on rats.[43] By the 1840s, however, it was clear to Töpffer that a priesthood inculcating humility, obedience, and ignorance was less dangerous than the radicals of "Young Switzerland" agitating for secularism, socialism, and atheism. In the *Voyages* much—too much—sympathetic space is given over to the simple pious exercises of Catholic rustics, and their crude religious theater.

Peasants and countryside

Retrograde religion, as we see, was characteristic of the peasantry, especially in Savoy, who inevitably became more of a political factor with the enlargement of the canton of Geneva. The reformers demanded universal male suffrage to include them, to give them more voice in the councils of state, and instead of the city running the canton, separation of administrations. In Basel, the city-canton conflict came to such a pass in 1832 that two separate cantons had to be created, which still exist as such, as they do in a more recent creation for Berne.

Class antagonism between peasant and bourgeois becomes a major stream of nineteenth-century comic strip and caricature (as of the novel), reaching full flood in the picture stories of Léonce Petit in the 1870s and 1880s. Töpffer, with his embryonic sense of this antagonism, may have toyed for a moment with the idea of a story based upon it, for the manuscript album of *Crépin* starts with four drawings showing the progressive attack upon a bourgeois type, his humiliation and total subjection by a peasant armed with a flail. The idea of developing a narrative from this kernel was probably too frightening. Töpffer himself could retire, later in life, in the summer to a country house, although he does not seem to have been a landowner or invested in land. Two at least of his protagonists, Crépin and Festus, evidently live on country estates, as local mini–lords of the manor, with peasants at their ser-

vice and patronage to offer. But this was not typical of the canton Geneva, largely occupied by independent, self-governing farmers with small properties. Unlike the Alpine dwellers, they were not poor.

The Voyages offer a more or less realistic panorama of very different conditions in the Alps. The Alpine peasantry fall into basically two groups: those now dedicated to living directly off the tourists and those happy, industrious folk encountered by chance going about their agricultural labors. Something of the moral spectrum of behavior among innkeepers and guides is given in a later chapter. Suffice it to say here that the sheer range of peasant qualities, as manifested in their treatment of tourists and travelers, was a source of aesthetic delight and much moralizing. As one would expect in a satirical medium, the moral range shrinks in the picture stories, where there are few virtuous, intelligent peasants (George Luçon seems to be unique, although others are depicted neutrally), and many who behave as we have seen in a foolish, superstitious, and cowardly manner. The Force Armée described above would probably be peasants—landless, vagrant, lumpen types recruited from the dregs of the population. The prose *Festus* has an embellishment that prefigures Léonce Petit's comic strip satires on rural litigiousness: in order to explain why the Primebosse villagers of Ginvernais leap upon the idea that the giant telescope washed up on their shores is a belltower, we learn that the commune was unable to pay for the new one needed because it had ruined itself in a lawsuit involving (à la Petit) a really trivial-seeming matter: the apple trees grown in one commune dropped its apples in the neighboring one. An escalation of mutual recriminations nourishes a seven-year lawsuit, at the conclusion of which justice takes all, even the apples.

Töpffer inherited the traditional urban condescension toward the peasantry mitigated by a Rousseauist idealization of their simplicity and piety. The urban heroes of the picture stories are profes-

1-20. Daumier: When you make hay, and try to inspect your haymakers too closely ("Pastorales," *Le Charivari*, 29 April 1846).

Töpffer lends substance to peasant life with credible-sounding names of individuals (unlike the anonymous "burgher" in *Pencil*) and locales, and the depiction of real, useful rural occupations that contrast with the mentally aberrant existence of the townsmen. In a familiar topos, the town is the mind or head of the rural body. The urban mind of Festus, however, is the crazy and useless one that screams in twenty-two different languages against the raw physical reality of a saw biting into his toe, as it cuts the tree where he lies hidden (26). Only his pain is real. Dr. Festus escaping into a corn shed and hiding in a corn-sack that is carried by peasants for grinding to a mill enacts, comically of course, a literal kind of reinsertion of the urban into the rural, which compounds the chaos. The ensuing alarm and fear of the devil reveal a countryside destabilized by the very force, religion, that is supposed to bind them together. Violence and vindictiveness follow each other in a folktale (or Molièresque) pattern: the humiliated miller Claude Thiolier beats his wife for saying she did not see anything, the miller's wife beats the boy for having said he saw something, and the boy beats the ass for having caused all the misfortune (33, fig. 1-21). In fact, of course, it is Festus the townsman who causes the misfortune, unwittingly, and it is the invasion of the countryside by urban misfits that sows dissensions and violence among the ranks of the peasants, exacerbated by their natural superstition. Like the corn-sack and the haystack, the windmill, another symbol of rural life, by throwing Festus and the Armed Force into the air acts to reject the alien urban body.

The rural guards (*garde champêtre*) were established in 1817 by law, given uniforms by the state, and responsible to a mayor. Their function is similar to that of the Armed Force (also essentially a police force), with the difference, in Töpffer, that they are not ridiculed and shown to be stupid automata. We see one exercising a major function, preventing hunting without a license[44] in *Albert* (10), and

sional men who, when they venture out of town or out of their country estate, brush with the peasantry and thereby are capable of being led, like Dr. Festus, into dream and nightmare states, as if the countryside, far from fulfilling its purpose of relaxation and inspiration, was apt to play strange tricks upon them (fig. 1-20). Comic strip and caricature in the nineteenth century are full of this. The townsman is never prepared, psychologically or physically, for rural conditions—even in little Geneva, so close to its canton, and with open fields within its town walls. Festus's "educational tour" (*voyage d'instruction*) into the countryside nourishes only fantasies and hallucinations.

Quand le village s'est éloigné, Claude Thiolier bat sa femme pour avoir dit qu'elle n'a rien vu.

La Meunière bat le garçon pour avoir dit qu'il a vu quelque chose.

Le garçon bat l'âne pour avoir causé tout ce mal. Après quoi la paix revient dans le moulin 33

1-21. Claude Thiolier beats his wife for saying she saw nothing. The miller's wife beats the boy for having said he saw something. The boy beats the ass for having caused all the trouble. After which peace returns to the mill (*Festus* 33).

in *Crépin* (37–39) where, under collective upper-class urban (and urbane) insult, he deftly gathers evidence and brings the petty juvenile delinquents to book. In French caricature of the age, the garde champêtre is the constant reminder of the vulnerability and incompatibility of the petty bourgeois in the countryside.

The Duel

European countries tried from time to time to prevent and criminalize dueling, in France to least avail. The duel, comic duel, and non-duel were staples of romantic literature, romantic literary clichés in themselves. Many leading French figures fought duels, and some died in them, like the brilliant young mathematician Evariste Galois, aged 21 years, in 1832, and the famous journalist Armand Carrel in 1838. Alexander Pushkin, who wrote his famous verse novel *Eugene Onegin* to condemn the practice, was killed in a duel forced on him by enemies in 1837. Töpffer would have known that his patron and favorite correspondent, the soldier and writer Xavier de Maistre, composed his most famous work *Voyage autour de ma chambre* (1794), which is deemed to be a model for Töpffer's *Bibliothèque de mon Oncle*, under house arrest for fighting a duel. The English, meanwhile, having illegalized it in 1803, succeeded in actually deterring it by hanging some victors of lethal cases. The French, in mockery of repeated laws, were the worst, with 228 known duels ending in death in the period 1826–34; the mania was ended only by the First World War.

Many duels were faked, meant to satisfy honor, not to take a life or even injure. A duel Töpffer reported to his parents from his student days in Paris involved two legislators who in the Chamber considered themselves insulted, and arranged a duel at which both fired in the air—honor satisfied.[45] The French had a term for it: *duel pour rire*. The pretext could be of Töpfferian absurdity: in 1837 two professors at the law school in Paris challenged each other over whether a passage in the *Pandects* of Justinian should use a colon or semi-colon.[46] Jabot, likewise, demands satisfaction over a pun. The duel is a central satiric butt in *Jabot*, where the hero provokes five duels in one evening, which are satisfied (31) by pistols loaded with bread-balls. "Swords at ten metres distance" is the title (more or less) of a picture story by Léonce Petit.[47]

Suicide

The author himself confessed to occasional suicidal thoughts. There is suicide and suicidality in all of Töpffer's picture stories (and in some of his prose work); arch-romantic lover Vieux Bois attempts suicide five times. It too was a consecrated romantic theme. Béranger deplored it, Vigny poeticized it, resurrecting the poet Chatterton, who poisoned himself at the age of eighteen. In the later eighteenth century there was a European-wide epidemic that some blamed on Goethe's *Werther* (1774) and that was reflected in fiction. Suicide often afflicted the Byron-Shelley circle, which was for a while so close to Geneva: Mary Shelley's half sister and the poet Shelley's wife Harriet both committed suicide, Mary's mother Mary Wollstonecraft tried twice, and died giving birth to her, leaving her with the notion that childbirth is itself suicidal. In Mary Shelley's great fictional creation *Frankenstein*, which she wrote on the shores of the Lake of Geneva in 1816, Victor Frank, father of the monster, is a Genevan who nearly drives himself mad and becomes

suicidal with his scientific mania, like the astronomers in *Festus*.

The real-life incidence increased again in the 1820s and 1830s, rising in France by 70 percent in this period.[48] *Werther* was banned, to the approval even of Goethe himself. There were some dramatic suicides of prominent people: Baron Antoine Jean Gros, the favorite painter of Napoleon, after his art was criticized, threw himself into the Seine 1835; Adolphe Nourrit, a singer, who at thirty-eight suddenly lost his voice; Victor Lescousse and Auguste Lebras, nineteen and sixteen years old, after their play was hissed in 1832 (they became the "official representatives of romantic suicide").[49] Genevese too: Imbert Gallois, a nineteen-year-old arriving in Paris with some insignificant poems, which were rejected, killed himself in 1828. As a youth in Paris 1820 Töpffer learned of the suicide of a school friend in Russia. In Geneva in the late eighteenth century there had been a wave of suicides, far outnumbering homicides. Suicide was not decriminalized in French civil law until 1791; Geneva had done this by 1764, when Beccaria appealed for such a humanitarian measure.[50]

Three of Töpffer's characters are suicidal for love. The senselessly jealous Jolibois, in *Pencil*, is deterred by the depth of the lake, and thus the prospect of succeeding. A second attempt when he is airborne is frustrated by his shirt opening like a parachute and a wind blowing from below (6, 8). Elvire, the frustrated lover of Cryptogame, heroic to the last, self-explodes in a jealous fury. Vieux Bois is the gourmet of suicide, choosing in turn five of the principal means: by hanging, by the sword, by poison, by jumping out of the window, and by drowning. All fail, despite the hero's conviction otherwise (6, fig. 1-22). He is exceeded only by Dickens's Mr. Mantalini in *Nicholas Nickleby* (1839), who tries to poison himself seven times. There are no figures on the ratio, then, of unsuccessful suicide attempts to successful ones; today it is calculated at about ten or fifteen (registered—many more

1-22. Mr. Vieux Bois thinks he is dead for 48 hours. Returns to existence very much thinner. Changes his shirt (*Vieux Bois* 6).

go unreported) to one. Of the various options, hanging was considered the least honorable for its criminal associations; the sword, associated with ancient Roman heroics, was considered noble but the hardest to effect. Vieux Bois is, of course, mad with love; suicidality was believed to be an extreme and the most tragic form of madness. His attempts punctuate the course of his love like their antidote, changing his shirt, which gives him a new lease on life. Vieux Bois's hapless rival in love also shows suicidal tendencies.

Another common cause of suicide was professional failure and vanity: this is exemplified in Fadet, the failed tutor in *Crépin*. He overcomes his suicidal despair, however, and actually dies a martyr to his vanity and to fashion, strangled by tying his waterproof crinoline cravat too tight (87, fig. 1-23). This may be read as a metaphor of the strangulation effect of his and others' educational systems; but those with an eye on the *chronique scandaleuse*

would have known of the controversy surrounding the death of the last Prince of Condé in 1830: was his being found hanged murder, suicide, or perhaps accident?—the latter resulting from a fetish for the masochistic pleasures of semi-strangulation, the milder effects of which from a very tight cravat were enjoyed, it seems, by some dandies of the period, like Fadet (as today in sadomasochistic game-play, which can also go wrong).[51] Astronomer Apogée in *Festus* is another victim of what he deems a professional failure, the loss of his asteroid, and descends into madness (64, fig. 1-24), the symptoms of which are given in some farcical detail, before succumbing altogether "of a repressed asteroid."

The most interesting suicidal madman, and another case of professional failure, is the Mayor in *Festus*. His attempt at suicide, Roman style, by means of a sword run through his breast (56, fig. 1-25) is an opportunity for Töpffer to display his pathognomic skills in a series of sketches he expands from

Au bout de onze mois Craniose meurt de misère un Jeudi matin, au septième étage. Il laisse un testament olographe par lequel il lègue sa théorie au monde, et son crâne à la Science.

Nul ne réclamant leur succession Craniose est porté en terre, et avec lui, Ses trente six crânes de gredins.

Au bout de cinq ans Fadet meurt un Samedi matin, pour avoir trop serré sa crinoline imperméable.

(87.)

1-23. Death and burial of Craniose with his thirty-six rogues' skulls. Fadet strangles himself by drawing his waterproof crinoline cravat too tight (*Crépin* 87).

Alors Monsieur Apogée leur lance ses pommes sur le nez, et les vingt huit prennent la fuite en criant: Sauve qui peut!...

64.

A cette vue Monsieur Apogée rit avec une telle véhémence, qu'entraîné en faiblesse il tombe du pommier sur le terreau, où il reste empreint comme un bronze dans du plâtre frais. C'est là que Madame Apogée en peignoir retrouve son époux en caleçons.

1-24. Astronomer Apogee throws his apples at his twenty-eight assistants, who flee. At the sight of which Apogee laughs so much he falls from the tree (*Festus* 64).

1-25. The Mayor remembers what he owes his commune, and throws away the weapon with horror. Then remembering he has no commune, seizes the weapon again and enraged again, directs it towards his breast. Then, realizing there is no one to register his death, place the seals, and proceed to burial, he renounces his project and resumes the path to his commune (*Festus* 56).

the manuscript, dwelling upon the mayoral agony of indecision between what he owes his citizens and the realization that he has none, but deterred above all by the bureaucratic consideration that if he does die there will be no one to certify his death, affix the seals, and proceed to interment. Töpffer also adds in the published version the renewed despair of the Mayor finding his commune deserted; like Apogee, he indulges in a debauchery of madness, an antisocial orgy, which in its final, military spasm, involves the death of his Armed Force (two persons) as well as himself. All this, on the part of a (relatively) high government official, may owe something to the incidence of crime and madness among the upper classes in France in this period.

The follies of science

Science has not yet taught us if madness
is or is not the sublimity of intelligence.
—EDGAR ALLAN POE

Geneva was known internationally for its science rather than arts or letters. The *Bibliothèque Britannique*, which under the Napoleonic occupation had managed to break the continental blockade against Britain and maintain a vital cultural and scientific exchange with that country, had been grandiloquently renamed the *Bibliothèque Universelle de Genève* by the time Töpffer joined it, becoming a very prolific collaborator and editor on the magazine. A man of Töpffer's catholicity of intellectual taste embraced the chance to join a scientific community gathered in the magazine, and he counted among his closest friends scientific colleagues at the university where he taught literature.

Geneva had made its mark in the development of various sciences, notably in botany, physics, and astronomy. In botany, the name of Nicolas-Théodore de Saussure (1767–1845) was famous throughout Europe, and considered a model of experimental science expressed in rigorous, limpid terms. He was a pioneer in plant nutrition and photosynthesis, and his investigation of carbonic acid gas (carbon dioxide) is of the kind that underlies some of Töpffer's references to "subterranean gas" (actually, those emanating from a toilet) in *Pencil* (5). Töpffer added the scientific touch to increase the comic effect, when (in an 1840 addition to the 1829 manuscript), he improved the original "loud snore drawing the trunk-lid down on Festus asleep inside" to a "heavy intake of breath creates a vacuum and brings down the lid."

Saussure *père*, Horace Bénédict de Saussure (1740–99), who introduced the word geology, taught philosophy and meteorology and was also a distinguished botanist who appealed particularly to Töpffer the excursionist for his achievement in being the first to ascend Mont Blanc in 1787. Plant physiologist Jean-Pierre Vaucher was a friend with a vast publication record who managed also to run a boarding school, like Töpffer, at which Charles-Albert, the future king of Sardinia, was a pupil. Augustin-Pyramus de Candolle (1778–1841), professor at the Academy from 1816, created a Botanical Garden in Geneva, presided over the Société des Arts from 1823, and was Rector of the Academy from 1832. Having greatly increased the taxonomy of plants, he made the (to us) amusing error of grouping *Cryptogames vasculaires* with the *Monocotylédones*[52]—amusing for the coincidence of the name Cryptogame, Töpffer's most popular comic hero (actually named after the Greek, meaning secretly married), who was in the

first version of the picture story an amateur botanist chasing tulips, before he became a butterfly hunter.

The very preponderance of botanical science in Geneva may have deterred Töpffer from botanizing anew in his travel writings, a genre where commentary on the local flora as well as fauna was traditional. In *Festus* he mocks the quest for new species, which as discovered there seem to oscillate between the vegetable and animal domains, and arouse the pretentious ignorance of scientists as well as the greed of museum curators.

After botany, astronomy was the most Genevan of sciences. The first observatory in Geneva was set up in 1772, and a new one created in 1830, from which attempts were made (by F. W. Bessel, among others) to determine the distance of the closest stars: 61 Cygne was measured at 10.25 light-years, or 657,000 times the distance of the earth from the sun.[53] The magnitude and precision of such calculations, of course, staggered belief, perhaps Töpffer's too. Astronomical observations in Geneva were very much geared toward industry, to the point that commentators on the Genevan cultural scene would note, primly, that all science in Geneva served industry, and therefore mammon.

The uses of astronomy to watchmaking, the principal industry in Geneva, were patent, and the calculation of sidereal time helped establish exact terrestrial time. The calculation that tidal action on the earth was slowing down its rotation at the rate of two milliseconds a century would have struck many, including Töpffer, as simply comic. The observatory, directed by Marc-Auguste Pictet from 1790 to 1819, served both chronometry and meteorology, the latter of intense interest to the Alpine wanderer like Töpffer, although, again, his description of the weather nonetheless remains poetic and visual rather than scientific, and the predictions he encountered were folkloristic rather than scientific.

New planets were being discovered, notably Neptune in 1846, and Halley's comet passed close to the earth in 1835, eliciting observations still useful when it returned in 1986. There was a total eclipse of the sun in 1842, visible in southern France and northern Italy. The Genevans knew all about the discoveries of the famous Herschels, a name that appears on the telescope in the manuscript of *Festus*, to be later deleted. The claim of human inhabitants and constructions on distant planets, posited by Herschel himself, was taken seriously by some.[54] Rapidly advancing astronomical science gave zest to the folk imagination that had always wanted to believe in extraterrestrials, as it still does, and the "man in the moon" was even conjured up by the likes of William Blake. The idea of a creature landing from some strange planet, which the Professor names Psyche and its denizens psychiots, lies at the core of *Monsieur Pencil*.

Time in modern physics is now regarded as no absolute concept, but dependent on a frame of reference. Fictional time has always relied on this. Time in Töpffer's comic albums is a malleable substance, as it would be in Lewis Carroll and Einstein. It seems, as with the great musicians, to be both compressed and dilated. The Swiss throws into chaos the ideal notion that the physical laws of the universe, such as those governing planets, winds, gravity, and human motion in space, behave like clockwork mechanisms. Rodolphe married into a family of watchmakers, and his own father started out as engraver for watches. Watchmaking was poetically described in a Société des Arts précis as the "art of representing by the movement of a little machine, the perfectly uniform revolution of our planet earth upon itself, despite the contention of a multitude of variable interferences which tend to disturb the regularity of this movement."[55] Töpffer saw the constitution and institutions of Geneva as fitted with "wheel-trains (*rouages*) that have the perfection of the watches that are its renown." With the local looming revolution, alas, "this chosen piece, of so rare a manufacture, with its ingeniously arranged mechanism [threatens to] fall into the hands of brutal men ten times as likely to break it as perfect it or

improve its movement."[56] But his own handling of time in the comic strips is perfectly anarchic.

Sometimes Rodolphe gives time intervals with excessive precision, and comic-epic exaggeration; always, to be sure, an easy way to get a laugh. Otherwise, and in general, time in the picture stories is atmospheric, vaguely flowing in different directions and apt to play jokes in the form of bizarre coincidences that serve to bring together characters accidentally or arbitrarily separated by twists of plot. The twists of time can have the most unfortunate effect, as when the time (surely short, but deliberately unspecified) taken for Vieux Bois to return home, let out his dog, and then return to the church where he is to be wed, results in the bridal party abandoning the church, and the wedding altogether. A more curious instance, that of time running as it were in two separate dimensions, one fast, the other slow, is found in the same story. The dunking of the Rival on a waterwheel, which cannot realistically last more than a few minutes at the most, is intercut in a prolonged (and most perfectly cinematic) fashion, with the escape of Vieux Bois and the Beloved Object from the river, the disposal of the chaise, retreat up into the hills, and the prolonged enjoyment of the pastoral life, allowing time for the Beloved Object to get so fat that she has to return in a custom-built palanquin—all this before the Rival can free himself of the waterwheel.

Fancifully, one might see in the consciously wavering and trembling ductus of the frame-lines, which should be straight and were straightened in all the unauthorized copies, and which represent time intervals, a fracturing of the normal sensation of passing time. The occasional eruption of these frame-lines into squiggles and even little doodled faces suggest, subliminally, the suspension or diversion of time, a "time-out."

Töpffer's satire is of course directed against a certain kind of scientist rather than science as such, against their gullibility, timorousness, egotism, and proneness to monomania and madness. Competi-

Le Maire leur dit que c'est des bêtes d'eau sa-
lée, et qu'il y a quelque chose à gagner, mais
il ne leur en offre rien, ensorte qu'ils vont
à Prévot l'écrivain public.

Prévot, l'écrivain public, leur dit que c'est
des fausses couches de Baleine, et que
ça ne vaut rien à manger, par rap =
port à ce que ça n'a pas eu son excrois-
sance, et qu'on ne mange le veau qu'a-
près huit mois. Ensorte que, moyennant
trois sous, il leur écrit une lettre pour
Favras le Botaniste, qui demeure à huit
lieues de là.

Favras, le Botaniste, leur dit que c'est une pulpe fila-
menteuse qui a recouvert une noix du Micisispi, et il leur
en donne deux écus patagons.

76.

1-26. The Mayor tells them that they [the wigs] are salt-water creatures, and sends them on to Prévot the Public Scrivener. Who tells them that they are aborted whale foetuses. Sends them to Favras the botanist, who tells them that they are the filamentary pulp covering a Micisispi nut, and gives them two Patagonian écus (*Festus* 76).

tive in the worst way, they can be totally crushed by the slightest reversal to their hopes. There is embedded here a mocking perception of the role of science in society, with its public, competitive aspect that Töpffer saw as corrupting the Parisian literati. This perception must have appealed to Goethe, the scientist and critic of science, when he saw the manuscript version of *Festus*. Astronomers, of all scientists, may be said to literally keep their heads (or eyes) in the clouds, and were a favorite butt of caricaturists, eyes glued on the telescope lens, for instance, while their assistants made out with their wives behind their backs.

In *Festus*, the astronomers are logically exploded into the sky where they dwell in their hearts and minds, astride their telescope. The scientific debate that any important scientific discovery or theory, however crackpot, could engender is coded by Töpffer as a quarreling as mindless and instinctual, in its way, as the Pavlovian behavior of the Force Armée in the same story. But this flailing of competing hypotheses in the sky turns into natatory motions in the water when their furious proponents finally descend into the sea, which keeps them afloat and saves them, perversely, from drowning (69). It is their continued fighting on land that disturbs the peace and puts them in jail—would that one could thus shut up the real-life disturbers of intellectual peace.

Meanwhile, a trio of washed-up astronomers' wigs—themselves symbols of old-fashioned thinking—becomes of a controversial scientific interest among the public at large in a way that parodies the market mechanism apt to attach value to anything novel and exotic, raising it progressively up the social and scientific hierarchy and turning fanciful hypothesis into absolute truth. The peasants who fish up the wigs recognize their possible value as scientific curiosities and take them to the local mayor, who identifies them, vaguely, as saltwater creatures but who offers no money, so they go to the Public Scrivener, who interprets them as inedible whale foetuses and sends them for a fee, with a letter of recommendation, to a distant botanist who tells them that they (the wigs) are the filamentary pulp-covering of a Mississippi ("Micisispi") nut, and pays the peasants "two Patagonian écus" (76, fig. 1-26). The botanist then takes them to the head keeper of the Royal Museum, who recognizes them as three hitherto unclassified magnificent crustaceans and buys them for twelve patagonian écus each. The head keeper sells them to the (his!) museum for 1,000 écus each, where they become the admiration of distinguished foreigners.

The delusions of the astronomers are severe, but ultimately harm only themselves. Those of the Professor in *Pencil* cause great mental and bodily harm to the poor Monsieur Jolibois. This comic chain starts innocently, and poetically enough, in an image easily understood as a metaphor of the flight of the poetic imagination: Monsieur Pencil, artist as his name implies, finds his landscape drawing whisked off by a playful little zephyr (i.e., chance, fate) that goes on to suck up heavier, human bodies, leading to the Professor's delusion that an inhabitant from a new planet he calls Psyche has landed like a meteor among his lettuces. He puts his scientific data into a cage, prepares to dissect him like a corpse, scientifically interprets his natural human reactions as demonstrations of extraterrestriality, then sends him in a crate to a scientific congress in Paris, causing him to suffer despair and fumigation en route, which results in his being treated as a monster when he escapes from the crate. Himself a physical and moral coward, the Professor shows no

remorse when he discovers that his Psychiot is in fact a normal human being and someone's lost husband, and when finally disabused, simply and childishly expresses his being "fed up" with his "difficult" subject.

He behaves somewhat like the mad scientist of popular culture, which originates in the Romantic era with Mary Shelley's *Frankenstein* (1818), written in Geneva. This Gothic novel offers a panegyric on modern chemistry, pays tribute to the power, indeed the terrifying, demonic power of science, which claims new and limitless domains, commanding thunder and earthquake, ascending the heavens . . . as does literally the mad ambition of the astronomers in *Festus* and the Professor in *Pencil*. The escape of Jolibois from the crate, and being taken for the Beast of Gévaudan, is comparable, in its comic way, to the escape of the monster from the clutches of his creator Dr. Frankenstein. (In the Kenneth Branagh film version of 1994, incidentally, the Creature is taken for the cholera in person by the townsfolk of Ingolstadt.)

Apart from a youthful stay in Paris, Töpffer never himself traveled very far: to Genoa, Venice, and Milan at the furthest. He may not have dreamed of exploring the sources of the Nile, like Trictrac, but he must have envied those able to visit London, the home of Hogarth and Cruikshank. In his writing, he exoticized on a smaller scale the Alps near Geneva, where you could get lost, suffer privations, and encounter primitive and sometimes hostile tribes with strange habits. Trictrac's adventures, which spin quite out of control and in which the hero himself gets strangely disappeared in the jungle of a plot, parody the unpredictable twists and turns of chance attending exploration of distant parts. Töpffer rather liked the idea of getting lost, and it is not hard to see his caricatural novels as the imaginary travels of a relatively sedentary hometown and housebound schoolmaster.

Medical doctors, with lawyers, among all the professions (discounting politicians) offer the broadest butts to cartoon and caricature. Hogarth viewed them (indistinguishable from quacks) with something like venom, as Töpffer must have known. Stendhal, for one, thought Geneva had good doctors and hospitals, although the Académie included no medical school, which is why it did not call itself a university. Dr. Maunoir, an ophthalmology specialist, was a friend, although Töpffer did not let him treat his own poor eyesight. Unlike his disciple Cham, who was a hypochondriac sucker for patent medicines, Töpffer's attitude was very much let ill alone. At the very end, when the symptoms were frightening, he consented unwillingly to depart for the baths at Lavey and Vichy, the waters of such spas then being considered a panacea. They did his enlarged spleen no good at all, and only increased his suffering.

It may be that there was a now lost medical *Dr Saitout* (Dr. Knowall), for Töpffer listed the title as one of the several stories he had done or in progress in 1831.[57] At the end of his life, while he was taking the waters at Vichy, he was being discreetly encouraged by his cousin Dubochet in Paris to use his observation of the many doctors there as the material for some comic tale. He was, alas, too weak even to start one. As it is, we have only a jab at lethal chiropody as practiced by Albert on the run, and a series of planned episodes from the text-only, full-length scenario of Claudius Berlu, involving giant poultices, cataplasms, fumigations, pills and draughts, and a mumbo-jumbo of assorted diagnoses and remedies.[58] There is a sinister moment when Berlu, the nominal protagonist (the real protagonist may be a poultice), gets stuck in prison as a thief, and the more he tries to explain himself and tell what has happened, the more he is treated as delirious, in effect mad. The incarceration of inconvenient relatives was a continuing scandal of the time. The Claudius Berlu scenario may have been abandoned in favor of *Trictrac*, where there are similar switches between real and supposed thieves, and a similar and funnier comedy of medical affectations. Unlike his colleagues in Hogarth, the doctor in *Trictrac* is not visually caricatured but his methods are. Faced with a "simple" matter of a switched identity, he gabbles away, always claiming (when identities are switched again) that he expected the change, and if anything goes wrong, it is someone else's fault.

In Töpffer's comic strips there are three incidents of people flung into and traveling by air: in *Pencil* by the uplift of a subterranean wind, and in *Festus* twice, by the force of the arms of a windmill and then by a steamship explosion. Like Cyrano de Bergerac in mid-seventeenth century, Töpffer used fantastic aerial travel to satirize astronomers. Closer to home, the skyborne antics in *Festus* and *Pencil* were surely stimulated by the real-life travel in balloons initiated by Montgolfier in 1783, and the considerable public attention, manifested also in caricature, that these fantastic, courageous, and perilous enterprises aroused. The ridiculous peasant attack on the giant telescope descended from the skies in *Pencil* had a real-life precedent in the early (1783) unmanned flight of a balloon launched in Paris that landed in a field at some distance, and was torn to pieces as a live monster by rustic scythes, flails, and pitchforks.[59]

There is a curious, unpublished pictorial precedent to Töpffer's fantasy in a series of narrative pictures by the English caricaturist Edward Burney, who planned a scenario for which nineteen pictures but no text survive, except the title *Adventures of Q.Q. es'Qre* (Q.Q. Esquire). The hero in his homemade aerial machine is launched by cannon-blast into the air, where he remains suspended by means of a huge umbrella. Like Cryptogame he lands on a whale and is cast adrift in the ocean, before being picked up by sailors in a Viking ship.[60]

One cannot but wonder whether Nadar (after Cham Töpffer's best imitator)—who characterizes Montgolfier's as a "sublime and execrable discovery," became the first balloonist-photographer, and referred to the "zigzag" researches of balloon science—was not touched by Töpffer's hapless ethereal travelers.[61]

Chapter Two

GOETHE, TÖPFFER, AND A NEW KIND OF CARICATURE[1]

The repressive Restoration Europe of the 1820s was not conducive to caricature or freedom of the press. Even in England there was a decline in both. The Revolution in France of July 1830, promising new freedoms, injected new energies to which Töpffer, who had already embarked on his picture stories, responded in his own way. At first hesitant to publish, Töpffer found a sponsor in an unexpected place, and by chance: Johann Wolfgang von Goethe in Weimar. It is a remarkable fact that Töpffer's little hobby, his new branch of narrative caricature, first practiced to amuse schoolchildren, family, and friends, should have found imprimatur in one notorious for his hostility to caricature, largely for its association with personal, social, and (worst of all) revolutionary polemics. Despite the all-encompassing generosity of his mind, Goethe, as he grew older and more conservative, became increasingly averse to a branch of art that seemed to negate the beautiful and the classical, his most cherished aesthetic precepts. There were of course different kinds of caricature, but Goethe tended to suspect them all. Despite its success as a kind of social parlor game, Goethe feared portrait and social caricature as a socially disruptive force, and his heroization of Napoleon, by far the most caricatured figure of the era, deepened an instinctive prejudice. He could not even bring himself to like Hogarth,[2] such a favorite in Germany and celebrated by Lichtenberg's extravagant commentaries; not even his friend and associate J. H. Ramberg's harmless social game of impromptu caricature could shift him from his view that "sa-

tirical caricatures" were "greatest destroyers of art, taste and morals." In his monarchical conservatism he was not unhappy to see the journal of his fellow Weimarian F. J. J. Bertuch, *London und Paris*, which systematically ran small versions of Gillray cartoons, expire under the savage Napoleonic censorship that could be lethal.[3] The "Napoleon of European Letters" applauded Bonaparte's conquest of Germany, lamented his defeat, and proved indifferent to the terrible slaughters, atrocities, and suffering Napoleon had caused, even when they affected Weimar itself.

There is little doubt that Goethe's praise of Töpffer was sincere, and not given just to help the friend of his friend Soret. Goethe enjoyed his role as a patron because he believed that literature, like Napoleon's army, was a "career open to talents." Like Napoleon he liked to promote the worthy, seeking out the marshal's baton in the corporal's knapsack. Toward the end of his life, however, he became less accessible—even so attractive a young talent as Thackeray had difficulty getting access in person, as we note below—and bringing Töpffer into the great man's mental sanctuary took the combined efforts of his literary factotum and secretary, Johann Peter Eckermann, and Frédéric Soret, a former school friend of Töpffer from Geneva, now tutor to the duke of Weimar's children and translator of Goethe's *Metamorphosis of Plants*.

Eckermann, after traveling to Italy with Goethe's son, returned to Weimar via Geneva, where he met Soret's friend Töpffer, and encouraged Soret when he was, somewhat later, also in Geneva, to

127.

128

Cependant, Mr Cryptogame fait neuf fois le tour du pont sans trouver d'issue.

auvenue sur le pont, Elvire se met à la poursuite de Mr. Cryptogame.

132.

133.

134

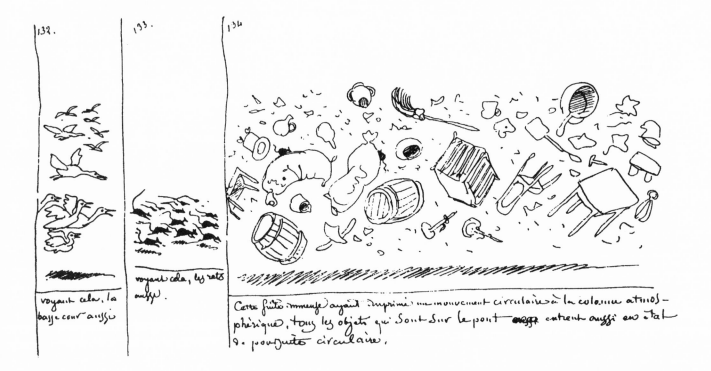

voyant cela, la basse cour aussi

voyant cela, les rats aussi.

Cette fuite immense ayant imprimé un mouvement circulaire à la colonne atmosphérique, tous les objets qui sont sur le pont entrent aussi en état de poursuite circulaire.

2-1. M. Cryptogame runs around the deck, Elvire chases him, the Abbé flees and chases at the same time, without understanding anything. Seeing which the Moors too. Seeing which, the domestic animals too. Seeing which the farmyard animals too. Seeing which, the rats too. This immense flight lends a circular movement to the atmospheric column, all the objects on the deck enter into the state of circular chase (*Cryptogame* 127–34).

bring back some of Töpffer's works, which he had seen lying on a salon table in the author's house. Amusing travel diaries and funny picture stories seemed just the thing to distract the lonely octogenarian during the long winter evenings of 1830–31, when he was still depressed after the recent French revolution. The response was immediate and favorable: "*Cryptogame* arrived at the moment when Eckermann was with the old Patriarch," Soret wrote to Töpffer at the end of January 1831. "M. de Goethe found your nature-lover very amusing, and what seemed to strike him most, apart from the originality of the drawings, was your talent for exhausting a subject, for getting the most out of it, for example, when all the inhabitants of the vessel down to the furniture follow the rotatory movements of Cryptogame, when everything freezes and unfreezes as it were in the spirit of imitation . . ." (fig. 2-1).[4]

Festus, which Soret presented personally on December 27, was also a great success. "We looked at Töpffer's drawings together, his *Adventures of Dr. Festus*, which gave his Excellency extraordinary pleasure. 'That is really too crazy,' he kept repeating, 'but he really sparkles with talent and wit; much of it is quite perfect; it shows just how much the artist could yet achieve, if he dealt with modern [less frivolous][5] material and went to work with less haste, and more reflection. If Töpffer did not have such an insignificant text [i.e. scenario] before him, he would invent things which would surpass all our expectations.'"[6] Goethe seemed to return to Töpffer's albums as a respite from the pain of the recent death of his son; he came to regard young Soret in a filial light, and listened readily to his report on Töpffer's life and character, stressing his youth, his lack of ambition, his humble schoolmastering, his skills as an amateur artist and playwright-actor-director—all miniaturized versions of tasks Goethe himself had performed as minister of culture and theater director of the duchy of Weimar.

Goethe kept the two albums a few days, "looking at only ten pages or so at a time, resting afterwards, because, he said, he risked getting an indigestion of ideas." Pressed to render a written (dictated) judgment, he praised the artist warmly as "the most fertile inventor of combinations," for being able to "draw multiple motifs out of a few figures" and for his "innate, gay and ever-ready talent."[7] From the context it is evident that Goethe was more interested in Töpffer's caricatures than in his various prose pieces. He even promised, busy as he was, to cast on paper some ideas that the caricature albums suggested to him, but nothing came of that. Soret also showed the albums successfully at the ducal court and to his pupil, the young prince, then about thirteen years old, who "spent whole hours making faces à la Cryptogame"; but Goethe does not seem, oddly, to have asked Soret to show them to his grandchildren, about the same age.

This approval from above, reported back to Töpffer, inspired him to complete two new albums, which he offered to send but held back, probably unsure whether certain political jibes in them might cause offense and whether more serious work in prose was not called for. Finally he sent both, *Jabot* and two *Voyages*, that he illuminated specially. They arrived, happily, the day after Christmas and in time for the New Year (1832) festivities. Prodded to comment on the landscape drawings, Goethe seemed to prefer *Jabot*, even showing signs of wanting to keep it for himself, somewhat to Soret's alarm. He expatiated on the "strange" and "witty" album, the "little baroque novel," with its "spook" (*Gespenst*) of a hero capable of "always producing his impossible personality anew in the most varied forms."[8] Soret added, in his report back to his friend, some detailed remarks of his own, particularly praising the scene of Jabot's public fart—which Töpffer cut from the published version.

Meanwhile, Töpffer made his first public literary hit back home, a whimsical, Sternean semiautobiographical reverie called *La Bibliothèque de mon oncle*. He sent a copy of this to Goethe, embellished with drawings made specially, but it arrived too late:

GOETHE, TÖPFFER, AND A NEW KIND OF CARICATURE

Goethe had died six days before, on 22 March. But Goethe's imprimatur of Töpffer was soon printed in a long article by Soret and Eckermann in the last, posthumous issue of *Kunst und Alterthum*, a journal Goethe edited and co-wrote. The article is true to Goethe's own, prophetic preference for Töpffer's caricature, in that although entitled "On the pen-drawings of Rodolphe Töpfer [sic]" it deals almost exclusively with the caricatures.[9] It does so in a way that bridges the gap between the patriarch's antipathy to most caricature and his approval of this new and innocent newcomer. With no other purpose than to amuse his extended family, his inner circle of boys and friends, in a spontaneous and imaginative recreation where all participated, it was all part of a convivial game, so different from the socially and politically hostile English caricature.

Goethe's imprimatur of Töpffer, while it was quickly published in *Kunst und Alterthum*, did not make it, as it should have, into Eckermann's two-volume *Conversations with Goethe* when they appeared in 1836. Töpffer must have been disappointed and puzzled. The reason seems to be that the panjandrum's possibly odd enthusiasm for a still largely unknown artist and writer did not fit in with Eckermann's grand scheme of presenting the "great, healthy, true Goethe" that Carlyle recognized in Eckermann's portrait.[10] The omission was made good in a third, oddly fated volume of more *Conversations with Goethe*, a bric-à-brac volume that came out only in 1848, after Töpffer's death. It is, I suspect, Eckermann's original omission that prompted Töpffer to publish his own, ironic self-review of *Jabot*, published in Geneva the previous year (see below, p. 60).

A new kind of caricature

Töpffer's was indeed a new kind of caricature, in style, spirit, and narrative form, all apt to tickle Goethe's fancy. It was more innocent than Gillray

but retained some of the impishness and whimsy of Cruikshank, who was much admired in Germany and France. The immensely versatile Goethe must also have appreciated the versatility of the young Genevan, artist, writer, and artist-writer in one, new medium. He would have admired the spontaneity and ease with which he wrote and drew, the freedom of his stroke that he admired in Delacroix's lithographic illustrations to his *Faust* and that he considered the very hallmark of creative genius. For all that they gave him "an indigestion of ideas," Goethe must have valued the improvisatory, digressive, parenthesis-prone qualities that Töpffer's writing and particularly comic albums share with Laurence Sterne, whom Goethe admired exceedingly. Sterne himself, in his masterpiece, *Tristram Shandy*, drew a whimsical diagram of his crazy narrative line which fits Töpffer's too:

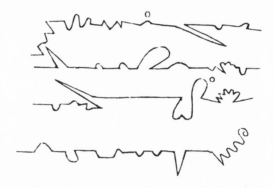

Did the very name *Festus* strike a chord with Goethe, as he worked on the second part of his *Faust* (completed July 1831)? Both Goethe's *Faust* and Töpffer's *Festus* are engaged in a quest for knowledge, both are wanderers cast adrift from society; both are at the mercy of uncontrollable forces. Although one hesitates to press comparison between such totally different works too far, there are formal and philosophical similarities between *Festus* and *Faust II*: lack of unity, a certain willful incomprehensibility, maybe a touch of mysticism in Goethe comparable to Töpffer's absurdism. And there is even a shared reluctance to publish for fear of critical misunderstanding.

Certain broad (impersonal) satirical themes must also have appealed to Goethe: scientific vanity and fraud, the perils of excessive ambition, and the social disorder resulting from these. Goethe, the brilliant scientific amateur and controversialist, had met his share of vanity, obstinacy, and ignorance of the kind Töpffer ridicules in *Festus*, as he had had his fill of Jabot-like social upstarts. For Goethe the real revolution in Paris July 1830 was not the one that toppled king Charles X, but the triumph in a great debate of Geoffroy Saint-Hilaire over Georges Cuvier, which promised to be Goethe's own. As precursors of Charles Darwin, who in fact paid tribute to their work on the origin of species, Geoffroy and Goethe were links in the chain of a theory that was to have decisive effect on the development of the picture story and comic strip in the second half of the century, notably in the very Darwinian Wilhelm Busch. It is almost as if the fledgling Geoffroy–Goethe theory of evolution were refracted, crazy-quilt-like, through Töpffer's visual narratives, which adapt to environmental circumstances and accidents, developing, spiraling, metamorphosing in so complex an interrelation as to defy rational investigation.

Goethe encountered *Festus* at the very moment he was preparing for observations of Halley's comet, as well as being occupied with the Geoffroy–Cuvier debate. Töpffer's mockery of the astronomers' furious flailing of rival hypotheses, which became a scientific phenomenon in themselves, echoes Goethe's own sentiments about the egoism of scientists. "The questions of science are often questions of existence. A simple discovery can make a man famous and establish his career. Which is why in science too there reigns this great bitterness and this tenacity and jealousy over the discoveries of others."[11] Scientists idolized their errors, became blind and deaf through excess of erudition and hypothesizing. This is what Töpffer is saying, too.

Goethe the botanist must have personally known the likes of Monsieur Cryptogame, whose passion for tulips sends him off, abandoning all, to America. The primary propulsion was of course the urge to escape his fiancée, and the breathless concatenation of causes and effects that succeed each other is a parody of physical laws and obeys a certain logic of its own. By a perverted law of physics motion is contagious, like a disease. One episode infects the next, and frenzied energy is transmitted like an electric current from person to person, and person to object, in an ever-descending hierarchy. This process is spectacularly illustrated by the pursuit around the ship's deck, and the episode when Cryptogame leaps overboard, to be followed in turn by Elvire, captain, crew, animals, and finally rats (fig. 2-1). Both episodes were cited at admiring length by Eckermann and Soret in their *Kunst und Alterthum* review, and noted by Goethe.

The idea of "rotatory movements" following each other "in the spirit of imitation" certainly relates to Goethe's theory of plant morphology. The whole narrative method of Töpffer, which is not linear, so to speak, but spiral, might fancifully be related to Goethe's controversial theory of the spiral tendency of plants, which so preoccupied him in his late years, a theory extended, by Goethe himself or his followers, to encompass historical evolution in its broadest sense. Goethe the botanical theorist seems to have been intrigued by the way Töpffer allowed incidents to unfold layer upon layer like the petals of a flower, "draw[ing] multiple motifs out of a few figures" in the most "fertile combinations," leading to an "exhaustive" kind of self-fulfillment.

Another chase in *Cryptogame*, in which the Abbé, fleeing with a beam tied to his leg, causes a forest fire, which causes a stampede, and so on (fig. 2-2) summons up the laws of chain reaction and friction. And what happens when, in the old conundrum, an irresistible force (Elvire) meets an immovable object (Cryptogame)? A terrible explosion. Alternatively, one may see the absurd spec-

GOETHE, TÖPFFER, AND A NEW KIND OF CARICATURE

2-2. The Abbé fleeing in fear of being hanged, the friction sets the beam on fire. The fire catches the grasslands, and the lions leave their lairs. All the inhabitants of the countryside flee towards Algiers, unnoticed because people are busy electing a new dey (*Cryptogame* 164–67).

tacle of the sexes reacting on one another like opposite poles of a magnet as the necessary corrective of the romantic cliché of perfect fusion. Goethe, who had transcended the romanticism of his youth, would also have enjoyed Töpffer's mockery of a tired romantic scenario, when it is not by any intentionality but only by a preposterous chain of accidents that Jabot achieves his goal of marrying an aristocrat.

Given the differences of political outlook to be expected between the liberal-republican Töpffer around 1830 and the conservative-aristocratic Goethe, it is worth considering what Töpffer chose *not* to send to Weimar, notably the anti-militarist *Monsieur Pencil*. This, with its proposition that the accidental waggling, by a little dog, of a telegraph could precipitate economic chaos, strikes by starving workers, widespread social agitation, and murderous repression by vicious soldiers, all referable, of course, to the real revolutionary agitation of and since July 1830, could have appeared downright frightening to the nervous old sage, troubled as he

was by that revolution and its aftermath. The antics of the Force Armée punctuating *Festus* are mere farcical interludes compared with the sustained threat of European war in *Pencil*.

Indeed, there may have been an element of active reassurance, to a conservative like Goethe, in showing soldiers who are more likely to stick their bayonets into trees than people. They act like automata (in *Pencil* they act with cruel deliberation), and as mindlessly as the whole village populations who in *Festus* throw themselves into the lake. The self-destruction is so extreme and arbitrary that it loses its threatening aspect. The groundless arrest of Mayor, Milord, and Milady for not having passports, their condemnation as Carbonari conspirators to perpetual imprisonment (42), and their miraculous escape succeed in defusing otherwise alarming ideas.

Some elements of religious satire in the albums seen by Goethe would also have been congenial to him and his Protestant, mildly anti-Catholic heritage: the superstitious, murderous monks in *Festus*, for instance, and the stupid, ever stupefied Abbé whom Cryptogame tries to inveigle into marrying Elvire.

Whatever the mixture of fun and satire, and however seriously the satire may have been meant or received, Goethe and other readers clearly appreciated the lack of real political malice à l'anglaise. Goethe would surely have agreed with a fellow German aesthetician, Friedrich Vischer (see Appendix B), that "the malice, the bitterness" associated with caricature is "volatilized in the light champagne foam of humor."

Chapter Three

JABOT, CRÉPIN, VIEUX BOIS

The praise of Goethe and the long notice in *Kunst und Alterthum* were not enough to persuade Töpffer to start publishing his comic albums. As his father had discovered, there was a very real risk to becoming identified with a genre of such low and dubious status as caricature, especially for one who had ambitions to become established as a serious, moral writer. Rodolphe's father had been very careful as to which of his satirical caricatures he had engraved and distributed; most of them, done in watercolor, circulated privately. He made enemies anyway, and he did not have his son's social ambitions. The flattering sobriquet attached to him early on as the "Genevan Hogarth" was meant to raise his status as a genre painter rather than satirist. His landscape and genre paintings were now less in demand, partly because of the new school of landscape painting his son was himself fostering as an art critic, and Wolfgang-Adam was beginning to be known as the father of Rodolphe.

For Rodolphe to go public with his comic albums was to jeopardize his reputation as a schoolmaster and educator. And he was now to acquire another, grander title: that of professor at the Genevan Académie, a university-level institution of high repute especially for its law and science faculties. When it was decided to improve its offerings in the modern humanities (that is, literature), Töpffer's initial appointment in 1832 as *chargé de cours* in *rhétorique et belles lettres* (modern literature), the equivalent of assistant professor in the United States today, was upgraded in 1835 to titular (or tenured) profes-

sor. The appointment, which some thought should have been opened to public competition, did not go through easily, for the candidate did not have demonstrated breadth in French literature; nor was he known for his classical learning, despite an undistinguished edition of Demosthenes he published as a very young man. In these circumstances, the likes of *Jabot* and *Festus* were little less than a handicap, and his opponents would deride him as the author of nothing better than caricature albums.[1]

An attack from outside, of the kind to which the Genevans were normally sensitive, reflected a strand of opinion prevalent for some years inside Geneva. In 1837 the Prussian Baron Adelbert von Bornstedt published a book of travel impressions called *Basreliefs*.[2] After the usual praise of the little city of Geneva for its geographical situation, political constitution, and culture, he passes to "Genevan criticism," its representative organ, the *Bibliothèque Universelle*, and its principal arts critic, Töpffer. Infuriated by Töpffer's attacks on French romantic literature, the Prussian inveighs at length against the "corner author [*Winkelautor*] who walks around on stilts," and is capably only of "little books" (including no doubt *Jabot*), "little phrases [*Sätzchen*] and little stylistic flourishes etc. . . . [and] lachrymose-moral pathos."

The Bornstedt attack cannot have much surprised the victim, who evidently met the man when he circulated in Geneva the previous year and excited in Töpffer instant loathing. A passage in a letter to his friend Auguste de la Rive can only be described as caricature in a Dickensian-Daumieresque mode: "It was like Satan fallen among saints. The glaze of his porcelain eye was crackled. Rogue [*gredouille* = *gredin*?] of a man. False gaze, pallid cheek, forehead like a firecracker, tartuffian smile, 19-bladed tongue tipped with darts and bile, pointed chin, face-puller, like his soul. Fossilized, impious, moralist and licentious, friend by calculation, hateful, naturally jealous, important and useless, egotistically devoted, incomparably egotistic like no one, pious, ladies' man, slanderous fellow, venomous, cordial . . . all the masks! Ouah!!"[3]

In May(?) 1833 Töpffer lithographed the whole of the *Histoire de Mr. Jabot* and printed some copies; these he distributed among selected friends but withheld from the bookstores.[4] He planned a more general distribution the following year, but again held back, partly because the printer and the printing were causing him trouble. A legal dispute with his printer, Freydig of Geneva, who meanwhile moved to Berne, over money owed and over drawings apparently spoiled that Töpffer wanted to exchange, testify to an ongoing, if hesitant and sporadic, concern for the birthing of his "problem child" during 1834 that came to a head early the following year.[5] Although he had printed and paid for several hundred copies, the author delayed until the summer, becoming quite angry with his printer, whom he accused of prematurely publicizing the book by letting a copy get around. This the printer indignantly denied, indicating that, having refused requests from reliable friends to take away the one copy he had retained per contract, "in order to show it to some ladies," it could be that this copy had been purloined from his office.[6] Töpffer seems to have been making a great fuss over small matters, but he was taking the question of distribution of his new invention very seriously. Just before the book went into the bookstores he was telling a correspondent, a state councillor no less, who had asked for copies of *Jabot*, that he could not gratify him in isolation because he "realized too well how much the high price of my scribbling [*barbouillage*], by keeping it rather rare in private houses, will really encourage pretty lucrative sales. So I have postponed the pleasure of giving it a distribution among friends which would throw twenty or so prematurely into circulation." At about the same time, he contemplated sending a dozen to Weimar, remembering how well the original had been received there.[7] A little suspense would pique curiosity and help sales.

In the course of 1836 we find him cheerfully admitting, almost boasting how little the album cost him compared with what he sold it for (ten times as much), and soliciting his friends and contacts for sales in distant parts—France, Germany, and England. It was a convenient way of cutting out the middleman, the bookseller, tiny as that markup was (one franc per ten-franc copy—40 to 50 percent is normal today). Becoming one's own publisher-distributor had worked well with Hogarth exactly a century before, less profitably for William Blake, and was always an aspiration of Cruikshank. "Keep the public hungry" was Töpffer's motto (*on a plus faim quand le gigot est petit*), with small quantities handed (sold) from friend to friend. We do not learn what his friends thought of this rather exploitative procedure for smoothing *Jabot*'s entrée into the world; but he, Jabot, would get on (in Paris) anyway, "thanks to his good manners."[8]

Jabot appeared with a pretense at anonymity, but with every page prominently initialed RT in a double scroll. Anonymity was a common form of alluring mystification adopted, for instance, by Walter Scott in his Waverley novels, when all Edinburgh knew the identity of the author, as all in Geneva knew who RT was. The protection of some pose of authorial modesty or reticence was certainly another factor with Töpffer, if not with Scott. He would, however, prove no more modest than Jabot himself. As a common social type Jabot was, to a degree, self-persiflage of the author, who compared himself to a Jabot who went around boasting of a

JABOT, CRÉPIN, VIEUX BOIS

11.

malheureusement Mr Jabot glisse au plus beau moment.

Ce qui cause du dérangement dans le reste de la galope.

3-1. Jabot slips at a critical moment. Which disturbs the galop (*Jabot* 11).

copy of *Kunst und Alterthum* in his pocket. Töpffer was not exactly a social upstart but, grandson of an immigrant tailor and son of an artist who never hid his petty-bourgeois status, he had married the daughter of one Geneva's wealthiest watchmakers, risen by his talent into the grande bourgeoisie, and indeed, through the Académie, into the ruling elite itself. *Jabot*, although not the first-drawn of Töpffer's picture stories, was a natural choice to make his public debut into caricature.

Jabot the social upstart was a safe, broadly recognizable satirical target, a familiar stereotype of Restoration satire, which sought revenge against the "career open to [low-class] talent" of the Napoleonic era. Society figures in *Jabot* as it was in reality, a finely regulated and delicately balanced dance; the satirist in Töpffer also sees it as a galop that a single literal faux pas can bring down like

dominoes (fig. 3-1). Society, diffused as a blithely hostile physical environment in which furniture and people are accomplices against any intruder, takes its revenge, in an impetus both collective and individual, by knocking the interloper about—as will ever be the destiny of petty-bourgeois ambition. We know that Jabot, the little buffoon rising from below, is out of place from the start, for he is in the first part of the story the only figure who is caricatured; and he himself caricatures the very language of politesse and romance. The ladies, and to a degree the gentlemen also, whose social milieu is that of Töpffer's own readers (with the inevitable complement of English aristocrats), are rendered in a pleasant, almost idealized form. Töpffer could not be accused of taking on society 'as a whole' like the radicals. As for the ridicule of a specific social abuse such as dueling, this would have struck a

3-2. Mr. Jabot cleaves the throng (*Jabot* 24).

Mr. Jabot fend la presse.

3-3. George Cruikshank, *Inconveniences of a Crowded Drawing-Room*, 6 May 1818, detail.

chord with many, and particularly Genevans, who had no sympathy for such follies.

But the familiarity of the satire and farcical development in the first part—we see echoes of Cruikshank's 1818 etching *Inconveniences of a Crowded Drawing Room* (figs. 3-2, 3-3)—yields in the second part to a chain of incidents that transcends conventional comic situations, becoming absurd and surreal. Small dogs—ever favorite characters in Töpfferian caricature—drag Jabot's bed into a Marquise's bedroom and back again; Jabot drinks candle-wax and tries to get into the Marquise's clothes. A conventional structure of courtship becomes overwhelmed by waves of mistaken identities and purposes and bizarre accidents. Here satirical logic devours itself, rather as the little mutts devour each other.

Jabot remained a favorite with the author, who frequently brings him on stage by name and in drawing in his *Voyages* (fig. 3-4)—three times in one of 1837[9]—as a pretentious and obnoxious type relying, clearly, on his general notoriety. Cautiously, Töpffer watched *Jabot*, an intruder of a new genre, seep into the public domain. Deciding its success was assured, he put a jocose review (by himself, signed with his initials) of the album into his magazine, the *Bibliothèque Universelle*, only in June 1837, probably in connection with his preparations to launch two more stories upon the public, *Crépin* and *Vieux Bois*. The review was crafted to assert and explain their originality with amusingly false modesty, in a wittily self-disparaging tone, and is worth quoting at some length, for it represents the first description we have of the new genre:

> This little book is of a mixed nature. It is composed of a series of autographed line drawings. Each of these drawings is accompanied by one or two lines of text. The drawings, without this text, would only be obscure in meaning; the text, without the drawings would mean nothing. The whole constitutes a sort of novel, all the more original in that it does

JABOT, CRÉPIN, VIEUX BOIS

M. JABOT de SEYSSEL 1833

3-4. Mr. Jabot de Seyssel, 1833; RT and co. met this little fellow who officiously gives contradictory advice, in Seyssel in Savoy (*Nouveaux Voyages en Zigzag*, 1854).

not resemble a novel more than anything else. The author of this little oblong volume has not made his name known. If he is an artist, his drawing is feeble, but he has a certain practice in writing; if he is a literary type, his writing is mediocre, but he does have, on the other hand, in the matter of drawing, a pretty amateur talent. If he is a grave man, he has some singularly funny ideas; if he is a funny man, he is not lacking on the serious side.

The review as a whole tries to transcend the critical norms, whether for literature or art. It wavers between the grave and the tongue-in-cheek and teasingly shifts the grounds of its argument. After citing the "anticritical" epigraph that prefaces all of his picture stories—"Go little book, and choose your public, for with crazy things, whoever doesn't laugh, yawns; whoever doesn't yield, resists, whoever reasons, is mistaken, and whoever wishes to keep a straight face, is free to do so"—the author makes a plea for a new kind of comedy that resides

not only in the character of the situation, but also in the briskness of the drawing itself—in other words, he calls for a new graphic aesthetic.

Crépin and education

Töpffer's is a graphic and narrative aesthetic that emerges by accident: the doodled head of the hero, which the author then interrogates for its potential. In his *Essay on Physiognomics* the author explains the system underlying the method of his drawing and how the idea of a story came to him, using the example of his systematically anti-systemic *Story of Mr. Crépin*:

> What gave us the idea of doing the whole story of Mr. Crépin was having found in a single stroke of the pen and quite by accident the face you see opposite. "Hey," we said to ourselves, "here is most decidedly a character one and indivisible, by no means good-looking nor cut out to be a success by his face alone, and of an upright rather than open intelligence, but a pretty good fellow otherwise and not a bad sort, endowed with some common sense, and who would be firm if he could trust his judgment, or be free enough in his proceedings. Beyond that, paterfamilias of course, and I'll wager that his wife frustrates him. . . . We tried her out, and indeed his wife did frustrate him in the education of his eleven children, falling in turn for all the foolish tutors, all the crazy methods, and all the phrenologists who happened by. And there you have the whole epic issuing much less from a preconceived idea than from a [facial] type and by chance.[10]

Mr. Crépin (lithographed by 29 July 1837), like *Jabot*, also has an a priori, readily identifiable target: education. This was a natural, of course, for one who earned his living as a school principal. Education was the buzzword of the day throughout Europe, as secular forces struggled for control against the church, as reformers sought democracy by educating the masses, and practical subjects like science and business were pitted against the ancient predominance of the Greco-Latin classics. The state tried to expand public education for all, both as a perceived good in itself and as a means of disciplining a restive population. Primary and secondary schoolteachers were generally badly paid and often badly trained and poorly motivated. Teaching at this level was, for many educated and semi-educated sons of the lower middle class, the profession of last resort. Daumier's series *Teachers and Kids* (1845–46) shows the teachers as narrow-minded, jesuitical petty tyrants, assistant teachers (*pions*) as contemptible, and the boys as oppressed and naturally rebellious (see fig. 3-7). But Daumier's cartoons are set in a low-class suburban or provincial public school, while Töpffer posits, at the end of *Crépin*, the upper-class ideal of the small private institution such as he himself operated, followed by the public *collège*. Monsieur Crépin eventually finds such a school in the teeth of the foolish educational antics of a series of private tutors hired by a gullible wife for his pullulating brood. It is a private tutor who is hired by the benevolent uncle in Töpffer's most celebrated story, *La Bibliothèque de mon Oncle* (1832). He must represent a figure known from Töpffer's youth: a pathetic, tyrannical figure called Ratin, prudish to absurdity, whose only redeeming feature is facial, a hairy wart on the nose that provokes in his pupil his favorite indulgence of "crazy laughter."

Without Daumier's humorous condoning of childish rebellion, Töpffer's distaste for conventional learning was such that, at one point in his *Voyages*, he virtually summons youth to rise against the tyranny of the classroom and take over the government. He does this in the euphoria of the mountain air and the relief of escaping schoolroom exercises that he must have sometimes felt as stifling as did the boys. The Alps are the real educators; "watch out governments, watch out schoolmasters, let their grammars

and manuals and dictionaries practice their trade armed to the teeth and seconded by police."[11] The officious guides and sterile guidebooks (the *itinéraires*) are a kind of infestation of "schoolmasters and schoolbooks" for tourists that should be driven out like bearers of contagious disease.

In a Geneva and a Switzerland attractive for its schools and rife with new educational theories, *Crépin* could not fail to strike a nerve. Töpffer, ever railing against systems, whether social, political, religious, or pedagogic, probably doubted even his own, insofar as he had one or admitted to one. The intelligent schoolmaster at the conclusion of *Crépin* claims no more than to apply common sense, to do his best, and to ask the students to do likewise. Töpffer the teacher is something of a mystery to us; we know him better as a kind of anti-teacher. The prolific author is remarkable, in a life full of autobiographical writing, for his reticence as to how he ran his school and taught his classes; he seems to have limited his own instruction to the classics and modern French literature, which he also taught at the Académie, without arousing much enthusiasm and without daring to admit more humor than some sarcasm. Töpffer taught in an age that was beginning to question the value of the classics as the alpha and omega of learning, echoing at every level the famous cry *qui nous délivrera des grecs et romains*. Deliverance had not come by the present writer's school days, when we were ground to a fine dust in Latin language and grammar—Latin literature did not exist—as a requirement for Oxbridge entrance. Töpffer himself, trained in the classics as the only route to the private tutoring that, as a youth, he expected (and feared) was to be his future, seems to have, halfheartedly and pro forma, resisted the reforms tending toward more a modern and practical education. A passage in one of his *Voyages* enlarges upon the evils attending too much classical learning, which was botched in a hurry, crammed students with too much too fast, and turned children into a mental hurdy-gurdy.[12]

Mr Bonichon met aussitôt les Crépin cadets à sa méthode qui consiste à étudier la physique dans les *Aventures de Télémaque*, à la manière Jacotot.

Mr Fadet met aussitôt les Crépin aînés à sa méthode qui consiste à tout réduire en nombres fractionnaires, selon un Système dont il est l'inventeur. 21.

3-5. Bonichon sets the younger Crépins to his method, that is, studying the *Adventures of Télémaque* in the Jacotot manner. Mr. Fadet also sets the elder Crépins to his method, reducing everything to fractions, according to a system he invented (*Crépin* 21).

Töpffer's attitude to the sacrosanct ancient imperial civilizations was marked by a deeply rooted patriotism and republicanism, and no doubt a certain iconoclasm: in Aosta, he denounced the ancient arch erected to the "divine" Augustus "to perpetuate his triumph over the Salasses, that is the enslavement of a proud, free and courageous people to the great brute of a people who regarded the universe as its legitimate prey, and the independence of others as an insult to its rights."[13] He preferred Arminius to Scipio, barbarians to Romans.

Töpffer resented being what he calls an academic "Fadet," kept in school supervising until ten o'clock while his friends dined and enjoyed after-dinner conversation. Soon a member of the ruling political as well as educational bureaucracy of Geneva, Töpffer saw himself as being ground down by petty academic tasks and disputes within the Académie, which he did his best to avoid—sometimes with ornate jesting, as his correspondence shows. The idea of any kind of systematic educational reform filled him with dismay, partly because it would require more bureaucracy. *Crépin* is the precipitate of that acute discomfort, which came to inform his whole aesthetic philosophy (or anti-philosophy), with the systemic thinking that lent itself to ossification, manic exaggeration, and intellectual and scientific (or pseudoscientific) intolerance. *Crépin* brings the earlier satires on physical scientists into the realm of pedagogic science—or pedagogic "science." The international success of Swiss and German educational theories failed to convince Töpffer that many of them were not bogus. Geneva itself was praised at the time as a pedagogic laboratory.[14] But fanaticism and intolerance had brought this experimentation into disrepute, with outrageous claims that one system—and one, its inventor's alone—was the panacea for all social ills.

Töpffer's angle is both broad and narrow. In *Crépin*, for instance, the Institut Parpaillozzi conjures up the famous Swiss Heinrich Pestalozzi; and the Farcet institution's method of using toys to "instruct by entertaining" (75) must refer to the innovations (still honored in schools bearing his name today) of Friedrich Fröbel, who had recently spent five years in Switzerland. But Töpffer's farther aim is to ridicule certain methods reducible, as Pestalozzi's and Fröbel's were not, to slogans such as that of the first (unnamed) tutor for the Crépin family, whose trick was to "proceed from the general to the particular." This kind of sloganeering is reminiscent of the Joseph Jacotot Method of Universal Instruction, the publicity for which featured the motto "All is in All," and which promoted learning by rote and the simple transference of principles, ideas, and facts from one domain to an entirely different one. Thus Töpffer shows the tutor Bonichon teaching the Crépin children physics using Fénelon's *Adventures of Télémaque*, "a la manière Jacotot" (21, fig. 3-5). In a *Voyage*, Töpffer notes in passing a mulberry tree "stunted by the Jacotot method."[15]

Crépin was certainly a provocative venture at such a time and in such a place, written as it was from within the pedagogic hierarchy, by one who relished the prospect of scandalizing "that band of hateful pedants" among his colleagues.[16] One such colleague duly scandalized by Crépin was the famous, notoriously humorless Swiss educator and agronomist Philipp Emmanuel Fellenberg, to whom Töpffer—mischievously?—sent a copy of *Festus*.[17] This "pontiff and missionary of the new pedagogic church" had been the object of several watercolor caricatures by Wolfgang-Adam done during Rodolphe's youth (1807–14), and it is worth dwelling a while with this figure as representative of progressive, "scientific" agricultural reforms twinned with repressive social and educational attitudes. Töpffer *père* had attacked

Fellenberg, already renowned in Europe for his model school and farm in Hofwyl near Berne, and for treating agriculture as an "object of [material] interest, amusement or speculation."[18] With the apparently laudable aim, more open to criticism now than then, of making agriculture more productive, he instituted a regime of military discipline among his workers, one "abusively paternalist" and highly centralized with an "observation tower" to facilitate constant surveillance, as in the new prisons. The school was oriented toward producing submissive, pious, fatalistic laborers. The Fellenberg reforms clearly threatened the ancient patterns of rural life, which were to be disrupted by a scientific agricultural revolution (the origins of today's horrendous factory farming) geared to profit the big gentleman farmer rather than the traditional small-holder. The peasants themselves were not consulted, and suffered. Fellenberg educated them to suffer in silence. This was the kind of "progress" Rodolphe, with his romantic idealization of rural life, abhorred. And yet Monsieur Crépin (or his wife) seemed to justify Fellenberg's dramatic charge that "parents are totally incompetent to educate their own children"[19]—or even choose a tutor for them.

With *Crépin* Töpffer engaged in an indirect form of self-advertisement not only for a school that does seem appealing to us today (and the brochures for which he parodied in his correspondence) but also for the Swiss type of small private school that stood in contrast to the archaic system of private tutoring with its vulnerability to pedagogic eccentricity. After running Maria Edgworth's *Practical Education* in twelve successive issues of the *Bibliothèque Britannique* 1798–99, the editors concluded by preferring a school to home tutoring. Fortunately for Mr. Crépin, the private tutors all discredit themselves before they can do permanent damage, and Crépin *père* finally, belatedly summons the strength to assert common sense and paternal authority against the nervous crises and idiotic enthusiasms of his wife. Madame Crépin is a satirical target in

Craniose etant descendu pour reprendre ses cranes de gredins est re=
poussé avec perte.

Craniose se refugie dans la loge du chien et les jeunes Crépin continuent leur partie.

3-6. Craniose come down to recover his rogues' skulls, is repulsed with losses. He takes refuge in the dog kennel, and the young Crépins go on with their game (*Crépin* 66).

PROFESSEURS ET MOUTARDS.

Un surveillant obligé de fermer l'œil sur la conduite de ses élèves.

3-7. Daumier: An assistant master obliged to turn a blind eye on the conduct of his pupils (*Le Charivari*, 24 December 1845).

Pour s'assurer de l'amende, le garde champêtre, enfile d'un coup de sabre les onze chapeaux et s'enfuit.

N'ayant plus leur chapeau, les jeunes Crépin jettent leur lorgnon, perdent leur tenue ; et font de mauvaises manières en retournant chez eux. [39]

3-8. To assure himself of his fine, the rural guard skewers the eleven hats and makes off. Lacking their hat, the young Crépins cast aside their lorgnettes, and cause chaos on their way home (*Crépin* 39).

herself, embodying some of the characteristics of the ill-educated nouveau riche: along with her husband, perhaps nouveau riche himself, she thinks private tutoring confers social status. Finally, after so much travail allowing for a good dose of knockabout farce, Monsieur Crépin seeks out a small private school and, after rejecting several that look as fraudulent as those mounted by the arch–caricatural fraudster of the age, Daumier-Philipon's Macaire, finds that of Mr. Bonnefoi (Goodfaith). There, rather than applying any system at all, teacher and student simply follow instinct and common sense.

In terms of the ascendant bourgeoisie's demands for cheap (or free) and practical education, Töpffer's satire flows in two, one might say contrary, directions: it opposes an economically extravagant, none-too-efficient, archaic, and aristocratic educational system, that of the private tutor, and at the same time ridicules methods devised for mass public education. The small private school, *type école Töpffer*, sought a happy medium between these two. The English boys at his school should have been happy not to be stuck in the English so-called public (i.e., large private boarding) school, where bullying by older or stronger boys and savage beating by the masters was still rife. This was the kind abhorrent to sensitive spirits such as Charles Dodgson (Lewis Carroll). Töpffer, whose sympathy was always with the children (so unlike Wilhelm Busch later!), shows them taking a just and semi-violent revenge on their oppressor (fig. 3-6).

Children, like adults, are both good and bad. A normal dose of high spirits and a pleasure in mischief can degenerate into the torment of sober citizens facing a mini-riot in the street (fig. 3-8) when the symbol of discipline, their hat (like the Mayor's uniform in *Festus*), is suddenly removed. This scene follows a series of travesties of "correct" behavior in society, which is reduced to a mechanical uniformity, military-style, of bowing, attitudinizing, the covering up a superior's fart or applauding his joke, handling of a lorgnon, and all the body language expressive of social hierarchy in which Grandville made his mark. The tutor whose expertise lies here (and only here) is a satire on education designed to produce all form and no substance, such as was associated with Jesuit schools.

Crépin, its first half a satire on educational systems, then turns to take issue with pseudoscientific theory whose potential social effects transcended the domain of education and shook the sacred Christian foundations of philosophy and religion themselves. Phrenology or craniology, or bumpology as it was also vulgarly called, claimed a theory based on the work of Franz Joseph Gall in the early years of the century, which purported to show how fixed character traits might be read from the protuberances of the skull. Overlaid upon, and in a sense even superseding, the well-established physiognomic theories of the eighteenth century relating to the shapes of the face, it had become a craze by the 1830s, only to resurface later in the century in the theories of the criminologist Cesare Lombroso. *Le système des bosses est éclos sous la bosse des systèmes* (the system of bumps was hatched under the bump of systems), as a Gavarni caption put it.[20] A critique of 1836 avers "It is, especially nowadays, a new psychological doctrine which claims nothing less than to renew the facts of science, of society, and virtually the world, and which, seeming to break all relations with the past, sets itself up as a sort of fiat lux."[21] The caricaturists, who could never dispense with physiognomic theory (and Töpffer had his own, new version of that), had a field day with phrenology; witness Cruikshank's *Phrenological Illustrations* of 1826 and Daumier with several series in the 1830s (fig. 3-9). Dickens, too, had his fun with a "phrenological" disquisition on doorknockers.[22] Somewhere between pseudoscience and

3-9. Daumier: The Cranioscope-Phrenologistocope. "Yes, that's it! I have the bump of ideality, and the causality of locativity, it's a prodigiosity" (*Le Charivari*, 14 March 1836).

popular social entertainment, phrenology was used like astrology is today. Lecture series, as Töpffer shows, were vastly popular, in Geneva as elsewhere. Aesthetically, phrenology exerted irresistible charms. Major writers like Balzac were fascinated by it and it seems that George Sand was seriously worried that her traveling companion, the scientific Genevan Adolphe Pictet, wanted to check her bumps.[23]

The pretensions of the phrenologists, like those of some pedagogues, reached absurd proportions, and the implications of the theory, especially in the domain of criminology, seemed to threaten the very concept of free will and the divinity of creation. Töpffer shows how the tutor Craniose, after being ejected from the Crépin household, descends to the life of the peripatetic lecturer and palpator of skulls among the stupid and vulgar. His doctrines lead to attitudes that could only foster and justify criminality, and in an adroit narrative link the murderer of a former Crépin tutor is acquitted by a jury under the influence of Craniose's theory of criminal predestination. Here Töpffer gets all too serious, and his picture-driven mode breaks down, with a large chunk of text holding up to ridicule the atheistic-determinist arguments in defense of the murderer.

Les Amours de Monsieur Vieux Bois

The Loves of Mr. Vieux Bois (Les Amours de Monsieur Vieux Bois), first published in 1837, resurrected Töpffer's very first picture story, as drafted ten years earlier. Though much less focused as social satire, Vieux Bois was topical on two fronts: First, it ridiculed certain aspects of Catholicism, as we have seen. Secondly it was a timely parody of literary romanticism, targeting the more traditional, simple-minded and archaic features of the movement whose new aggressive and more realistic mode Töpffer resisted. The pastoral delusions, heroic emotionalism, and wild incredibility of the old romanticism were also easy targets.

But Töpffer's political and cultural critique, his starting point and leitmotif in Vieux Bois, is not structural but tends to dissolve narrative and satirical logic in the development of the unique Töpfferian mode: surreal, freewheeling comedy. If there is structure, it is that of two intercut rhythms: the emotional and the physical, movement of the heart and the body. The amorous hypersensitivity of Vieux Bois, parodic in itself, is rendered extra absurd (or maybe hyper-logical) in that its target, the Objet Aimé or Beloved Object as she is invariably

called, a nameless Romantic abstraction, remains totally unresponsive to it and the hectic adventures it provokes. He is as wildly energetic as she is passively torpid. He is an irresistible force meeting an (almost) immovable object. A Rival, that indispensable component, serves to frustrate the hero's intentions and inflame his passion, but his role is somewhat incidental. Rather, chance and capricious coincidence wholly determine the manner of the capture, loss, and recapture of the Beloved Object, as well the sequence of Gothic paraphernalia: several elopements and abductions, a duel, a ghost, five attempted suicides, two attempted murders, plus an auto-da-fé, a burial alive, resuscitation, and two imprisonments, one civil and one monastic.

This is razzle-dazzle stuff that defies summarizing and mocks rational analysis. Let us limit ourselves to noting some improvements that the author made in the three versions, of 1827, 1837, and 1839, the last serving also to undercut the Aubert piracy that appeared that year. The published versions reinforce the parody of amorous susceptibility through comic emotional kaleidoscopes and refrains. They also emphasize the extent to which individual emotional self-indulgence can lead to a kind of frenzy, possibly (self)violence, where the hero, pleading his case, goes literally overboard (see figs. 1-12, 1-13). His jail sentence is correspondingly increased from one year (1837) to two (1839); and the judges who condemn him have increased in number and absurdity of expression, possibly under the impact of a famous Daumier design (figs. 3-10, 3-11). The social disorder caused by the beam from which Vieux Bois tries to hang himself and then drags into the street (first introduced in 1837) is much extended in the second edition, reaching the forces of order themselves (fig. 3-12). The beam seems to symbolize his desperate passion, as that tied inescapably to the leg of the Abbé in Cryptogame does that character's stupidity.

Here we first meet the pre-cinematic Töpffer. He improved upon certain brilliant graphic inventions, such as the refrain of the Rival being dunked by a

Mr Vieux Bois change de linge

Les héritiers ayant porté plainte, Mr Vieux Bois est arrêté comme prévenu de tapage diurne.

Mr Vieux Bois plaide lui-même sa cause. Il débute par un exorde rempli de calme et de noblesse.
41.

3-10. Mr. Vieux Bois changes his shirt. The heirs complain and Mr. Vieux Bois is arrested for daytime disturbance. Mr. Vieux Bois pleads his own cause. He starts with an exordium full of calm and nobility (*Vieux Bois* 41).

3-11. Daumier: The Legislative Belly (*Le Charivari*, January 1834).

Ce qui cause du désagrément au bourgeois.

10.

Et non moins à la garde nationale.

M. Vieux Bois touche presque à l'Objet aimé.

11.

3-12. Mr. Vieux Bois causes unpleasantness to the citizens. And no less to the National Guard. Mr. Vieux Bois almost touches the Beloved Object (*Vieux Bois* 10–11).

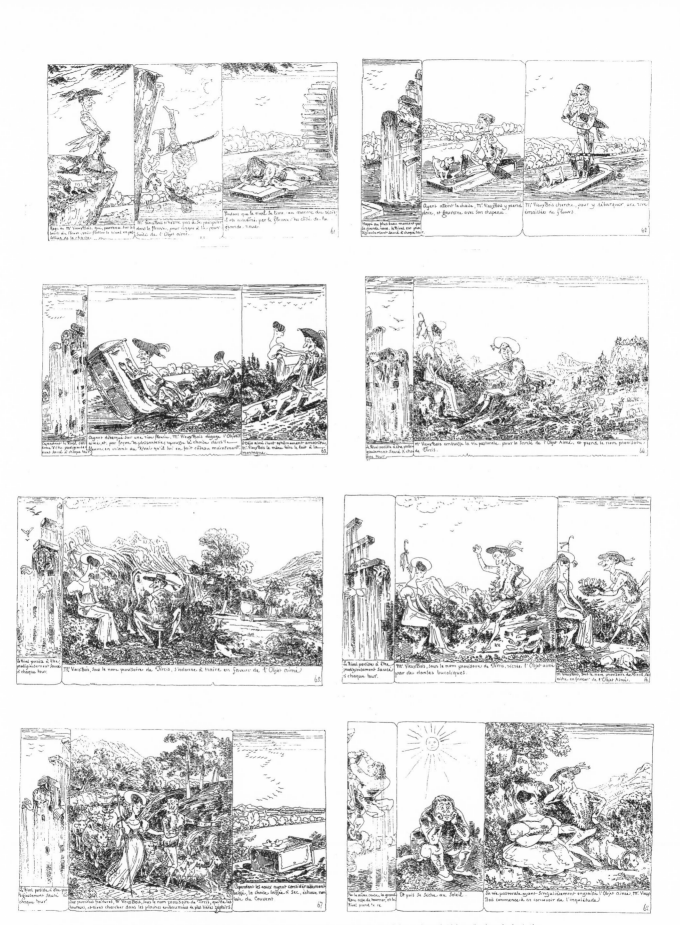

3-13. In a jealous rage Vieux Bois plunges after the Rival on the chaise. Charmed by the story of the Beloved Object (in the chaise), the Rival is caught in the waterwheel. Vieux Bois takes over the chaise, seeks a flowery bank, pushes the chaise back into the river, and with the Beloved Object embraces the pastoral life. Meanwhile, the Rival gets dunked at every turn of the waterwheel (*Vieux Bois* 61–68).

A

B

C

3-14. M. Vieux Bois introduces himself by the chimney into the bedroom of the Beloved Object, who is much afraid (versions from, left to right: the 1827 ms, the first printed edition of 1837, and (below) the revised edition of *Vieux Bois*, 1839.

waterwheel, intercut with graphically larger scenes of Vieux Bois pursuing his triumphant journey: humiliation confronting triumph. Added as a quartet of almost identical scenes in 1837, in 1839 this refrain became a septet (61–68, fig. 3-13). The counterpoint offered by Vieux Bois's ugly little mutt of a dog has also been enhanced. When he is the unwitting cause of his master's missing his wedding and losing his bride, he shows his feeling about it all by lifting his leg against the church wall. His behavior and expression on the roof,

where he runs the gamut of canine pathos—at first horribly emaciated, then grotesquely paunchy—is almost a subplot in itself (51–53). Abrupt changes of shape, to which the Beloved Object is also subject, an embryonic device here of cartoon animation, are the counterpart to the sudden emotional transformations.

Comparison of three versions of the scene where the hero descends the chimney into the Beloved Object's bedroom allows us to track not so much improvement as the author's fear of violating decency. In the drawing the Objet Aimé, animated for once, hiding under the bed exposes to the full her thinly draped backside; in the 1837 edition she is partly protected by the bed coverlet, and in 1839 more completely so (fig. 3-14).

Designed, as Töpffer says in his second *Jabot* self-review of 1839,[24] to counter the deplorable Aubert piracy, the second edition of *Vieux Bois* with *des changements et des augmentations considérables* also testified to Töpffer's increasing self-confidence in his new genre and his sense that it had made its wider mark. *Jabot* was perhaps too tightly organized to allow of changes and additions in a second edition, although he did intend to do one to replace the original edition, now sold out, as soon as he had finished refurbishing *Vieux Bois*.[25] Töpffer deplored, at some length, the "honorably boring and faithful manner" of the piracy. But the real Jabot had inserted himself successfully into society, entered the drawing rooms of the public world. Originating in a private and restricted social conviviality, *Jabot* with *Vieux Bois* was braving it out in the Parisian salon against an impostor. Jabot the prototypical social upstart and *Jabot* the new artistic genre were both social catalysts reflected in and reflecting upon each other. Töpffer ends his first *Jabot* review "All in all, M. Jabot is an amusing book, poorly printed, very expensive, and in its place above all in a salon. For in a salon, all men become more or less Jabots, all, more or less, *think they ought* . . . and it is very entertaining to contemplate them as they laugh, or *think they ought* to laugh at the little story. Like a pleasant fellow who laughs to see his own face in the glass, taking it for someone else's."

Chapter Four

TÖPFFER LAUNCHED, COMIC STRIP DEFENDED, LITERARY FAME, *FESTUS*

The year 1839, that of the second *Vieux Bois* edition, of the Parisian piracies of Töpffer's comic albums, and of the first imitations of them by Cham, all of which signaled the wider acceptance of the new genre, was also—coincidentally?—that of Töpffer's emergence onto the Parisian literary scene. *Le Presbytère*, expanded now into a full-length two-volume novel, was hailed by the essayist Xavier de Maistre as a "third Héloïse, better than Rousseau's." De Maistre, now an octogenarian at the Russian court, who had long since made a splash with a short, Sternean piece called *Voyage autour de ma chambre*, recognized his affinity with the young Genevan who had sent him anonymously some of his stories in prose and picture. The older man used the younger as a confidant, adopted him as a literary heir, wrote him at least fifty surviving letters without ever meeting him personally, and recommended Töpffer's latest novel to his publisher, Charpentier, in Paris. It was from de Maistre, who also loved the picture stories, that Töpffer learned of the plagiaries, first the copying of *Jabot* in Philipon's *Charivari*, where, however, it was quickly suspended after one installment (was it intended as a kind of advertisement for the coming album?), and then the wholesale piracy of not only that album, but *Vieux Bois* and *Crépin* by the associated firm of Aubert, the big caricature specialist in Paris. None of these piracies carried any indication of origin.

Thus was launched Aubert's famous and longlasting Albums Jabot series, to which Cham and Gustave Doré were to contribute. Aubert's piracy was commonplace and, in the absence of an inter-national copyright law, not illegal (Töpffer's father had contributed to a plagiary of the French *Encyclopédie* by a Lausanne publisher). Belgium was known as a regular nest of pirates—and of books censored in France. Rodophe left himself open to piracy by not avowing himself the author of the albums and, above all, by not supplying his Parisian distributor with sufficient copies of the original. He watched the advent of these copies with a mixture of annoyance and relief (at their poor quality), and was surely a bit flattered. Later, when he saw that Aubert continued to capitalize on the "albums Jabot," he was ready to "break his neck."

More important, Töpffer was roused to publish the following year (1840), in improved redrawn versions, his *Docteur Festus* and *Monsieur Pencil*, both of which he lithographed in Geneva but which carry very prominently the Paris address of Abraham Cherbuliez, who advertised them in the normal way.[1] Meanwhile, the Charpentier edition of Töpffer's *Nouvelles Genevoises*, short, sentimental stories of traditional Genevese life, was out, soon to be reviewed, on de Maistre's recommendation, in a long and highly laudatory essay by Charles-Augustin Sainte-Beuve in the prestigious *Revue des deux mondes*. Sainte-Beuve had given advance notice of the review in his essay on Xavier de Maistre.[2] He probably knew of Töpffer independently of de Maistre, having lectured in Lausanne, which lies near to Geneva on the lake. Töpffer was ecstatic at the review. His Jabot alter ego had really made it. The provincial had made it into the metropolis. He had been launched into the Parisian literary world—much of which, ironically, he affected to despise—by the biggest critical gun of the age, as the latest in a highly distinguished ten-year-long succession of writers in French: Hugo, Lamartine, Béranger, Musset, Chateaubriand, Balzac, de Staël, de Maistre, Vigny, Nodier, Sue—and now Töpffer.

But only Töpffer the writer of fiction, the prose stylist. Sainte-Beuve distances himself at the outset from the *albums humoristiques* that he misleadingly implies were barely known or available in Paris. His purpose is to laud the Swiss, by contrast with the "infected" work currently fashionable (Balzac and Sue, also anathema to the prudish Töpffer), as the purest of *littérateurs* imbued with a "sweet and healthy *saveur*" uncorrupted by overweening ambition or literary industrialization of the Parisians.

With respect to the picture stories, what seemed to him an "impure" literary-pictorial cocktail of Töpffer's invention, Sainte-Beuve was in a quandary; he designed his essay as biographical as well as literary-critical, and Töpffer had been particularly forthcoming, in the autobiographical sketch he had furnished to the critic in advance, on the subject of his comic albums, their origin, and the role they played in his life and current reputation. Hitherto skittish on the subject in public, Töpffer now freely acknowledged his pride in their authorship and popular success. But Sainte-Beuve was put off by the examples Töpffer had sent him and refused to enter into any discussion of this, to him dubious, aspect of the writer's oeuvre. He did not shift his position subsequently; indeed, he downplayed the albums even further in one of the obituaries he wrote for the Swiss and did not even mention them in the other.[3] He discouraged Töpffer's widow, who wanted to do a new edition, "which would be to the detriment of the memory of her husband." In this first review, using Töpffer's own description ("crazy stories mixed with a touch of the serious"), Sainte-Beuve recounts briefly their origin, character, and favorable reception by a condescending Goethe (who, as the French critic puts it, "did not disdain anything human"), evidently in order to cast his, Sainte-Beuve's, role as patron of the *writer* as the fulfillment of one first assumed by Goethe à propos Töpffer as a mere caricaturist.

In a deft evasion, the critic dismisses the albums as at once indescribable to anyone who has not seen them and beyond criticism—one can only taste them, praise, and laugh. He skillfully justifies this attitude by means of the critical disclaimer with which Töpffer always prefaced his albums: ". . . whoever reasons [over the tales] is mistaken." Sainte-Beuve applied his reasoning, above all, to the moral timbre of the prose writings, and his criteria were accepted for the next half century down to the major biographies of Blondel and Relave, who did not much value the picture stories either. Such criteria virtually excluded appreciation of the albums' unique qualities, which did not serve the stereotype of purity and simplicity, of the provincial homegrown virtues of naïve, innocent household morality, attached to Töpffer's prose fiction.

In 1841 Töpffer began to reach another public, broadly middle-class and French, with articles on Geneva and Genevan art in the *Magasin pittoresque*, France's first cheap, general-interest illustrated weekly, modeled on the English *Penny Magazine*. With increasing awareness now of the special social role his picture novels might play, a piece called "Le Marchand d'images"[5] tries to place his new invention in a didactic and popular graphic tradition uncorrupted by market forces in an industrial society. Sainte-Beuve had recognized that Töpffer's comic albums were "dans le genre d'Hogartt" (sic), and although the themes they treated were hardly popular in the same sense that Hogarth's were with his very broadly upper- and middle-class audience, Töpffer places his own mode of graphic narrative somewhere in that broad space between Hogarth and the Imagerie d'Epinal, the pictorial broadsheets telling simple traditional tales that sold cheaply in country street and fairground, and appealed to the simple emotions and piety of the illiterate villager, semiliterate townsfolk, and children. Ironically, the example he gives, a broadsheet entitled "Story of

4-1. *History of Robinson Crusoe*, popular woodcut, Martin de la Haye, Lille, between 1802 and 1833 (*Imagerie populaire française*).

Cécile, daughter of Fitz-Henry, seduced by Arthur, dedicated to tender hearts, in four tableaux: Seduction, Flight, Repentance, Reconciliation," evokes just the kind of popular romanticism he parodied in *Vieux Bois*. The sequence of themes is also precisely replicated in four sentimental pictures updating Hogarth by George Morland in England.[6] I have not found the story of Cécile in the very considerable literature devoted to French popular imagery, or the model for Töpffer's own rendition from the *Voyages*, done in a contour style akin to his own (see p. 82), but I reproduce a very common type of adventure story, as such a more Töpfferian choice[7] (fig. 4-1). The parallel between Töpffer's kind of graphic naïveté and that of the truly unschooled and awkward Imagerie d'Epinal—the "byzantins d'Epinal" as he called them—whose "precious lack of skill," "clarity of expression," and "power of intention" all betoken sincerity, is in fact, very misleading. Töpffer's draughtsmanship is a highly sophisticated product of considerable schooling, and his themes are innovative and intellectual.

Ending the article with a demand for more moral, popular serial stories, Töpffer seems to be appealing to other artists to stake out some sort of middle ground between, on the one hand, his own highly sophisticated and intellectual comic fantasies, published in relatively expensive albums and destined for a restricted, rather upper-class and well-educated audience and, on the other hand, cheap (single-sheet), crudely moralistic imagery for the uneducated, Imagerie d'Epinal–style. The subsequent history of the comic strip occupies this middle ground, but inclining more to Töpffer than imagerie populaire. Early Wilhelm Busch, who at first published in broadsheet, that is popular imagery (*Fliegende Blätter*) format, raised it to a level attempted in no other country.

Essai d'Autographie

Töpffer intuited the future of his invention, and provided for it by choosing at this time (1842) to reveal, in his *Essai d'Autographie*, the technical "secret" of his own reproductive procedure, which had so many practical advantages over wood engraving and regular chalk lithography. Engraving and etching on metal required special training impossible to weak eyes. Wood engraving required drawing directly on wood, which would also have been hard on Töpffer's eyesight, and then cutting into the

wood by other more or less capable specialist hands, as would necessarily be done with *Cryptogame*. He tried this on one occasion, to no-one's satisfaction, and so did his father. It also required printing in reverse, as did normal lithography. The author may by this time have already been considering his own ability to draw, be it picture story or landscape, at an end, hindered by what he feared was a terminally deteriorating eyesight, other health problems, and by the equally rapidly deteriorating political situation in Geneva; he refers to both in his long explanation of the *Essai* in the *Courrier de Genève*,[8] the polemical journal he helped launch earlier in the year to combat the Genevan radicals.

The *Essai d'Autographie* is composed of twelve plates of landscape and twelve of *drôleries*, that is, caricatures of such types as he used in his picture stories. The combination demonstrated the versatility and flexibility of the "autographic" method, as well adapted to the rendition of finely hatched shadows and atmospheric effects as to the simplified contours of his caricatures, to which he added (vis-à-vis the manuscript versions) quite evocative landscape effects. When text was required, the method offered the inestimable advantage of reproducing writing directly, that is, by a double reversal, while the usual art lithography, if a caption or internal inscription was needed, required recourse to a calligrapher trained in mirror writing. It was absolutely essential to Töpffer that his captions, and indeed the often quirky frames, be in the same handwriting as the sketches above and within. This gives a singular unity to the page design, which the copies (except those precisely traced in the later authorized editions of 1846 and 1860) can never emulate.

Töpffer, tongue in cheek, claims to have a "humanitarian" purpose in proposing "an invention, a discovery, at least one of these little nothings as big as others with which, today, one changes at any moment the face of the universe and the future of humanity."[9] He might, justifiably, be referring to that world-conqueror, the comic strip as such, rather than the technique he developed expressly for it. As it is, his aim was to have raised a humble technique, hitherto reserved for advertising circulars and grocers' bills, to the level of art. This may have been the situation in Geneva, which hardly knew "art" lithography anyway, but in England, always experimental in printing techniques, Töpffer's method was known as transfer lithography and "is now so generally adopted, and its utility so thoroughly acknowledged" for all kinds of purposes, among them the writing of music, making facsimiles of manuscript, and cheap children's books, notably Edward Lear's first *Book of Nonsense* (1846), which retained the author's own scribbled handwriting. The quotation is from the 1832 edition of *A Manual of Lithography*, which insists, as does Töpffer, that a steel-nibbed pen made from watch-spring be used.

Töpffer describes the process as follows: "The lithographer gives you a stick of ink, and a piece of paper spread with a layer of glue starch. You dilute the ink, dip your pen in it, you scribble on the paper . . . [and] send the page to the lithographer. He wets it on the reverse side, lays it on the stone and subjects it to pressure, and here is your design transferred from paper to stone. It has then only to be fixed by means of the usual preparation, inked and printed it in as many copies as you want." By this double reversal, the page comes out printed as you wrote it. *A Manual of Lithography* specifies a rich recipe for the transfer ink: "Shell-lac, Wax, Tallow, Gum-mastich, Soap, Lamp-Black."[10] It adds that it is possible to make changes, to scratch out writing with a special scraper; Töpffer cannot or does not bother to do this, so that signs of small errors in the captions of his picture stories remain. Printed at four pages per stone, the cost of printing was only a little over the cost of the paper, which gives us an idea of the relatively low price of labor compared to the high price of materials in those days. Töpffer paid his printer a total of 853 francs for 800 copies of *Pencil*, which he sold for ten francs each—a tidy profit!

Töpffer sought, first of all, to justify (to himself) the publication of such a "frivolity" in the midst of the political turmoil around him. He did so in a cantankerous way, pretending that even his innocent artistic invention is infected by the dreadful corruption prevailing. His pleasure at having intuited a "transcendental physiognomics," a sort of "superior phrenology" (a theme he was to develop more systematically in his 1845 *Essai de Physiognomonie*), is marred by his concern that perverted reformers would use his "system," as they had used other physiognomic and phrenological theories (vide *Crépin*), to antisocial purpose—"to prove that virtue depends on the shape of the nose, and stupidity on the curve of the chin." The author feigns to accuse his little demonstration of all the vices of the age: superficiality, scandalousness, and "an abject materialism" appropriate to a country careening into democracy. The paradox of this self-deprecating stance derives from his flailing simultaneously against enemies who are in no sense comparable: the new social ideas on the one hand, and on the other, critical rejection of his comic albums, the status of which vis-à-vis those new ideas he was not disposed to clarify. Töpffer knew that his whole modus operandi in the albums served to undermine traditional rationalist and materialist concepts, insofar as the latter were based on order and logic, and that his method of random physiognomic and narrative invention, far from justifying determinist phrenology, contradicted it.

After weaving his way through successive contradictions of this sort, Töpffer justifies his comic albums in commonplace fashion as a necessary "escape from the chains of reality." Angry at being distracted by ugly politics from the pleasures that were his true métier, he offers his graphic fancies as an uncontaminated island where politics and critics are excluded, where reigns a new anti-utilitarian aesthetic philosophy of "pure creativity," of "creation for the pleasure of the creator," transcending notions of glory and public success. Yet was this not close to the doctrine of "art for art's sake" that he professed to abhor? If so, it was better than politics for the sake of politics—and politicians.

Festus: Picture story and novelette

We have dealt with *Festus* above, as it was received by Goethe, with its satire on science and scientists that must have had a special appeal for the poet who was also something of a scientist. Suffice it here to single out some of the considerable changes the author made to the 1830 version, without changing the basic structure. We may regret that he cut a hilarious bit of extended farce, showing how the Mayor escaped from prison, stretching like rubber and through a hole much too small (fig. 4-2; the whole excised episode is reproduced in our facsimile edition)—in 1840 (39) he merely bashes the jailer on the head with a water jug—but otherwise the changes are happy extensions and interpolations. The artist built in, as was his wont, backgrounds, landscape, and settings. He lengthened the sublime episode of the Armed Force obeying the Mayor's disembodied uniform (11–13). He made Milord a more (mock-)heroic figure in stature and more mythic in behavior: he sends the Armed Force literally flying with his cudgel instead of (in cowardly fashion) beating them while they lie on the ground. He added the hilarious notion of piglets being born to the sows that, flung up by the arms of a windmill, spend three weeks airborne (fig. 4-3). Festus and a chalk-whitened peasant taken for ghosts, more mayoral suicide attempts, and more civic chaos caused by mayoral absence are further embellishments. But these pale before the apogee of fifteen added scenes of the madness of astronomer Apogee, his attack on his assistants, his depression and death (see fig. 1-24), the extension of the mayor's surreal bureaucratic dream, the placing of the telescope on the church, and interpretation of the washed-up wigs.

Fearlessly, I tried comparing the two versions involving the initial tangle of switched clothes and identity. From the 1827 version I deduced the following: Milord Dobleyou (for thus he is named here), robbed of his clothes by the two brigands who stole Milady's trunk with Festus in it, after fighting and defeating the Mayor and his Armed Force, dons the Mayor's uniform; while the Mayor, left in his shirtsleeves, encounters Milady, strips her of her clothes, and dons them. Milady finds and dons the Mayor's uniform left by Milord on a riverbank while bathing (23), and encounters her husband wearing her clothes. At this point (to cut the gordian knot of confusion) she should be able to simply switch with her husband, but for the mechanical stupidity of the Armed Force which "defends the uniform" at all cost, so that the Mayor in Milady's clothes goes off with Milady in his uniform, to the jealous rage of Milord, in his shirtsleeves again, who beats up the Mayor taking him for Milady. Clear so far? There is evidence that Töpffer confused even himself. Now the 1840 version is different. . . . Meanwhile, meanwhile . . .

Let us just say that later the 1840 Dr. Festus gets into the quick-change act. Finding Milady's clothes (i.e., the Mayor's uniform), he dons it, while the Mayor, in Milady's clothes, is relieved of them, while sleeping, by their rightful owner. Is this all a dream? Well, no, because while Festus is apt to dream, he is dreaming whatever (we suppose) is really happening to him; it is the Mayor who gets the real-life bureaucratic dream, one of a spectacularly surreal or psychedelic kind. This coherent fantasy comes as a relief. It is easier to follow the changes of clothes and identity in *Trictrac* than here.

When *Festus* was in Weimar Soret wrote to his friend in Geneva offering to do what Goethe had thought for a moment of doing himself, that is, compose a short novel on the basis of the *Festus* captions. Not unnaturally, Töpffer, *incornifistibulé*, did not take to this idea, knowing the limitations of

L'adjoint croit bien faire. Le Maire s'allonge par bas.

Le concierge ayant surpris le maire en état d'évasion s'étale d'arrêter le mal. Le maire s'allonge du haut.

L'adjoint triomphe. ayant pris un fort élan il saute au cou d'son ami. et lui témoigne sa joie — Cependant le concierge ne lâche pas.

4-2. The Mayor's adjunct pulls, the Mayor is stretched from below. The porter surprises the Mayor escaping, and stretches him from above. The adjunct succeeds, and jumping round the neck of his friend, expresses his joy. But the porter holds on (*Festus* ms, 67).

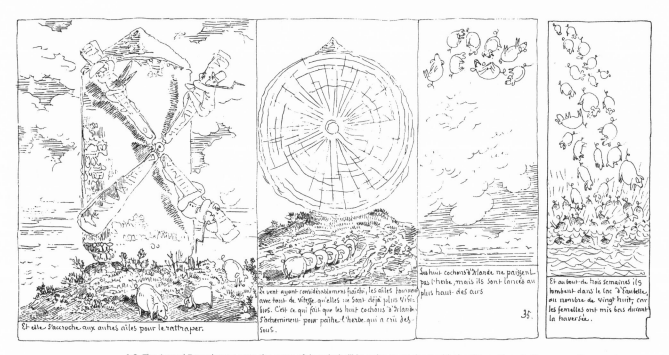

Et elle s'accroche aux autres ailes pour le rattraper.

Le vent ayant considérablement fraichi, les ailes tournent avec tant de vitesse qu'elles ne sont déjà plus visibles. C'est ce qui fait que les huit cochons d'Irlande s'acheminent pour paître l'herbe qui a crû dessous.

Les huit cochons d'Irlande ne paissent pas l'herbe, mais ils sont lancés au plus haut des airs

35.

Et au bout de trois semaines ils tombent dans le lac d'Santelle, au nombre de vingt huit, car les femelles ont mis bas durant la traversée.

4-3. The Armed Force hangs on to the arms of the windmill in order to catch up with the Mayor. The wind increases, the arms turn faster, and attract eight Irish pigs, which are swept up into the air. After three weeks they descend into the lake, now twenty-eight in number because the females have produced litters meanwhile (*Festus* 35–36).

his friend's literary talents, and that such a project would not, as he (Soret) seemed to hope, "make a Rabelais of him."[11] But why should Töpffer himself not try it? The idea had worked in England, where William Combe had "written up to" Rowlandson's *Syntax* illustrations. The prose Festus was probably written soon after the sketchbook returned from Weimar but, even more satirical and much more scatological, was not considered publishable any more than the sketches were.[12] In 1840, as he refurbished the pictorial *Festus* for publication, the writer-artist returned to his prose version, insisting, for cause, that it appear after the picture story.

The prose *Voyages et Aventures of Dr. Festus*, at 160 pages and with twenty-two specially made illustrations, some of incidents not in the picture album, was somewhat bowdlerized by the author, and published with some expectations on his part. But the work received little attention then and not much since, although it has been republished in our time. The sequel he virtually promised at the end never appeared. The question whether there was a market for this brand of simple, foolish humor in this form, a kind of Rabelais for children, seemed to have been answered. He did not repeat the experiment.

The preface to the prose *Festus* observes that "in two similar things, the differences between them change what they have in common." The two modes of *Festus* are certainly similar in that they follow the same plotlines and repeat many of the same incidents. At the same time, pictorial crazy-paving of plot merging with subplot might not work so well in "traditional" prose format, and Töpffer seems to have tried to rationalize the labyrinth.

The differences are those of a man released from certain constraints, most obviously on picture captions that must be kept short, but also on decency. The preface confesses a lack of taste and incorrect language fit to horrify the purist. Of all Töpffer's prose works, his prose *Festus* is the most licentiously, verbally Rabelaisian in its sheer excess, in its delight in exaggeration, numerical, chronological, and oneiric, in its hyperbolic effusion, in its devotion to lists of things (where Rabelais meets schoolboy, and bureaucracy), and the constant (perhaps tiresome) ebbing and overflowing of (pseudo-) philosophical learning and learned allusion—of which last Festus himself is an incarnation. The book is also Rabelaisian in a certain moral license, otherwise repressed, in "broadening" his humor—the scatological, the schoolboy stuff, such as we encountered in Jabot's fart. There are several sniffs of this excluded, for reason, from the picture story: the *mouche bovine* (bovine gadfly) that enters the rectum of Festus's mule just at the moment he is arranging the major of a syllogism of which he has already the minor, and which causes the mule to gallop for five hours nonstop. The w.c., discreetly diminished, as we noted, in the comic album of 1840, is now more pervasive, with its "alkaline miasmas" and "odorous particles." The petition to commute the Mayor's death sentence is used by the king to wipe his bottom (81).

As in Rabelais, the higher reaches of mental cognition are brought into collision with the base bodily realities. As in Rabelais, there is a constant tension between knowledge theoretical, acquired through books and expressed in verbiage, and knowledge practical gained from experience. Festus has read everything but cannot for a moment understand what is actually happening to him. He is the omniscient ignoramus who knows useless things in twenty-two languages, and the narcoleptic dreamer who cannot even figure out whether he is dreaming or not, for whom the composition of syllogisms and dancing of hordes of neo-platonists is more real than being sawn up in a tree. He knows all the sciences, natural history, botany, and astronomy, but he is the last person you would want leading you on an Alpine excursion. As for the professional astronomers—they are, in the cusp of their professional careerism, madder than Festus, and die deservedly.

Some jokes and comic incidents would not appear in the picture story because they were hard

4-4. "Histoire de Cécile" (Voyage à la Grande Charteuse 1833, *OC* vol. 5, p. 59).

to represent pictorially, such as the furious battle between a squirrel and a mouse in Festus's pocket, who end up devouring each other. The feistiness of Milady who, in the prose version in perfect English and broken French, violently insults and physically attacks her accusers and judges and needs seventy soldiers to subdue her, makes a welcome change from many passive and foolish females in Töpffer (78). Her stout resistance to tyranny is entirely missing from the picture story.

Greater space means magnification of comic effects, which are all too often enumerative and cumulative. What is treated briefly and deftly in the picture story is pumped up in the prose version. It is easier, perhaps, to laugh at a picture and caption quickly scanned than at an overloaded verbal passage that (whether so intended or not) invites slower and steadier consideration. The greater violence, pain, disease, and death in the prose version have an uncanny effect. Is this really funny or not? The humor is gallows humor, for the jester's cap donned by Töpffer permits an elaboration of gruesome

medical and anatomical detail that appears (coming from the picture story) gratuitous, even cruel, and would have (must have) been found repulsive by some, as Töpffer found Balzac's physical realism repulsive. The pigs that land on Ginvernais territory introduce the red Irish pig which multiplies at the expense of cattle and sheep, causing the people to eat too much pork sausage, which heats their blood, renders their faces pustulent, makes them beat their wives, and die of wrath prematurely (59). The two sawyers who in the album are merely scared by Festus exiting the tree trunk, die of pulmonary exhaustion; Taillandier, after falling into the chalk-bin, is not simply taken for a ghost but is injured and deformed, which deformity is inherited by his descendants who have difficulty finding a wife. The bullet Luçon receives in the neck, described with surgical precision, is, by contrast, a godsend: it puts a brake on his alcoholism and helps him become, eventually, mayor of Porelières (51). The efforts of the three astronomers to immobilize, that is, annihilate each other is also given in superfluous anatomical precision: as with evil doctors their learning is homicidal. Worst of all, the very sacred act of laughter turns sour: Milord laughs so much at seeing the dead brigand that he cracks eighty-two jokes, which ruptures his diaphragm, making his voice hollow and his laughter abdominal. Töpffer is playing at the coldhearted, pedantic, bureaucratic chronicler who may omit nothing. This shows on occasion in the album too, as when he has Festus, exiting his sack, admire the beauties of nature while the miller's wife "falls on her nose and breaks three teeth, that is two incisors and one eye-tooth" (31).

Is the pain in *Dr. Festus*, either version, if it is dream-nightmare pain, less real?

Chapter Five

POLITICS AND ABSURDITY: *PENCIL* AND *TRICTRAC*

Of all Töpffer's picture stories, *Monsieur Pencil* bears the clearest imprint of the July 1830 revolution in France. The most polarized of his comic albums, playing the most absurd fantasies against emphatic injections of political actuality, it is at the same time balanced, and was tempered by the experience of a decade between its composition in 1831 and the rather different version published in 1840.[1] It is, I believe, Töpffer's aesthetic masterpiece, although it has not been his most popular story, and is even omitted in some editions. The manuscript was executed between March and July 1831 and, although lacking an ending, was soon circulated among the inner circle, as is evident from the complaint in the preface dated 31 August 1831, addressed presumably to the schoolboys, about clumsy, dirty fingers disfiguring the pages.

Pencil was infected by the disillusionment following the July Revolution in Paris, and follows the wave of caricature by Daumier and company that mocked two (among so many other) political issues foregrounded in *Pencil*, the parliamentary debate and repression by the National Guard. The parliamentary debate reflected a spectrum of political positions, as shown in *Pencil*. Töpffer goes further, showing *consequences*, how a national fractiousness impacts the international balance, how inherent instability and mutual suspicion among the European powers can lead to ministerial panic, civil discord, and the threat of a European war compounded by that of cholera, which, in turn, brings science into disrepute and by implication the very concept of sci-

entific social improvement dear to so many reform-minded politicians. This escalation of disasters starts with the most trivial of accidents in communication: a little dog making the arms of a telegraph waggle at random. Töpffer, still the political liberal in 1831, kept intact in 1840 his sympathy for the workers, shown unemployed, going on strike, and violently repressed (30–31), victims of economic crises met by a lot of hot air from demagogues of various stripes. Strikes among Genevan tailors and locksmiths were among the earliest in Swiss history; the workers of Saint Gervais would make the revolution of 1846.

The idea of a European war was no joke when Belgium, Poland, and Italy experienced nationalist rebellions that were hugely popular and liable to suffer Great Power interventions. Switzerland too was affected: in late 1830 and early 1831 in nearby Neuchâtel and Lausanne revolution threatened, which Töpffer feared would spread to Geneva. For the moment, however, Geneva seemed a haven of peace and as such, conducive to the pursuit of Töpffer's little hobbies. Writing to a pastor friend in Neuchâtel, Töpffer assures him "I am *liberal as can be*, but I am fed up, stuffed, indigestified [*indijectionné*] with politics."[2] He goes on to list all the picture stories he has recently executed or has in progress, and then returns to the subject of Geneva's happy preservation, for the time being, from the crises, expressing mock pique at the French ("clumsy people!!") for not waiting for a few years before making their revolution so that he could buy his house in peace.

This is the language of extreme ambivalence. The *romans en estampes* had always been Töpffer's escape from realities both near and far, yet they bore the marks of what he was escaping from, which was also what he was attracted to. Töpffer starts *Pencil* with a sketch wafted off by a capricious wind, which surely represents the gusts of artistic imagination, but it is also this wind that sets in motion a chain of accidents that bring on major political near-disasters. It is as if art, which should rise above politics, could not escape it, as Géricault and Delacroix discovered and demonstrated.

Pencil's sketch might have been a cartoon. The new regime of Louis-Philippe, especially in its first five years, was one of the most abundantly caricatured in history. The great caricatural spasm in Paris came at a moment of "movement and resistance, revolutionary stress, status-quoism, a chain of cabinet crises, street disorders, noisy chambers, press laws, and public trials, in which tribunal became theater"[3]—theater of the absurd, theater of caricature. Much of the disorder, specifically in the tribunals, was due to the government's reneging on that very freedom of the press that had brought it to power in the first place. In the four years between August 1830 and October 1834 there were, in Paris alone, 520 press trials, with 188 condemnations amounting to 106 years in prison and 44,000 francs in fines.[4] In Geneva the press felt itself to be relatively free, although some self-censorship was expected in order to avoid offending foreign governments and Swiss political neutrality.

The Romantic assertion of freedom was translated by French graphic artists into a political militance and social critique conceived on the model of English caricature of the Golden Age, with which Töpffer's father became familiar on his visit to England. It is not clear how much of this Rodolphe knew, apart from a volume of Hogarth given to him by Wolfgang-Adam, but he was surely inspired by the example of Philipon's *La Caricature*, founded in November 1830, the first weekly newspaper to pub-lish regular cartoons. With this magazine and its successor, the daily *Charivari*, the history of caricature underwent a mutation as the genre entered the sociopolitical mainstream through journalism, arguably the most potent force henceforth in the formation of public opinion. The journal was certainly available in Geneva—Stendhal saw a copy of it there on 24 June 1837,[5] and there was a very short-lived (four issues, unillustrated) weekly *Charivari Genevois* in 1837. Töpffer must have followed the fortunes of the Philipon journals, which publicly conducted their "auto-martyrography," and boasted a galaxy of talent including Töpffer's favorite Grandville. The Swiss must have known of the numerous raids on the Aubert shop, the prison sentences meted out to Philipon and Daumier, and been an armchair spectator of the whole struggle between press and government culminating in the draconian press laws of 1835 that stifled French political caricature altogether. Henceforth French caricature, in its political pinch, overflowed, diverted, and broadened into a panorama of social issues including business, law, and industry. The spectacle of this other kind of "enforced" freedom must have encouraged the young Swiss to throw into the public domain, at last, his own peculiar "little follies" in social caricature.

Töpffer sensed what was apparent all over European culture: the age of illustration, the "cult of the image" (Baudelaire's term) had arrived. All the major French writers were affected, Balzac, Hugo, and Sue massively. Illustrated journalism was born; so was the newspaper and magazine serial novel, the *roman feuilleton* that was to revolutionize sales of every kind of newsprint, and reading habits. Literature, as Töpffer had cause to complain, became an industry.

But the particular political turmoil of the years 1830–31 had by 1840 abated, and the revisions to *Pencil* reflect this change. Töpffer cut back radically on the text-laden satire of French parliamentary antics in order to preserve the pictorial dominance, and avoid repetition and monotony. In the process

5-1. Mr. Jolibois goes crazy with jealousy. The Professor writes . . . great at swearing . . . burning climate. And upside down also. The Professor writes: . . . walk equally well on feet as on their head. And in swimming fashion. The Professor writes: . . . and they jump like carps. And whirling around. The Professor writes: . . . they whirl around like Demons (*Pencil* 17).

of raising aesthetic considerations over the political satire, the author heightened certain graphic effects, notably by doubling the rhythm of the Professor writing his memoir intercut with the unhappy object of that memoir, Jolibois struggling in his cage (fig. 5-1). The whole effect here is akin to that of a musical score.

In another major graphic enhancement that is woven into the narrative in three phases, Töpffer ascends the brightest heaven of invention. The manic Professor sends his "psychiot" sample packed up in a crate to the Royal Academy, to serve as material data for his report. But the crate is stolen from the post-coach by brigands and eventually falls by the wayside. The idea of animating this unpromising oblong object, influenced possibly by Grandvillian fantasies, attains in 1840 a hilarious triple develop-

ment. When Pencil delivers Madame Jolibois from her crated and crazed husband by cutting off her skirt, he inside his crate is left in vain pursuit and melancholy reflection upon his predicament. He (it) abandons him- (it)self to a characteristically Töpfferian gamut of emotions, from jealousy to despair, all the more impressive for the reduction of the expressive elements to a pair of pathetically gesticulating forearms and eyes that, through the airholes in the crate, somehow manage to look lugubrious. Trapped as he is, like other neurotic heroes in Töpffer, Jolibois abandons himself to suicide: perforce by hanging, from one hand, to the branch of a tree and then, sublimely, "he changes hands" (fig. 5-2).

After further narrative twists, Jolibois, in another enrichment of 1840, engages from his crate in a surreal and unequal battle with his persecutors.

Captions within the image:
N'ayant pu atteindre sa femme, mr. Jolibois accuse le ciel et les hommes.

Après quoi il se livre aux bords d'une jalousie effrénée.

Après quoi il s'abandonne au suicide par pendaison.

Et il change de main.

46.

5-2. Unable to reach his wife, Mr. Jolibois accuses the heavens and man. After which he surrenders to the bounds of frantic jealousy. After which he abandons himself to suicide by hanging. And changes hands (*Pencil* 46).

With the aid of his stick he manages to fend off the cowardly Professor, but the Maid, less easy to intimidate, proves too much for him (fig. 5-3). Later she courageously recaptures him after he escapes during the fumigation at the frontier, identified as he is as the Cholera in person (see chap. 1). At this point terror is written all over him, and one wonders whether it is entirely accidental, within a mode that avoided both speech balloons and direct speech in the captions, that under this frame the base line, hitherto impassively straight, suddenly breaks into a kind of speech, a gurgling "a e i o u" (fig. 5-4). Is this just silly doodling, or an expression of pain emanating from the vowels of Jolibois's tormented soul?

Pencil is balanced between twin determinants of human affairs: fate and politics. It is an instrument of fate, of timeless, placeless nature, a sportive wind whisking away the Pencil drawing and depositing a little dog on the arm of a telegraph, that first threatens the social equilibrium; but it is the neurotic selfishness of propertied people at a particular historical moment, consumed by their immediate material concerns and panicking at the garbled telegraphic news, that makes the danger real. War is rumored imminent, the stock market takes a dive, bankruptcies are declared, workshops close, workers assemble ominously. In the face of all this, the government calls for a debate on the forest code. The deputies will have none of it, but even as they engage the national crisis, their sectarian manner of dealing with it only makes it worse. A babel of interruptions and eruptions corresponding to a uniquely French political spectrum ensues, and all ends in a fistfight. After a suspension, the session reopens with a repetition of the earlier pattern of complaints, demands, and insults.

5-3. [Jolibois] seeing that the Maid is getting involved, makes off. The battle is engaged. And victory declared (*Pencil* 62).

5-4. At the sight of the cholera in person, the health officers take the bit between the teeth. And the male nurses likewise. And the female nurses likewise. Fortunately the Maid realizes that it is her master's escaped Psychiot, and she soon recaptures him (*Pencil* 65).

5-5. The National Guard persuades the mob to disperse (two versions from *Pencil,* as printed 1840 and ms 1831).

Most of this block of fourteen scenes with their long captions, together with a similar interlude later, was cut in 1840. Had he been closer to events, and minded to engage in caricature of individual politicians like the English earlier, or the French after 1830, with Daumier's now-celebrated portrait-masks of deputies and ministers, Töpffer might have restored visual interest to what was becoming mere illustrated text. But he was, indirectly, justifying the Genevan political system, conducted with decorum in private by the tight little oligarchy immune to the vulgar glare of publicity and accusations of corruption surrounding French parliamentary procedure. Töpffer gleefully reveals

a corrupt *process* rather than the isolated moment: this is of course the genius of the comic strip as opposed to the single-picture cartoon, and why the former genre was chosen by the German followers of Töpffer who created *Piepmeyer* as a satire on the failed but wordy Frankfurt parliament of 1848–49 (see below).

Radically reduced as it was in 1840, the parliamentary speechifying and demagoguery in *Pencil* display a keen awareness of rhetorical cadence and financial manipulation, with allusions and observations as incisive as those of Philipon in his captions to the later (1836–38) *Robert Macaire* series. He brings on stage a "M. Rotschild" (sic), his pockets

POLITICS AND ABSURDITY: *PENCIL, TRICTRAC*

5-6. Feeling cold, the Professor dresses and goes off to write up his discovery of a brand-new subterranean wind. Ms. continues: Having a little apparatus which registers the existence of a wind blowing from below. He immediately classifies it among the subterranean winds (two versions from *Pencil*, as printed 1840 [5] and ms 1831 [12]).

bulging with banknotes, cynically calculating the relative profitability of war and peace (the Rothschild family fortune was founded on profit from the French revolutionary and Napoleonic wars). In the 1840 *Pencil* the Rothschild name was expunged.

"The workers continuing to go hungry," retained in 1840, stands forth, refrain-like, as the irreducible fact amid the oratorical blather and testifies to Töpffer's continuing or at least residual sympathy for the French (if not Genevan) working classes; such sympathy seems to anticipate the ter-

ribly repressed upheavals of unemployed and striking workers in Lyons November 1831 and in 1834. The mobs of "workers continuing to go hungry," despite the panaceas of the politicians, meet with the classic government solution: violent dispersion ("persuasion") by the naked bayonets of the National Guard, typified by a portly, bespectacled (that is, socially myopic) figure (31, fig. 5-5). He is the petty bourgeois turning against the class from which he may have risen and into which he fears to fall back, a grocer-guardsman perhaps of the type ironically celebrated by Daumier and Grandville in the 1830s—where Töpffer may indeed have found him, for he is a conspicuous addition of 1840.

Rather like the telegraph sending out random messages, the narrative line in *Pencil* zigzags back and forth between the various groups of characters that divide and coalesce in a geography both momentarily precise and yet left open—as in a dream. The telegraph, the new communications technology of the age undergoing expansion and improvement, particularly in England and the United States, where electrification was being introduced, but lacking in Switzerland and all the more wondrous-seeming for that, was another kind of fate—or a warning how technological progress may be suddenly sent crazy by a quirk of nature, embodied in the little dog precipitated on it.

Pencil, like *Festus*, is a satire on scientific pretension and delusion. After broadening into panoramas of political chaos, Töpffer narrows his focus back to the expired scientists, in a brilliant conjunction of the two main satiric strands threads he has been spinning, the political and the fantastic. The expired scientists, left asphyxiated much earlier by the fumes of the Professor's bottle of newly discovered "subterranean gas" (actually taken from a latrine, and thus loosely representative of the sewergas theory of disease), are diagnosed as having died of cholera, the political agency of which we have already noted. Töpffer tried to mitigate the all-too-obviously commonplace, unpleasant source of the gaseous wind, in the final version—see fig. 5-6.

With the chief protagonists, including the Professor's servant, reunited in detention at the frontier hospital, the manuscript version ends—and the dénouement in the published version begins. This follows a classic dramatic pattern, a last mini-crisis of jealous despair and fury on the part of both Madame and Monsieur Jolibois, who are finally pacified by mutual explanation "so that the light bursts forth in torrents." There is reconciliation and embracing all round (the ever egotistical Professor happily hugging himself), the Burgher and his dog

are finally rescued from the telegraph, and Europe is rescued from the threat of cholera. The general pacification is signaled by the telegraph returning to normal, after which "the cholera ceases and the affairs of Europe are becalmed." Was Töpffer thereby also becalming himself and fellow Genevans in the face of the rumbling that would break forth into a political cacophony the following year?

The solution came to the author only after a struggle, and he left evidence in the manuscript of the various alternatives that might best impose some structural sense on so much nonsensical matter. It is not hard to see M. Pencil as representing the author himself, the author-artist whose capricious imagination (symbolized by the little zephyr), and the product of his imagination (symbolized by the sketch), give the first shake to the kaleidoscope of adventure. And like an author who wants his story to stand as an autonomous chronicle, he disappears from the story. Although he intervenes "authorially" at the end to straighten out the tangle, Pencil is in fact only the progenitor rather than the recorder, much less editor, of a self-propelled fantasy that imbibes sketch and paper and human bodies alike, willfully suspending gravity and disbelief before letting all down to earth again. Töpffer would not have worried that despite the title (which he could easily have changed), the tale is not really about artist Pencil at all (and he even contemplated for a moment further reducing his role), any more than Sterne's *Life and Opinions of Tristram Shandy*, which inspired the free-floating digressions in some of Töpffer's prose works, is about that titular gentleman.

Monsieur Trictrac

The protagonists of Töpffer's picture tales are, so far, basic social and satirical types: upstart, lover, educator, scientist, artist, bureaucrat, politician. To this list we may add thief, who plays a leading role, in various guises, in *Monsieur Trictrac*, the gentleman bearing this name being, like Pencil, ancillary to the adventure. We have noted how the thief or criminal, petty or otherwise, held a firm place in Romantic and the new realist literature, and intrudes constantly in the nineteenth-century comic strip; here, as in so much else, Töpffer sets the example. The thief or petty criminal shadows the respectable citizen as a sinister alter ego. The thief–cop–respectable citizen thus involves a network of profound petty-bourgeois fears: that of losing property and discovering that the state is unable to protect that property or its owner; and worse, that of arrest and jail by the guardians of the state, who let the real criminal go free. The latter nightmare flows from the generalized anxiety of the lower middle classes about losing something more than the little property they had: social respect and status.

The scenario by which the blameless petty bourgeois is "exposed" (accused of a crime, found naked, itself an offense) plays on the shame and confusion surrounding the ethics of getting on—in business, in the world, where all is appearance anyway. *Trictrac* is Töpffer's comedy (or farce) par excellence of mistaken identities, his classic *vis comica*, involving abrupt and often involuntary switches of costume. These are symptoms of the flux of social roles in the real world, of temptations and pitfalls, of the need to appear as something other than what one is, or was, and the tendency to be taken for what one is not.

The petty-bourgeois fascination with the criminal, who stalks tall through the nineteenth-century popular novel, the man from the margins capable of great acts of power, like the Count of Monte Cristo, is a fantasy of those excluded from power, or given paltry symbols of it, like the grocer–national guardsman. To imagine oneself arrested as a petty criminal is thus a deterrent against, or advance punishment for, harboring criminal fantasies. Here lies the psychological appeal of those defiant petty criminals and grand mini-heroes of comic strip history, Busch's Max and Moritz. And surely the whole, huge genre of the detective story of our own times depends upon a similar mechanism: vicarious enjoyment of acts we would never dare to carry out in reality. At the same time, manifestly unjust arrest reproduces the immanent sense that society, with its laws, is altogether unjust.

Trictrac, like several of Töpffer's picture stories, was executed in the early 1830s and, having reached a goodish length, was left unfinished. Ironically, in his letter to Sainte-Beuve of 1840 the author refers to this very story about a thief as having been "momentarily stolen" (presumably lent out or borrowed without permission and not returned), and whether or not he failed to recover it, it remained unknown and unpublished until 1937.[6]

The story makes merry with the confusion and ambiguity inherent in the triangle thief–cop–citizen. The philosophical starting point is the fatalistic one underlying the comic view of law and lawlessness in general: theft is an accident of fate, a kind of natural disaster, rather than the typical manifestation of human depravity as in the rake's progresses of picture stories in previous centuries. A house suffers burglary as it might a fire; a coach suffers brigands as it might a broken axle. In Töpffer, theft precipitates the *natural* tendency of people and things to get themselves lost and their identities mixed up.

The theft of a trunk and the search for the thieves launches Dr. Festus on his crazy path of adventure. In *Pencil*, the theft of the Professor's crate with Jolibois inside spins off further narrative skeins. When fear of a burglarious noise precipitates the Marquise into his bedroom, Jabot (ironically the cause of the noise) "gallantly" acts the perfect cop by arresting the first person he sees, the innocent hotelier (46). The thief in *Trictrac*, together with the assumption of his identity by various other characters, determines the course of the plot. The story opens with a burglar, who has climbed down the chimney of Trictrac's house, being politely bidden to take Trictrac's place in bed,

5-7. The thief politely approaches Mr. Trictrac and begs him to believe that it was not him he intended. All suspicions fall upon the Lieutenant who suspects them all. After which the thief with as much dignity as he can muster enjoins the Lieutenant to return his clothes, and assures him of his pardon if he returns unresisting to an honest life. Profound astonishment of the Lieutenant (*Trictrac* 39–40).

5-8. The Reserve having made a *by the left flank* experiences difficulties in entering the street. Meanwhile the Thief is violently angry at the Reserve, finally shouting in order to make it disengage, Break ranks! The Reserve tries but is unable to, more because of the ladder than lack of discipline (*Trictrac* 58–60).

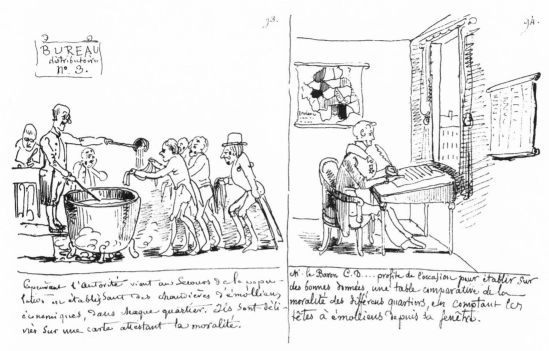

93.   94.

BUREAU
distributaire
nº 3.

Cependant l'autorité vient au secours de la population en établissant des chaudières d'émollients
économiques, dans chaque quartier. Ils sont déli-
vrés sur une carte attestant la moralité.

M. le Baron C.D. .... profite de l'occasion pour établir sur
des bonnes données, une table comparative de la
moralité des différents quartiers, en comptant les
têtes à émollients depuis sa fenêtre.

5-9. Meanwhile the authorities come to the help of the population by establishing soup kitchens of cheap emollients in each quarter. They are delivered upon certificates of good behavior. The baron C.D. . . . seizes the occasion to establish a reliable data base of comparative morality in the different quarters, counting the heads with emollients from his window (*Trictrac* 93–94).

while that gentleman, "devoured by science," sets off secretly on the virtually mythic quest to discover the source of the Nile. Naturally, he does not get far. The exchange of identity is complete and reciprocal, for just as the thief is taken for Trictrac, Trictrac is taken for the thief and apprehended on the roof of his own house (30) by the lieutenant of police. It is the World Upside Down; the thief, ever polite and gracious, pardons the police chief (39–40, fig. 5-7) (but later has him arrested), then takes his clothes and appeals to the reserve to rescue him from the rooftop. The soldiers, who clumsily tangle themselves up in the ladder (the drill-book does not detail a routine for ladders), cause escalating chaos in the town (figs. 5-8, 1-8).

Correctly blaming the police chief for the chaos, the citizenry seize the man they take to be the police chief—who is in fact the thief in disguise. Thus, when he encounters the real police chief in jail as a thief, the thief-in-police-garb is only too happy to recover his original clothing and sign an official

document declaring the other to be the "only true and indivisible chief of police"—which means that it is the real police chief who faces punishment after all. After a travesty of a trial, he is saved from hanging, in another ironic twist, by the thief who, having escaped from jail, agrees to unhang him and exchange clothes once more—under the threat, which seems quite idle under the circumstances, that the police chief will hang *him* if he refuses.

This simplified outline omits several detours in a labyrinth of reversals and counter-reversals of identities and roles. No solution seems in sight, although in one respect the wheel appears to have come full circle: the thief saves himself in the end by resuming his impersonation of Trictrac, thus also honoring his original commitment. The story is suspended on the image of the thief riding off as the putative son of Trictrac *père*, the epitome of a bourgeois respectability he has richly earned through his quickness of wit. He is still of the species Thief (having throughout no other name), but he has stolen nothing we know of except the limelight from the nominal hero, Trictrac *fils*, who has got no closer to the source of the Nile than the roof of his own house.

Here Töpffer paused, uncertain how, or perhaps even whether, to reintroduce Trictrac. The dénouement cannot have been far off, for the draft, with forty-one pages and 125 scenes, was already approaching the normal length of an album.[7] As a subversion of the concept of immutable law and order, it corresponds to the author's more liberal-radical stance around 1830. The interlude of mockery of petty civic regulations (in which Geneva was certainly not lacking) casts the story in an additionally anti-authoritarian light, which need not be taken too seriously. The critique of arbitrary justice condemning the innocent to death and frivolously losing the appeal for clemency may be taken as another of Töpffer's jibes at the neighboring absolutism.

Töpffer perceived his own Geneva as what today is mocked as a "nanny state," given to trivial protective regulation and misguided panaceas in emergencies. The social crisis unleashed by the militia stuck in the ladder is met by the establishment of a "soup kitchen" of emollient plasters (fig. 5-9), which universal cure is offered also to the thief. He prudently returns to the bed of Trictrac, to the delight of Trictrac *père*, who takes him for his son, returned at last and cured of his facial disturbance. The distribution of the emollient, which plays a conspicuous role in the plot and leads to further confusions of social identity (it gives the thieves who wear it the disguise of decent folk and opportunity to exercise their vocation to advantage), becomes a symbol of foolish and useless social welfare measures. Likewise, the well-meaning statistical efforts of the Baron C.D. . . . (fig. 5-9) are depicted as pointless at a time when governments staked their stability and reputation on the knowledge statistics were supposed to provide. Such knowledge can never compete with the quirks of fate.

Chapter Six

THE LAST YEARS: *CRYPTOGAME, ALBERT, AESTHETICS AND PHYSIOGNOMICS*

Histoire de Monsieur Cryptogame

The last two years vouchsafed to Töpffer were marked by a resurgence of attention to his picture stories, which he had neglected since 1840, and a concern to leave to posterity guidelines for his inventive procedure. The early 1840s offered the schoolmaster and university professor two additional distractions: the literary laurels with which he was crowned in Paris by Sainte-Beuve, to his delight, and the radical agitation in Geneva, which infuriated him. From early 1842 the threatening revolution consumed all his energies; he became, as some of his friends noted with regret, an *englué*, Genevan dialect for fanatic, and helped launch a twice-weekly newspaper, the *Courrier de Genève*, which he edited and co-wrote, in the wake of the first revolution of 22 November 1841. The magazine folded in defeat in March 1843. With his health and eyesight to worry about, Töpffer sought relief in a new, highly politicized picture story, conceived during a political lull at the end of 1844: *The Story of Albert*.

From 1843 he became actively engaged in negotiations for the publication of some literary works with his cousin, the Paris publisher Jacques-Julien Dubochet. Deciding that his latest piece of fiction, a long novel called *Rosa and Gertrude*, was not suited to serialization in *L'Illustration* or to the audience of that magazine (perhaps because of its relatively pungent libertine theme), he started toward the end of 1844 the *Histoire d'Albert*. Only comic in part, seriously and very locally polemical, this was no can-

didate for the Parisian magazine, but the prospect of the wider audience put him in the swing of graphic invention, and for *L'Illustration* he resurrected the last of his unpublished drafts, *L'Histoire de Monsieur Cryptogame*, which he had sent to Goethe in 1830. It ran in the French weekly from 25 January to 19 April. The magazine's circulation of 17,000 would have brought him five or ten times that number of potential readers. He described it in a letter to his cousin as "very funny in its extravagance, and briskly paced, inventive enough to win a happy popularity among people who liked to laugh at the impossible rendered comic, and sufficiently credible."[1] So enthusiastic was he, that he sent the drawings to Paris without even waiting for the publisher's approval. With its contemporary satirical target limited to a traditionally enemy culture, the Muslim (in Algeria), this otherwise innocently crazy spoof on unrequited romantic love seemed well-suited to the broad family readership of the *Illustration*, and constituted a complete novelty: *L'Illustration* was from the start (January 1843) devoted to caricature, but had never attempted a serialized graphic novel. Success was immediate, and imitators at much lesser length followed.

Knowing that his flighty drawings would have to be redrawn on and then cut into wood (lithography and type were not print-compatible), and that with his poor eyesight he was physically as well as temperamentally incapable of drawing on wood himself ("In order to get going at all, I have to burn the paper"), Töpffer fell naturally upon the new star

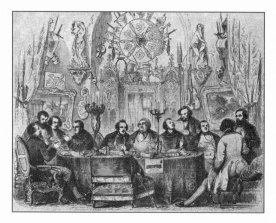

6-1. Workshop of the *Illustration* engravers at night and editorial board of the *Illustration* (both engravings from *L'Illustration*, 2 March 1844). The magazine here confesses to an invidious contrast between conditions in which the poorly paid engravers worked—a cramped, dark room, long, nocturnal hours, forced overtime—and the luxurious ambiance and evident wealth of the directors. The engravers would be those of the best firm in Paris, Hôtelin, Best and Leloir, who sign HBL on a *Cryptogame* design.

6-2. For his part, Mr. Cryptogame left to himself, dresses, locks the door, and leaves nocturnally for Marseille (two versions from *Cryptogame*: left, lithographic; right, woodcut in *L'Illustration*, 1845).

6-3. Where he begins to sound the depths of his situation. And he refuses to respond to the teasing of a superb Amphitrite (two versions from *Cryptogame*: left, lithographic; right, woodcut in *L'Illustration*, 1845).

of *L'Illustration* and the *Charivari*, Amédée de Noé, known as Cham. Cham had already published several Töpfferian albums since 1839 (see below), but was now, ironically, when called upon to translate original Töpffer drawings to the woodblock, moving away from Töpffer's sparse outline style toward a denser, blunter, more volumetric one, a miniaturization of Daumier.

Having pressed his project with comic urgency upon Dubochet, Töpffer courteously, flatteringly now deluged Cham with the most detailed instructions, urging him to be "free" and not slavish in his line, with a freedom (as Cham was supposed to intuit) that should be Töpffer's, not Cham's. In a copious correspondence with both publisher and artist, Töpffer "pestered" them (his word) with all kinds of little matters relating to the project, in an attempt to move it along and get it done right. Since wood engraving was not practiced in Geneva, he probably did not fully realize that there was in this craft—the actual cutting of the woodblocks being done by yet

a third party, and usually a team at that—a "house style" from which neither Cham nor the engravers could much depart. Töpffer nagged and, although duly grateful to Cham for his efforts and admitting the difficulty of keeping, for instance, physiognomic consistency in the facial features of the hero, seems to have been disappointed in the result—as so many artists and authors were in the nineteenth century who ill appreciated the technical difficulties, long hours, and poor pay of wood engravers (fig. 6-1). One can appreciate the loss, and sacrifice involved, by comparing the figures of Cryptogame about to engage in his nocturnal flight, where he looks amusingly furtive, while in Cham he becomes virtually expressionless, with eyes and mouth thrown into shadow (fig. 6-2). Likewise contemplating flight from Elvire (fig. 6-3): where Cham (and/or the woodcut carver) shows simple annoyance or anger, his more openly delineated, shadowless face in Töpffer invites a more complex and more fitting interpretation—deep and gloomy contemplation (as the caption in fact says) and the dilemma of temptation. And yet, the *Illustration* wood engravers proved themselves perfectly capable of rendering Töpffer's simple outlines when it came to reproducing his drawings for the *Essai de Physiognomonie*.[2] It was not the limitations of woodblock, but conscious choice that determined the style (see fig. 4-4).

The gift to Cham of a copy of *Albert* was clearly a reminder how Töpffer really hoped his drawings might look; Cham, rendering thanks, acknowledges how the Töpffer albums had inspired him to embark upon the career he was now embracing, but skirts the invitation to reciprocate with an album of his own, which he may have feared Töpffer knew was marketed as an "album Jabot," dismissing such work as a mere "sorry bauble [*méchante bamboche*] which was my first step in the noble art of caricature."[3] He may, moreover, have feared to be identified as the actual transcriber of the piracies, as a distinguished modern Töpffer editor has, I believe wrongly, supposed he actually was.[4] It is certain that Töpffer knew about the (anonymous) Cham titles in the Albums Jabot series, complaining as he does that Aubert "associates others with them (the Töpffer piracies) flat enough, *I am told*, to kill the genre" [emphasis mine].[5]

Even if he had not seen the imitations (see p. 141), he must have known Cham was responsible for them, as appears from his urging the Parisian to send them, which his "scruple of modesty" had regrettably prevented. Cham substituted his parodic illustrations to *The Wandering Jew* by Eugène Sue, the original of which Töpffer declared detestable without his having even tried to read it. Cham was understandably reluctant to give the master the means to make a direct comparison with his own, the disciple's experiments, original as they were. But Töpffer had already cast Cham as his successor, explaining the peculiar merits of the new genre and how to approach it, amidst particular instructions for improvements to *Cryptogame*. Recently acquired by the Geneva library, hitherto unknown and as yet unpublished, these two letters are worth quoting at length, constituting as they do something of a manifesto.

The first letter of 26 January 1845 reminds Cham that this is

> quite a new genre where a prodigious harvest is to be reaped, and where moreover by committing your pencil to the pursuit of certain aberrations (*travers*) while respecting all the usual decencies [i.e., not too much Parisian sex!], without depriving yourself of the least particle of amusing fun or comic effects, there is a way to making yourself at least as useful as the established novelists. You reach a lot of people and the graphic contour is after all a brisk, emphatic language and as for clarity, well it has no equal."

Töpffer goes on to recommend the study of Hogarth, the first master. Later (18 March, the success of the Töpffer-Cham *Cryptogame* assured), he gives more detailed instructions and suggestions which indicate that he already had an improved album edition in mind (not so many deadly black coats, fix the defective captions, show the Dey's scientists kneeling with their bottoms toward us and not standing), all preceded by a "philosophy" of comic reduction, that sublimation into "idea," intention, or essence of conventional appearances and action that lie at the heart of the picture story:

> First, for purposes of expression, you need the comic, funny stuff, to take risks, that is charge emotionally through the hundred thousand obstacles of real, familiar truth. That [literal] truth often comes off in this sort of thing as superfluous and chilling, almost always inferior to the truth of the idea, of the intention, which is the essential. Add to this principle the consequence that there must be an economy of accessories and only a lively and selective choice of the most characteristic among them, always in order to render the idea only in terms that enhance clarity and emphasize the sense of the

intention, adding nothing for the sake of [mere] description or completeness.

Second, for purposes of invention and composition you must likewise, if you wish to catch *any* action of the hop, begin by shaking off as far as possible the yoke of reality, and the logical drag of some conventional succession of incidents, in order to charge once more into an area of livelier, quicker, and easier relationships, those that the mind grasps between pictures bound to an idea; and then the graphic contour, with its power of illusion, almost never fails to gel into a whole with enough continuity of likeness, the bold or crazy, the fantastic or even absurd. Here again the truth of the idea, the charms of the intention, the apt, witty, or novel observation, may be stitched onto this slight fabric, becoming more relevant and more valuable than [literal] truth as such could ever be. Which is to say you let go on one side in order to pick up on the other, and also that you cannot fly without wings. This mental attitude is not to be called up on order, but one can lie in wait for it, and one must be prepared to woo it.

Cham did not heed this advice; he had already passed beyond it to a style more suited to woodcut and magazine illustration, less dependant on contour and more on shading, via Daumier perhaps, and hewing close to the "literal truth" of sociopolitical follies of the day.

Subsequent critics have been harsh on the *Illustration* translation, usually citing Cham, wrongly, as the engraver; for their part, as soon as photomechanical reproduction became possible, publishers of Töpffer editions preferred Töpffer's original drawings to the Cham version. It was, however, the latter that achieved great popularity and went into constantly revived editions in the years after Töpffer's death, thus keeping alive the Töpffer picture story which went otherwise out of print. And the drawings and story line of *Cryptogame* (bowdlerized) were turned, quite remarkably, into what has become an enduring children's classic in Holland.

But (Catholic) France was not (Calvinist) Geneva. A problem surfaced with the Abbé and the two Missionaries in *Cryptogame*, whom Dubochet decided to turn into a professor (*docteur*), and a mayor and his adjunct in order not to offend Catholics, particularly in Italy. But the publisher was able, just before the eleventh and final installment appeared in April, to pronounce the whole venture, in which he had as great a financial stake (having had to pay three parties) as Töpffer had a moral one (he got 1,000 francs), "a wild success with young and old, although contested by some." (The "contestation" was on grounds of sheer length.) It is therefore odd that the potentially lucrative album edition that was expected to follow immediately, in the manner of serial publications, should have been delayed, so much so that the specialist in comic albums in England, David Bogue, actually produced, from copies of the *Illustration* blocks he had received from Dubochet traveling to London for the purpose in June, his edition of *Cryptogame* that same year and long before the French album.

Yet as early as 7 April, even before the last installments of the story had appeared in *L'Illustration*, Cham was telling his mentor of the preparations for the album version and asking for specifications as to which designs needed to be redone; Töpffer, feeling very ill (and declining Dubochet's invitation to seek a cure in Paris), left the choice of substitute cuts to Cham, but wanted the Abbé restored, together with his wandering frame-lines, and some captions rendered more exactly. By 22 June, he complains "is it abandoned, dead, buried, or is it in production?" and he wants the manuscript back; a week later Dubochet assures his cousin that "Cryptogame is about to enter the lists in another form," but not ready because Cham still has to do some of the cuts crippled by the engraver, which required retaining the manuscript. By 30 July, all the while urging the sick man to try something new "of the Jabot, Vieux Bois, and Cryptogame family," Dubochet describes the album as "in press, appetizing, cheap." In

August more expressions of impatience arrive from Geneva, with concern not to drop the price below five francs (six was normal), and conceding that the Docteur stay instead of Abbé. But still the album did not appear, and it was not until the following 28 February 1846 that Dubochet is able to tell Töpffer that he is getting his manuscript back via Abraham Cherbuliez.

In fact, very little was done to the *Illustration* version, certainly not enough to justify the serious delay. The text was reset but virtually unchanged, and only seven scenes were redesigned and recut, the last of them so badly that one cannot believe it was drawn by Cham himself. Töpffer got his missionaries back, but not his Abbé, who remains Docteur, nor his wandering frame-lines. (I give more details in *Rodolphe Töpffer: The Complete Comic Strips*). A new title page was added (p. 119), including four small children peering over the stone bearing the publisher's name, three of whom are dark-skinned and one who wears a turban. The naughty suggestion here must be that Cryptogame has been otherwise busy in Algeria.

Was the delay the fault of Cham, or Dubochet, or the engraving shop? Was one of the reasons Dubochet's turning away from *L'Illustration* towards his uncle's gas company? Was Cham too busy with other work to perform this little chore for the master he so much admired? For it was not until 25/27 April, in a letter written in Kity's hand, when he was very close to death, that Töpffer acknowledges, briefly, receipt of *Cryptogame* (presumably the long-awaited album which bears the date 1846) and requests a copy of the English edition which Dubochet has (out of guilt?) failed hitherto to send him.

Töpffer wanted the manuscript back so that he could proceed with the lithographic version which he seems to have started even before he sent off the manuscript, for the latter as it survives today has lithographs pasted in at pages 9–16. How he imagined selling the two versions simultaneously is not clear. Genevan booksellers were pressing for another in the Jabot series, and it may be that he wanted the lithographic version of *Cryptogame* not so much to sell separately, as to join all the other albums in a collected edition for which he had sold the six existing stories to Kessmann by 14 October 1845. Kessmann brought out the first two installments, *Jabot* and *Crépin*, by March 1846, but the collection, which was faithfully copied from Töpffer, ended without the famous butterfly hunter.

When he returned to lithograph the first pages he incorporated some details from Cham, but he was by now very sick indeed, lacking in control of hand and eye, and the changes he made to the drawings are for the most part done for their own sakes, to differentiate them, I suspect, from the Cham version, and are not improvements. His covering the bare shoulder of Elvire (whom Cham had already tried to render more attractive) and showing the hero, originally drawn in his shirtsleeves, fully dressed was an unnecessary concession, surely, to the prudes. Physical pain ("toothache on his hip") and fear of time running out have blunted the old precision of control. He was even unable to rewrite a lithographic caption to incorporate the changes he wanted (fig. 6-2), and in *Albert* he let an obvious error (p. 37, no 2 for 20) pass him by.

The success of *Cryptogame* before the *bon gros public* Töpffer always aspired to must have been particularly sweet (or bittersweet) to the author, now gravely ill. In the spring and summer Dubochet was writing to his cousin in Vichy, where he was undergoing treatment for his swollen spleen and a general debilitation. A letter raising the question of a German edition of *Cryptogame* was written, *horribile dictu*, in his daughter's hand; Rodolphe, now too weak to use his pen, expressed the fear he would not leave Vichy alive.

News of the public success of *Cryptogame*, which reached many thousands who had never before encountered the author's work (he was billed in

L'Illustration as the author of *Jabot*, etc. and his fake anonymity was preserved in the album), prompted Dubochet to suggest discreetly that the author's experiences with the doctors at the famous spa invited some kind of medical satire. There had been some of this, to be sure, in the "stolen" *Trictrac* and, we surmise, in the (lost) *Dr. Saitout*, but this was otherwise virgin territory for Töpffer, who had managed hitherto to avoid doctors, even or especially eye doctors. He had during previous summer's "cure" contemplated a "Crépin à Lavey" (at the waters, in the bathhouse, in bed, taking coffee, playing whist), which went nowhere despite the success of some drawings shown around and presented to favored individuals at the spa.[6] Dubochet had suggested (16 November 1844) "the adventures and misadventures of a tourist during a season at the baths of Vichy, or elsewhere." And his hint now (16 April 1845) for a *série* on tourists, thinking of how amusingly Töpffer had mocked them in his *Voyages*, would anticipate the direction taken by the European comic strip in mid-century. The artist was more inclined to the medical satire, although the two topics could obviously have been combined, but any *bambochade* (bambocciata, humorous genre scene) was to be encouraged. Dubochet had followed up *Cryptogame* in *L'Illustration* with a strip repeating the African locale, which only underscored the uniqueness of his Swiss cousin's talent, as he pointed out, presciently: "You have created the genre and you haven't seen the last of your imitators."[7] Anxious not to importune a very sick man by demanding of him the slightest effort, Dubochet gently encouraged him in his medical satire, for which he even had a title or name of protagonist: "Vichy must be crowded with people great and humble. You have there a vast field of observation and you will have drawn there from nature more than one episode of M. Hydrophile." Some mockery of his own painful, useless, or counterproductive treatment might have brought psychological relief, but, alas, he could not even be-

gin to draw this or other ideas: "I have three stories in my head, of which two are almost written in captions [*Claudius Berlu* and *Lord Turneps?*—see *Rodolphe Töpffer: The Complete Comic Strips*], but there is no way that I can draw the slightest bit of a figure, nor apply myself to anything at all, other than drinking, soaking, digesting, vegetating, dragging myself round, to end up spending atrocious nights after 48 hour days."[8] He could still write, however, and with despairing gaiety, especially the long, daily letters to his wife. He died a year later, probably of leukemia or hepatitis.

Like *Vieux Bois*, *Cryptogame* parodies romantic love, but in reverse: instead of an ardent male lover indefatigably pursuing the torpid female against all obstacles, an equally ardent fiancée pursues an unwilling (and not at all torpid) male in the wildest adventures. Although as crazy and surreal in its incidents as any of the other Töpffer tales, *Cryptogame* is structurally more linear, borne along on a single narrative thread, with no "meanwhiles" that take us back in time and across space to where the author left another lot of characters. The lack of political or intellectual satire, apart from that involving Muslim Algeria, a target soft and safe, also made it suitable for children, as witness the much doctored German and Dutch versions, where Elvire is turned into a sister rather than fiancée.

The changes wrought by Töpffer (and Dubochet-Cham) in the various versions of *Cryptogame* between 1830 and 1845, not to speak of those made by plagiarists and copyists since, make a fascinating and complex story in which we can only point to some highlights. Töpffer's own changes between 1830 and 1844 add coherence and dynamism. Elvire, the dynamo who keeps the story revolving (and other figures in it as well, quite literally), acquires true mock-heroic stature through the addition of several important incidents. With superhuman strength she whirls the Turk, who has kidnapped her for his harem, around by the beard and into the sea (fig. 6-4).

6-4. Elvire frees herself and seizes the old Turk by the beard, swings him around and throws him into the ocean (*Cryptogame* 101–2).

6-5. Meanwhile Elvire turns the head of the Dey, who accedes to all her fantasies. Then at the given moment, like Judith, she thrusts her dagger into her Holofernes (*Cryptogame* 157–58).

Later (fig. 6-5), in immediate fear of ravishment, and with truly biblical courage, she reenacts Judith pretending to submit to Holofernes, the better to plunge a dagger into the tyrant's breast and escape. This scene, omitted in the children's versions, makes a startling contrast to the usual passive harem scenes so beloved of the painters and illustrators (Ingres and so many more); I have found only one French lithograph (fig. 6-6) showing a comparable counter-aggression. In 1830 Elvire adopted the much less heroic tactic of hitting the Dey in the head with a stone. She is on her own: Cryptogame and company make no attempt to intervene when she is abducted, and he even wears a smile of relief at the sight (fig. 6-7). This is consistent: he prefers slavery to the Turk to slavery to Elvire.

The reaction of Cryptogame to the overall increase in the mass and speed of his fiancée's onslaught is correspondingly and comically heightened. Töpffer much prolongs his iron resistance to the various means Elvire uses to unfreeze her lover onboard ship in a polar climate: all her ardent pleas, her hot toddies, her pectoral frictions, down to roasting on a spit, leave him—literally—cold. In 1844 Cryptogame tries actively to palm Elvire off on his companion the Abbé, impelled now by a double motive: fear of bigamy (not present in 1830) as well as of Elvire. And in the published version, in which the (celibate) Abbé has become a Professor, Cryptogame adroitly encourages his courtship of Elvire and marriage to her. The whole affair is enriched, in a classic, comically counterproductive maneuver, by Elvire's finding her own motive for encouraging the Abbé: to make Cryptogame jealous and thus (re)kindle his love.

The introduction in 1844, much earlier in the story, of Elvire's rival, the Belle Provençale, who celebrates her nuptials immediately and secretly in the belly of a whale (the name Cryptogame is actually Greek for "secretly married"), adds wings and credibility to the hero's flight, and a mythic dimension too: the hero finds his salvation (or so he

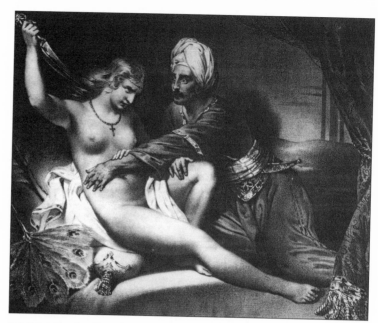

6-6. B. R. Julien after Alexandre Evariste Fragonard, *The Virtuous Odalisque*, lithograph, 1833 (from DelPlato).

6-7. The Dey's officers, hearing that there were three Christians on board, take possession of them, and begin with Elvire whom they destine for their master's seraglio (*Cryptogame* 142).

and we think) in "another world"; and belched up by the monster, whose digestive system is disturbed by the nuptial dancing, he is reborn as it were, like Jonah—and, we may add, like Baron Munchausen, perhaps an inspiration to Töpffer specifically here, as generally in the narration of comic impossibilia. In *The Adventures of Baron Munchausen*, that European best-seller, we find as in Töpffer the Turkish factor and oddities like a sojourn in a haystack.

The dénouement of the 1844 version is as violent as Elvire's temper and pursuit. Delayed by further adventures, Cryptogame's honeymoon has only just begun, when it is interrupted by Elvire. Her suicidal self-explosion eliminates her from the story, clearing the way for eternal bliss; this, however, in a last-minute twist belying the conventional and superficial, even ironic happy-marriage ending of several of Töpffer's other tales, prose and pictorial, proves to be short-lived, faced as the hero suddenly is with a hitherto concealed brood of brats from the bride's first marriage. He is glumly acquiescent, but we know his butterfly-hunting days are over.

For one whose eye was always on local Genevan affairs, Töpffer's use of the French occupation of Algeria seems extraordinarily well timed. Five weeks before he completed the first draft of *Cryptogame*, French forces invaded Algeria, beginning on 14 June 1830; he had preceded his picture story with a school playlet set in Algeria called *Les Aventures de M. Coquemolle*, Folie en 3 actes, written in 1829 and performed for the baptism on 6 September 1830 of his son François.[9] (It was successfully revived on the occasion of the bicentenary celebrations, Geneva 1999.) There is some thematic overlap. The barbaric behavior of Muslim leaders, toward their own people as well as the Europeans they massacred and enslaved, were topoi current in art and literature and sharpened by the Greek war of independence, while romantic lithographs and painters presented the attractive, erotic side to Muslim harem life. In

Töpffer, Arabs massacre the entire crew of a Norwegian whaler; the stupid and tyrannical Dey of Algiers capriciously hangs his court scientists; while the captured Cryptogame and company, avoiding the even more horrid fate of the galley slaves, are assigned to relatively congenial and painless tasks, Cryptogame as a gardener, the Abbé as a tutor to the Dey's children, and Elvire as harem maiden, a role she escapes as we have seen. Can the escape of our Europeans, under cover of the fire started accidentally by friction from the beam tied to the Abbé's leg, be seen as that of Europeans seeking to avoid the fire of colonial destruction? Lord Exmouth in 1816 threatened Dey Omar-Pacha with destruction of the town, which the invading French accomplished, in part, in 1830. Ali Khodja, elected the new dey after the assassination of Omar-Pacha, died of the plague at the moment he was considering abducting the wife and daughter of the Dutch consul for his seraglio—or so we are told by an *Histoire d'Alger* of 1841.[10]

"As for the slaves at Algiers, they are not indeed so unhappy," wrote a Frenchman referring to the household, as opposed to the galley slaves.[11] In *Cryptogame* the Europeans are treated better than the Algerian scientists, and in fact of history many captives ended up with decent jobs, as shopkeepers, gardeners (like Cryptogame himself), tutors (like the Abbé), and even as a kind of toy for children playing horsie, like the Abbé again (fig. 6-8). Many, like Cryptogame, "took the turban," embraced Islam as "renegades." Their lives in North Africa may indeed have been an improvement over life at home.

The climate of political and cultural criticism within which Töpffer first sketched the story was much aggravated by the time he came to publish it fifteen years later. The continuing war to establish French control, and the heroic resistance of Abd el-Kadr, kept Algeria and North Africa in the public eye. The fourth volume of *L'Illustration* (September 1844–February 1845) began a separate index category called "Scènes d'Algérie," so important had

145

146.

mais dès la seconde leçon, les petits Moustacha proposent à leur précepteur de jouer à tiens toi bien et l'instruction en souffre un peu

(dès la troisième leçon les petits Moustacha ne voulant plus que jouer à tiens toi bien, l'abbé s'y refuse, et l'instruction n'en va pas mieux

6-8. The little Moustachas suggest to their tutor a game of horsie, which prejudices the lesson. When the Abbé puts an end to it, the lesson is not advanced thereby (*Cryptogame* 145).

the country become in the public mind. Excitement mounted in 1844 with Biskra's expedition, the bombardment of Mogador, Bugeaud's victory at Isly, and the subsequent peace treaty—all featured and illustrated in the magazine. Algeria remained prominent throughout the months that *Cryptogame* was run; indeed the topic reached a climax in the very same issue that carried Töpffer's first Algerian episode (March 15), with a spectacular full-spread feature on Horace Vernet's "Capture of the smala [family headquarters] of Abd el-Kadr." This enormous, panoramic painting had been the sensation of the Salon that year. At the same time, beyond the conquest of Algeria, in the well-honed manner of imperialist cultural appropriation, Arab customs and exoticisms continued to excite the European imagination. Töpffer may as a boy have seen Ros-

sini's *L'Italiana in Algeri*, which had scored a great success in Geneva in 1813, and where the Bey of Algiers has a wife called Elvire, a name used also in Mozart's opera *Don Giovanni* for the abandoned female.[12]

The Genevan artist also projected into Algeria his experience of civil disorder at home. In 1844 he added a scene showing the terrible chaos caused by the janissaries' method of choosing a new dey (see fig. 2-2), meant surely to mirror the anarchy the author blamed on the electoral agitations of the Genevan radicals. Too busy fighting to notice that a fire is consuming the city, the Algerian citizens lose all chance of escape and are driven into the ocean. This replicates Töpffer's warnings in his polemical journalism: Genevan infighting would result in the ruin of that of the most perfect of structures,

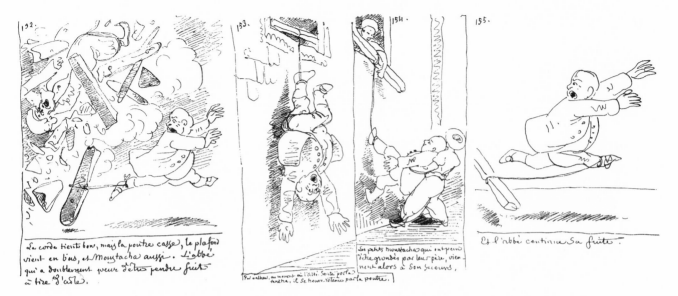

6-9. The rope holds fast, but the beam breaks, bringing down the ceiling and Moustacha too. The Abbé who is doubly afraid of being hanged flees pell mell. Unfortunately at the moment he jumps out the window, he is caught by the beam. The little Moustachas, afraid of being scolded by their father, come to his aid. And the Abbé continues his flight (*Cryptogame* 152–55).

the Genevan constitution. Otherwise, and, to his French public, the destruction of Algiers and its citizens was just vengeance for the long tradition of Muslim piracy, enslavement of Christians, and insults to diplomats.

Ironically, it is the dim-witted and otherwise torpid Abbé, employed to teach physics to the Dey's unruly children or be hanged, who, running off with the beam tied to his leg (fig. 6-9), illustrates the laws of physics, friction causing the fire that is the salvation of the Europeans. Or is the fire—another poetic justice?—the fault of the children of the Dey, who tied the beam to their tutor's leg? The beam becomes a virtual attribute of the Abbé, for he does not rid himself of it during all is subsequent adventures, down to the end, where the Belle Provençale's children fight over it. If the beam is viewed as a symbol of the Abbé's pedagogic martyrdom, as seems reasonable, one is tempted to see an autobiographical flourish here: Töpffer tied to the burden of his schoolmastering. More simply, the beam is the burden of life, and of the Abbé's stupidity.

Most of the Algerian episode survived intact from the 1830 version, gaining as we have seen in topicality. But a crescendo of movement of another kind, one that was particularly admired in Weimar, met with significant refinement. Starting from an almost true dead point—for when Elvire faints after a superlative fit of rage, the Abbé and Cryptogame prepare to throw her overboard, thinking her dead—a spark of energy from the suddenly reviving virago sets off a most wonderful chain reaction. Cryptogame flees and she pursues; but then, in 1844, through a witty reversal of designs Elvire, the pursuer of Cryptogame, appears to be pursued *by* him; and they, pursued by the Abbé, who both flees and pursues in imitation as is his wont, infect a descending hierarchy of crew, animals, and furniture, causing the whole ship to revolve and everyone to be pursuing and fleeing everyone else, in the kind of vertiginous mix-up dear to early movie farce (see fig. 2-1).

These are all additions. In 1844 Töpffer also made one small and one large cut. The small one is of rats, which in 1830 infest no fewer than twenty-

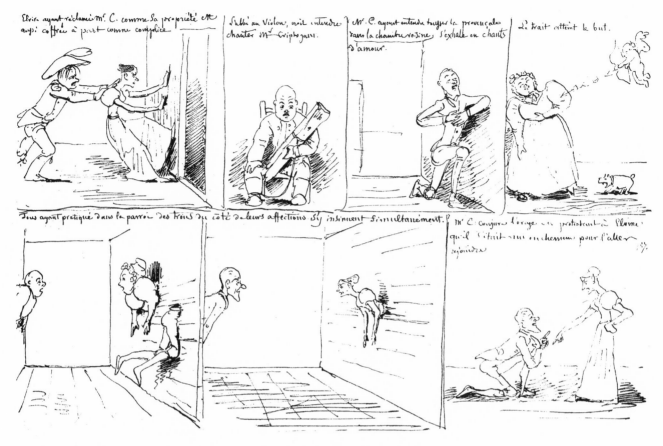

6-10. When Elvire claims Mr. C. as her property, she is also jailed as an accomplice. In jail, the Abbé thinks he hears Mr. Criptogame [*sic*] singing. Hearing the Woman from Provence coughing in the neighboring room, Mr. C. gives vent to love songs. The arrow reaches its target. Each having made a hole in the wall on the side of their affections, they insinuate themselves simultaneously. Mr. C. averts the storm by protesting to Elvire that he was just on the way to join her (*Cryptogame* ms, 1830, 181–87).

five scenes—fighting it out against the humans in the belly of the whale, clinging to the back of Elvire as she is hoisted aboard the Algerian brig, being eaten alive by the starving hero. Highly amusing, surely, to the schoolboys of the Pension Töpffer, but not to be risked with the mixed family readership of *L'Illustration.*

The larger cut, involving the last fifty-eight scenes of the 1830 manuscript (reproduced in our facsimile edition), is harder to explain. It affects the purest and most pristine, the most cinematic, funny, and physical of Töpfferian farce (fig. 6-10). Did the author deem it simply too silly for public con-

sumption? Or did this episode, with which Töpffer had left the story suspended in midair, threaten to prolong beyond feasible limits a story that must be quickly brought to its dénouement?

The change of format from small oblong album to large magazine (pictorial area 32 by 24 cm, roughly the format of a large modern comic book and graphic novel) was drastic. A series of crowded, full vertical quarto pages (to a total of twenty-two), such as became virtually standard with subsequent magazine comic strips, was new to Töpffer, whose oblong or "landscape" format albums with their ample margins helped propel and oxygenated a breathless narrative. The magazine also attenuated the forward impulse inherent both in the horizontal album shape and in the left-to-right movement of the figures, which Cham, culpably, did not bother to reverse. With the crowding of three rows of scenes per page in *L'Illustration* there is a loss of suspense and rushing air. Finally, the magazine's page format flattened out or obscured a characteristic break in rhythm: the *ritardando* of the single climactic or caesural scene spread over a whole page, followed by the *accelerando* of multiple, similar narrow scenes.

The "freedom" enjoined by Töpffer on his copyist Cham included that of leaving breaks in the lines of the face which contribute essentially to their mobility and openness of expression. Töpffer explained, at some length, how this worked in his treatise *Essai de Physiognomonie*, published soon afterward. This kind of abbreviation was a function of the speed with which the artist drew, and helped maintain continuity of a facial type, as any cartoonist today knows. Working for the "bon gros public" Cham was less willing to take his audience's comprehension for granted, and filled out Töpffer's sketches in order to achieve maximum legibility, which unfortunately entailed blurring psychological ambiguities and simplifying complex emotional states. And yet Cham's vulgarization of Töpffer for the masses is still much more lively than the dead hand of the plagiarists.

Meanwhile, at some time towards the end he was contemplating a "revision" of *Festus*,[13] presumably a second edition of the picture story, and fusing *Vieux Bois* with the "best of Criptogame" [sic], in which "he tells the Hermit his past, that is his loves with Elvire." This was, apparently, to be a novelette in the manner of the prose *Festus*, starting: "At 45 years of age, Mr Vieux Bois frequented the public promenades. It is about the age of forty-five that Mr Vieux Bois' star began to settle. This remarkable man was born under the sign . . ." (the manuscript here breaks off).[14] It may also be at this late period

that he started to write *The Story of Sébastien Brodbec*, a fantastic tale such as he had never attempted, which veered into the sexual and for that reason stalled (see Appendix A). On the verso of the last page appears a sketch for an Histoire d'une Maladie, with a page of notes for a story with elements of *Trictrac*. Finally, one may add a project mooted with Dubochet in May 1843–1844, to do woodcut version of *Jabot* and *Crépin*, the lithographic editions of which were almost sold out. Could they not be offered for wider distribution as cheap(er) woodcut albums that the big publisher Jules Hetzel might be interested in? Might they not be *traced* onto a woodblock, as they would be, afresh by another hand, onto lithographic paper for the posthumous collected editions? But the tests for a woodcut *Jabot* proved unsatisfactory.[15]

Histoire d'Albert

Töpffer's newspaper failed to check the progress of the Genevan revolution. Quite apart from his irreducible political convictions, the schoolmaster had another reason to fear social upheaval: it would jeopardize recruitment to his *pension*, a threat in actuality more than offset by the *Voyages* which served, fortuitously, to advertise it far and wide. His last new picture story was his symbolic revenge. *The Story of Albert by Simon of Nantua* was intended to be ready for the New Year 1845 gift market, and when this ambition was threatened by a delay at the printer's the author wrote him a sharp reproach.[16] *Albert* is didactic, polemical, and generally all too serious in tone; there are some graphic high jinks but little of the erstwhile comic fantasy. The tale is attributed on the title page to one Simon de Nantua, the fictional invention of Laurent de Jussieu, a very conservative writer for the young, who casts Simon of Nantua in the best-selling book (*Simon de Nantua, or the itinerant pedlar*) as a conservative,

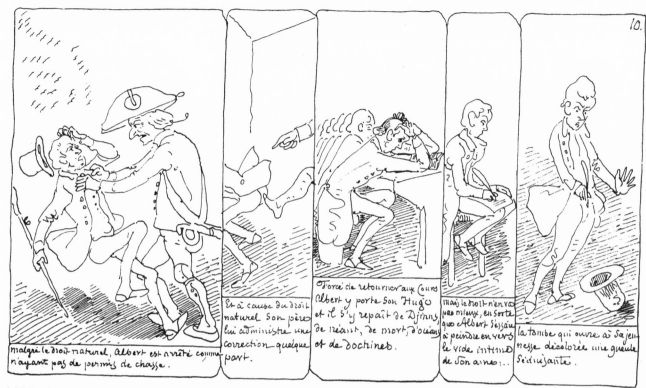

Handwritten text in panels:
malgré le droit naturel, Albert est arrêté comme n'ayant pas de permis de chasse.

Et à cause du droit naturel son père lui administre une correction quelque part.

Forcé de retourner aux cours Albert y porte son Hugo et il s'y repaît de Djinns de néant, de mort, d'océans et de doctrines.

mais le droit n'en va pas mieux, en sorte que Albert s'essaie à peindre en vers le vide intime de son âme:...

la tombe qui ouvre à sa jeunesse décolorée une gueule séduisante.

6-11. Despite natural law, Albert is arrested for not having a hunting license. And because of natural law his father administers a correction somewhere. Forced to return to the lectures, Albert brings his Hugo and feasts on Djinns, nothingness, death, oceans, and ideology. But the law does not improve thereby, so that Albert tries painting in verse the inner void of his soul . . . the tomb that opens to his washed-out youth a seductive maw (*Albert* 10).

disciplinarian moralist who preaches, for instance, that poverty is due to laziness.

Graphically, Töpffer's story is remarkable for its fertile technical devices: use of the pars pro toto, and (in the same scenes) the refrain-like repetition of Albert being kicked by his father and making strategic escapes from trouble (fig. 6-11). Despite its claim to be the first truly political modern comic strip, it has remained the least popular of Töpffer's published stories.[17] In Geneva it may have been engulfed by the events it satirizes; there were no reviews, and a friend sensed why it was neglected in Geneva: "It is a pity for your readers that so many things are momentarily escaping ridicule by dint of being odious or fatal, or rather that the ridicule which they really need as does every evil, hides under

horror and disgust; your gallery would be infinitely extended. . . . Our Switzerland is at the moment full of *Alberts*, but they are not yet fun at all; at least they are not yet having fun. Their hour will come. I wish the hour were already come to deliver up to ridicule this cross-eyed politics and its equivocal language."[18] Beyond the Alps praise came from none other than Count Camillo Cavour—with Mazzini maker of a united Italy—to whom Töpffer sent a copy (they had actually dined together in 1838). Cavour thanked Töpffer at some length: "The Story of Albert contains a subtle and witty satire of much of our current wrongdoing, it is a comedy of a Molière of today where instead of a Tartuffe of piety, you find so many tartuffes of industry, tartuffes of progress, tartuffes of patriotism etc. . . ."[19]

6-12. Unfortunately, bankruptcy is declared, and Jaques [= Albert] decamps. On behalf of a publisher-bookseller Albert is charged with placing the big edition of Metaphysics in Pictures, text and engravings, so that he begins to pester from floor to floor. Ground floor / first floor / 2nd / 3rd / 4th (*Albert* 25).

Albert attacks radicalism, opportunism, and political journalism. Its point of departure is a failed education, which is blamed not so much on the prevalence of false doctrines, as in *Crépin*, as on the individual moral flaw compounded by bad parenting. Old enough to be held personally responsible, Albert squanders his educational opportunities at the public schools (no private tutors for him). Of good bourgeois stock, alternately thrashed and kicked about by his father and spoiled by his mother, he is a dabbler, intelligent but lazy, inquisitive but scatterbrained, the kind of boy whom Töpffer must have known in his school. He is seduced by Romanticism and subsists for a while on a diet of jinns, void, death, oceans, and ideology (*doctrines*—a dig at Victor Hugo here [fig. 6-11]). He tries to launch himself as a romantic poet, with a collection of po-

ems called *Harmonies Orageuses* (Stormy Harmonies) for which he gets a preface from Mr. La Bartine (i.e., Lamartine), and puts up posters—just the kind of pretension and publicity Töpffer abhorred. So far Albert's only crime has been to hunt without a license, and absent the normal vices of youth that the literary stereotype of the wastrel demanded— drink, gambling, womanizing—his downward path is signaled by radical doctrines, contempt of all authorities, and flirting with the Carbonari.

The initially and theoretically secret society of the Carbonari (literally, charcoal burners) started in Italy, where it eventually grew to become the Giovine Italia and as such, eventually, midwife to the young unified Italian state. The Carbonari had been cruelly persecuted by the Austrians in Italy, and spread to France under the leadership of Lafayette, and elsewhere in Europe, totaling an estimated 60,000 members by the early 1830s,[20] with official, paranoid estimates for Italy alone ten times higher. Töpffer has the Carbonari satirically infiltrating the post of lamplighter all over France, from which vantage point a simultaneous uprising would occur and take over. In fact, there were in 1821 widespread plans in France for a simultaneous uprising in towns hundreds of miles apart, led by Carbonarists strategically placed in government positions. The plan was discovered and violently repressed. Töpffer's choice of lamplighter as the office of choice to infiltrate is partly absurd and partly symbolic: better street lighting was a generally demanded reform, and artificial light symbolized Enlightenment, to counter the obscurantism of the "Holy Alliance [which] loomed darkly over the whole of the continent," in the words of a history of secret societies of 1876.[21] The "Ultras" or worst reactionaries were called *éteignoirs* (light-extinguishers). A German satirical magazine called itself *Leuchtkugeln* (balls of light), an Italian one *Il Lampione*. Töpffer's choice of lamplighter must have amused Dubochet, who had begun to work for his uncle's gas company and sold company shares to his cousin.

Meanwhile, between his first flirtation and his active cooperation in Carbonarist conspiracy, Albert has tried himself and failed in a picaresque array of lowly trades: dentistry, podiatry, popular publishing, selling encyclopedias door-to-door (fig. 6-12), wine and groceries, manufacturing candles, and making chocolate without cocoa—this last an outright swindle of the *Macaire*-ish kind. The ease with which Albert floats from one menial job to another masks the real economic fact of high levels of unemployment and lack of job security. The ease was at the other end, that of the employers, who hired and fired workers at will. Töpffer identified members of the disaffected lower middle class, the class he had risen from, allied to equally discontented artisans, as the core of the radical and revolutionary movements. This was correct, although their ideologues

and activists were in reality also, often enough, upper class and aristocrats. Töpffer's Mangini, one of the three Carbonarists to whom he gives a name, is clearly Giuseppe Mazzini, son of a wealthy doctor and university professor, who became a lawyer and Carbonarist and was exiled to Geneva, where he befriended James Fazy and helped found the Young Switzerland society in 1834.

Discovered, Töpffer's conspirators flee France for Switzerland, where the free press, relaxed government, and hospitality to refugees from all over Europe offer fertile ground for subversion. The specific target in *The Story of Albert* (which was originally called *The Story of Jaques*) is the Genevan radical leader James Fazy (James is the equivalent of Jacques).[22] Son of a highly cultured, conservative, and important manufacturer father and Fourierist mother, James Fazy was educated in Paris, where he militated as a journalist for the 1830 Revolution and then against Louis-Philippe, for which he was jailed. He was associated, briefly, with Mazzini and the Carbonari. Back in Geneva in 1833, Fazy founded several journals, locking horns with Töpffer's own *Courrier de Genève* (15 January 1842–22 March 1843, with about 105 articles by the artist). Töpffer accused Fazy there, as in the figure of Albert, of engaging in unscrupulous agitation with selfish mercenary interests. While Töpffer spoke for traditional oligarchical (clerical-academic) rule, Fazy and his party, the Association du Trois Mars, represented major Genevan business interests with which the large, skilled, and long-disenfranchised artisan class (mostly watchmakers) identified.

Albert is modeled only partly on Fazy the individual, however. He is also a political *type*, the revolutionary as caricatured by the conservative, then as now, so as to conceal the true social forces behind revolutions and revolutionaries. For indeed, whether agitating above or below ground, the typical revolutionary or carbonaro was not—as in Töpffer—a shiftless coward, egotist, or drunkard who blabbed secrets to strangers in cafés, rhetorically brandished

6-13. "May an im-pure blood Qu-ench our furrows! Qu-ench our furrows!" No. 80 begs the powers to yield to the people their just demands. No. 90 begs the people to calm down, since the powers cannot refuse much longer their just demands. Meanwhile the people beginning to understand themselves and to be understood, the result is that the citizens fire on each other, the Constitution is overthrown, the town is in mourning, and business is ruined . . . (*Albert* 39).

daggers at meetings, and promised death to all tyrants and liberty to all peoples, sealed in an endless series of dinner-table toasts. Both Fazy and Mazzini, the Italian nationalist honored today with innumerable streets named after him, not to speak of a host of revolutionary leaders then and since, were men of the highest moral probity, brave and tenacious. Dubochet himself, in Paris with Fazy, had shown Carbonarist sympathies, for which he had been arrested in 1822. Where Albert is a fantast, a floater both in the realm of ideas and among people, Fazy was the epitome of pragmatism. Having outgrown utopian socialism, he strove to develop a moderate liberal position with respect to a free, competitive market economy and democratic procedures based on universal suffrage and parliaments such as other Swiss cities had had since 1830. This

was deemed the only route to stability and material progress. The constitution Fazy brought in survives in Geneva today.

While the purpose of *Albert* is to vilify the character of the revolutionary, to trivialize his plots and the very idea of revolution, the "revolutionary" tactics that are presented as the most dangerous, because the most successful, turn out to be journalistic and legal. The "revolutionary demands" in *Albert*, like Fazy's, are liberal ones, economic and political reforms directed from above. They resemble those of the French 1830 and 1848 revolutions, made by and for the press. Journalists were prominent in both, especially the latter, to which the insurrection in Geneva was a preliminary, relatively nonviolent tremor to a European earthquake.

In contrast to the comic-opera posturing and adventurism earlier in the story, apparently set in France, Albert's agitation in his and Töpffer's homeland of Switzerland/Geneva is conducted though "legitimate channels," in particular, an opposition press that appeals methodically to each aggrieved spectrum of the population, ranging from the big industrialists to the workers and lumpen types. The Genevan artisans in the watchmaking and allied trades, concentrated in the Saint Gervais district of the city, politically educated and traditionally combative, led the armed confrontations, as their fellow artisans in Paris did in 1830 and 1848.[23] It is these Genevese workers, then, who brought Fazy to power. Albert/Fazy's journal, after exploiting a generalized discontent that ensures its commercial success and good dinners for the owner, appeals to the government to agree on long-overdue constitutional reforms and long-ignored popular demands for economic improvements, and to the people to keep calm. But whether this is hypocrisy or well intentioned, it is too late, the damage is done, the purpose is achieved of arousing the people, who "begin to understand themselves and to be understood"—that is, in Marxian terms, achieve class consciousness—and violently turn the town upside down.

On 13 February 1843, an abortive attack on the Genevan town hall left three insurgents dead. In *Albert*, street fighting breaks out more as the result of open journalistic agitation than as a result of the Carbonarist conspiracy that preceded it (fig. 6-13). To this extent, Töpffer's satire is true to events. The momentary presence, in the 1830s, of Mazzini and Filippo Buonarrotti, another Carbonarist leader, seems actually to have left little impression. The Genevan revolution was strictly indigenous. As a projection of civil war, or total economic and political ruin, the fighting at the end of *Albert* is happily inaccurate: in October 1846, a few months after Töpffer's death, the workers of Geneva again confronted the city government, which refused to take extreme measures against them and resigned, leaving Fazy in power. The new regime introduced a period in Genevan history generally regarded as both prosperous and progressive; and in this new era, pace *Albert*, the change was not merely the occasion for the leader's enrichment, or escape.

Töpffer's aesthetic revolution: Theory and anti-theory

Töpffer lost against the political revolution at home; but the graphic and aesthetic revolution he pioneered and argued for was to be won in the twentieth century. His *Essai de physiognomonie* and his numerous essays on art, written serially over a dozen years beginning in the 1830s and gathered by Dubochet under the title *Réflexions et menus-propos d'un peintre genevois* (*Reflections and Small Talk of a Genevan Painter*, first edition 1848, constantly republished since), contain many of the seeds of aesthetic theory that have flowered in our own times. A modern critic has called them "the finest essays on aesthetics in French."[24] Baudelaire, who fails to mention Töpffer in his printed essays on caricature, knew of the Swiss,[25] probably through Théophile Gautier, the friend he called his master. Gautier's careful appreciation of Töpffer's *Réflexions* in the *Revue des deux mondes*[26] begins with a strenuous correction of Sainte-Beuve's disparagement of the comic albums, published six years before in the same magazine, and must have aroused attention.

The aesthetic ideas of Töpffer and Baudelaire have much in common, notably in rebutting the fundamental (traditional, classical) idea that the function of art is to imitate and idealize nature. Both anticipated the modernist idea that art transforms nature, does nature over, transcends and bypasses it, and that art obeys its own laws independent of nature. The Swiss does not go as far as to claim, with Baudelaire, that art may contradict nature. But art, being *independant* of nature, obeys its own laws. "Le mental zigzagging around. This is attested by the very form of Töpffer's meandering, digressive art criticism, as well as of the dreamlike flow of the picture stories and the "zigzag" philosophizing in the *Voyages en Zigzag*, themselves conducted in reality, as far as was practical, as semi-organized *flânerie*. Töpffer is the Montaigne of aesthetic reverie.

Töpffer's ideas were rooted, more than he would have cared to admit, in Romantic attitudes. The notions of caprice, chance, instinct, and the unconscious which inform both theory and comic album; the insistence that all artistic signs are conventional rather than more or less close approximations of nature; the special expressive value attached to naïve, crude, childish, and incomplete but "essential" forms, harking back (and over) to non-Western "primitive" art; the law by which any doodled face, "unable to exist without having an expression, must indeed have one" ("Töpffer's Law")—these ideas, although familiar now, were new then. Couched in a casual flow that seemed to resist being taken seriously, they have found a central place in E. H. Gombrich's analysis of physiognomic perception as a fundamental aspect of artistic illusion and representation.[28] The idea of the doodle as it were an act of nature herself may be traced back to Töpffer's discovery as a boy watching a cockchafer (*hanneton*) that had dipped its terebra in ink crawl magically about the page of an exercise book. In a famous passage from his partly autobiographical *Bibliothèque de mon Oncle*, he watched it make delicate traceries of lines, and taught it, with guidance from a wisp of straw, over a period of two hours, to write his name—"a masterpiece."

Töpffer is bubbling with theories that he cannot take seriously. He cannot, above all, imagine the reader taking him seriously for long. Like Goethe having to read *Cryptogame* bit by bit, he fears getting an indigestion of ideas, and losing the reader who may have wandered off on his own by now, or gone to sleep. The essays, which ramble on for 300

6-14. Duché de Vancy: Scene from Easter Island, engraving for La Pérouse (*Voyage around the World*, 1786).

beau de l'art est absolument indépendant du beau de la nature," was Töpffer's lapidary pronouncement.[27] But never for a moment, for Töpffer, still the Calvinist Swiss, was art to be independent of morality, that is social morality, and here Baudelaire parted company from him. While Töpffer took a polemical stand against the idea of "art for art's sake" (*l'art pour l'art*, of which Gautier's preface to *Mademoiselle de Maupin* [1835] is the manifesto), he and Baudelaire shared the aesthetic of negligence, of spontaneity—and particularly of *flânerie*, which may be translated, in Töpfferian terms, as casual pages, are wonderfully self-indulgent. Yes, Töpffer wrote and drew primarily to amuse himself. He will not attempt to define Beauty. Book 7, Chapter 1 of the *Réflexions* declares that to require him to do so would be to deny him liberty, and "try to strangle in my scrap of string this proteus of infinite transformations."[29]

The ugly, the monstrous are aesthetic criteria, after all. In his chapter (xx, Book 6) entitled "Where we deal with doodles" (*Où il est question de petits bonhommes*), he praises, as he did elsewhere, graffiti ancient and modern. He then goes on to evaluate the effect of statuary that very few people had ever seen, and was very little known: that of Easter Island, only discovered and reproduced in engravings in the late eighteenth century. He calls the statues "misshapen grotesques which in their rough breadth and deformed proportion hardly resemble anything but themselves, which resemble nothing . . . [they show] cruel, hard, superior creatures, brutal divinities, but divinities after all, of grandeur and beauty. They live, they speak, they proclaim" (fig. 6-14).[30]

The preference for the primitive, to use the title of Gombrich's last book, is deeply embedded in the rise of modernism, and is surely linked closely to Töpffer's theories, probably more indirectly than directly. The loose, incomplete touch became that of Impressionism; the appropriation of the childish, crude, and ugly became a norm of twentieth-century art; the rejection of the academic, the systematic, of rules became the rule. Caricature, and comic strip as its narrative form that gave this style of draughtsmanship unheard-of popularity, blended into modernism, as did the fantastic, the surreal, the dreamlike.

The tenuous line of social theory embedded in the *Réflexions* purports to serve as justification for Töpffer's "graphic follies." Being reproducible, they have a large potential audience; being simple-looking—and thus aside from their sophisticated content—they appeal to the "simple man," the masses of unlettered folk; conceived like Hogarth's engrav-

ings with a moral purpose, even if that is not always as clear as with the great English precursor, they serve social improvement. Unlike Salon painting, which is for the rich, and unlike *l'art pour l'art*, an absurdism leading to amoralism and anarchy,[31] Töpffer's "engraved literature" serves the people. While the citizen militates against it, the artist, *malgré lui*, speaks for democracy.

Essai de Physiognomonie

Published, with *Albert*, in January 1845, handwritten and drawn in auto-lithography, the *Essai de Physiognomonie* is as methodical, systemic, and rigorously logical as the *Reflections and Small Talk of a Genevan Painter* is randomly discursive, playful, and anti-systemic. The tone is also simply more serious, even solemn, scientific—as if his thoughts and theories about an essentially whimsical and entirely original invention demanded it, in a way his aesthetic theory in general did not. The fundamental importance of the *Essai* as an analysis of the very language or semiotics of art was first recognized by Gombrich in his pioneering *Art and Illusion: A Study in the Psychology of Pictorial Representation* (1960), in several pages of the chapter on The Experiment of Caricature. Töpffer thereby took his proper place in the history of art theory, but unlike the often reprinted *Small Talk*, the *Essai* was not reprinted until our own times.[32]

The point of departure was a polemical one recurrent in his thinking about narrative art: the *moral* usefulness of the hybrid form of pictorial literature which, practiced in the right, Hogarthian way, could act as a moral counterbalance to all the vicious literature of the Romantic school, of Sand, Balzac, and Sue. Töpffer himself, disingenuously, wishes (thinking back to the mild criticism of Goethe, perhaps), that his own picture stories had been more directed to serious moral concerns. He wants a picture story in praise, for instance, of mar-

6-15. *Essai de Physiognomonie*, title page, 1845.

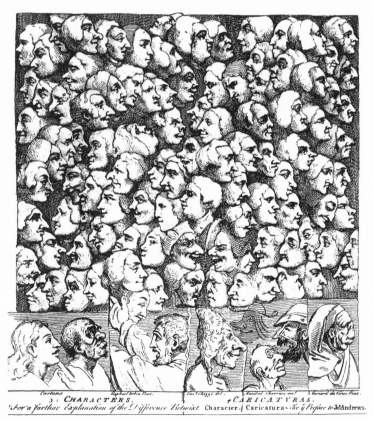

6-16. William Hogarth, *Characters and Caricaturas*, 1743.

riage, to counterbalance all the immoral seductions offered by the French writers named. Töpffer was too much the Calvinist to find adultery matter for artistic entertainment, although he must have recognized that Hogarth did just this in his six-part *Marriage A-la-mode*, which he mentions by name (and enlarges to "ten to twelve plates"). Töpffer imagines that Hogarth really spoke to the lower classes, as he believed the moralizing picture story should, to inoculate them against the poisons of Sue and company; his own clearly did not.

There is a final irony here. The very method that Töpffer proposes depended on an auto-lithographic technique excluded from popular imagery, which for economic reasons relied on woodcut. Töpffer's *Essai* is, moreover, written on a high intellectual level and is not the kind of text read by the simple makers of *imagerie populaire*. They were moreover under strict surveillance of a censorship quick to suppress anything politically untoward. Töpffer's stories really bear no relationship to the tepid folktales peddled to the masses.

The *Physiognomonie* booklet is, like the *Essai d'Autographie*, a how-to-do-it treatise, an appeal to the amateur who does not need to know how to draw in order to be able to draw. Simple contours allow for easy development and recognition of forms; artistic signs are conventional and need not depend upon nature, especially when linear (there are no lines in nature). Expressions may be arrived at by doodling, that is, allowing the free-flowing pencil, accident, and chance (we would say the unconscious) to take over, and interrogating random scribbles for expressive effects (fig. 6-15). Hogarth (fig. 6-16) insisted he was in the business of drawing credible characters and not grotesque caricatures (exemplified lower right). But Hogarth is also, in this plate, doodling and varying like Töpffer, but in his own, more finished way, while Töpffer allows himself the barest signifiers, flicks of the pen. Broken lines (fig. 6-17) are sufficient to render expression and character, and have the advantage of inviting what Gombrich called "the beholder's share."

6-17. "And note well that the least practiced eye supplies the gaps in imitation, with a facility and above all truthfulness which turn entirely to the advantage of the artist. There they are, heads, a gentleman and a lady who present broken lines in the highest degree, discontinuities of contour not a little monstrous . . ." (*Essai de Physiognomonie*, 1845).

We supply character or feeling, be the face never so crude, for merely by existing in lines on paper, a face must have an expression; it cannot indeed *not* speak to us, if only we listen. This is what Gombrich brightly codified into "Töpffer's law."

In a series of demonstration drawings Töpffer shows and explains how doodled faces can be systematically varied to suggest an infinite range of moods and characters, how changing proportions of different parts of the face relate to each other, and to a part of the face kept constant, which thereby itself changes; proving that we react to a gestalt, a pattern. Expressive facial types may be contradictory and incomplete. The artist distinguishes between the permanent and nonpermanent signs, the former being variable and fallible indices of character, the latter revealing reliable evidence of the emotions of the moment—what was called pathognomics. Here Töpffer returns to the critique he made in *Crépin* of phrenology, which is based on the assumption that the shape of the skull, particularly the upper part surrounding the brain, infallibly reveals character and even destiny. Physiognomics, the science of reading character and feeling from the signs, fixed or mobile, inscribed on the face, is "profound, subtle and mysterious;" phrenology, in theory and practice, was totally fallible, not even the beginnings of the science it set itself up to be. Töpffer skirts the fact that Lavater's *Physiognomic Fragments*, published in German, French, and English over the last quarter of the eighteenth century (and in a new French edition the year Töpffer's *Physiognomonie* came out), and deploying phrenological and physiognomic theory as it were divine truth, became a treasure trove of examples and stimuli for caricaturists and artists generally.

The face of *Crépin*, as we have seen, happened by chance, and was then briefly interrogated until a character and future blossomed forth. The doodled face thus allowed for the unfolding of a destiny—such a face on such a man was bound to give him wife- and children-trouble. Can we not add here that the physiognomic broken line which encouraged the beholder's share found its counterpart in the narrative broken line, with open space for a succession of accidents and unpredictables—the share of the artist himself as beholder, or that of a boy observing him at work, the share of the artist's unconscious? Töpffer does not say what I intuit here as the logical consequence of his graphic method, which, drawn out into the time dimension, creates unpredictable patterns of incident and non sequitur. Or, like temporary physiognomic marks on the permanent signs of character, the pattern may be varied by circling back to "permanent" comic refrains such as Albert getting kicked in the pants, or Vieux Bois changing his shirt, or the dunking of the Rival on the waterwheel.

Frames and captions

The only place where Töpffer mentions his method of framing is in letters to Dubochet wanting the *filets tremblotants* (the trembling frame-lines) introduced into the album edition of *Cryptogame*. This kind of frame actually complements the perfect unity of text and drawing design. Philosophically Töpffer was averse to the straight line, to rules and rulers. When hiking, too: he disliked the "ribbons" (*rubans*) carved straight through the Alps to facilitate the horse-drawn vehicles; they were boring and unnatural.

In his first sketched versions, Töpffer drew the vertical lines between scenes and horizontal ones to separate the captions freehand. In the lithographic versions, I would guess, he used a ruler as a rough guide for the maintenance of vertical and horizontal, but ran his pen loosely beside it, and often cast aside the ruler to allow for in- and out-dents necessitated by the overrunning caption, or letters like *p* or *j* that dropped below the line (e.g., *Vieux Bois* 51). He allowed the frames, like his characters, to take on a spontaneous life of their own, in squiggles, curlicues, and faces. Like his use of handwriting instead of typeface, the trembling, quirky frame line establishes continuity between image and word: in *Crépin* (see fig. 3-6), the frame grows a skull in sympathy with those being thrown at the phrenologist in the picture above, while in *Vieux Bois* 44 the bottom frame line seems to vocalize the squealing of a cat just above, as it sees Vieux Bois's dog appearing in the chimney. The frame becomes pictorial, and in so doing suggests a fluidity of time between scenes.

In another view, Töpffer's peculiar frame-lines, in denying the convention that multiple vignettes in a print should be boxed on a page as pictures are on a wall, aspire to the convention that paintings, when exhibited to the public, had a right to individualized framing. The squiggles become sighs and twitchings of discomfort and protest. At other times (e.g., *Vieux Bois* 46), Töpffer seems to be imitating the effect of a manuscript torn at the edges—as if in preemption of his schoolboy readers' mistreatment in handling the pages.

Playing with the frame has become a hallmark of avant-garde art today. Comic strip art has long been aware that the convention of the tight grid of boxes is only a convention, observed to be sure for much of the twentieth century, but now something to be varied, ignored, and joked with. This is part of the maturation of the genre. The mathematical regularity of the grid is satisfying, especially, it seems to children. This may have something to do with the custom of cutting out scenes and pasting them in to a book or on a screen, or it may respond to the feeling of the psychoanalyst and comic strip author Serge Tisseron, who as a child found happiness and safety in "space and time solidly partitioned: to every image, its frame, to every text, its balloon; each panel caught in the double embrace of its line and column."[33]

"Which comes first, text or picture?" is the question always asked of makers of comic strips. The answer is, as a rule, text, as in medieval illuminated manuscripts. But with Töpffer the captions were evidently composed or written after the drawing was done, with their overruns, crowding, blank spaces, and awkward word breaks, despite the many signs revealed by the sketchbooks of careful plotting of the scenario in advance. The pictures drive the narrative. If the round table at which the Crépin family sit in the valedictory scene impedes the normal rectangularity of caption frame, well, let the caption curve to table, and to rotundity of toast.

All this adds to the impression of spontaneity. It is not contrived; the author is letting us in on his creative process, where he himself does not know what will happen next. There are many small, easily correctable errors (notably the "Jaques" for "Albert," 25), and Töpffer makes no attempt to normalize his idiosyncratic handling of diacriticals. There is even a significant omission in a picture that it was left to plagiarist Aubert to make good: the missing hole in the roof in *Vieux Bois* (39). Rodolphe's son François, when he came to copy, by tracing, his father's designs for Garnier in 1860, is able to make the caption boxes look less crowded by writing them slightly smaller; he also smoothes out irregularities, corrects poorly defined accents, and generally enlarges the scenes sideways to equalize proportions, for which he adds bits of wall, furniture, architecture, and foliage where necessary. But he does not alter the eccentricity of the frame lines. The imposition of black boxes in certain German Töpffer editions (Nef 1887, and, even less excusable, Melzer 1975, copying Nef) condemns them outright.

Throughout the history of the nineteenth-century comic strip we find a deliberate, comic discordance between caption and drawing. This discordance reaches its apogee in Doré's 1854 *History of Holy Russia*, where the "straight," official historiography (caption) is made to collide with and contradict the cruel and cynical reality (drawing). Töpffer too plays on a discordance between the often stiff, solemn, banal, formal (and even archaic) phrasing of the caption (as it were, the official version of the mini-epic) against the spontaneous absurdity of the drawings (visualization of the imagined truth). It is the difference between what should be and what might be. The balance is perfect. There is here—as has been said of Wilhelm Busch, whose solemn moral platitudes in the verse highlight and contradict the author's evident delight in the mischief of the pictures—duel as well as duet.

Chapter Seven

TÖPFFER THE PROFESSIONAL DILETTANTE

We may be glad, as Töpffer eventually confessed himself to be, that his weak eyesight prevented him from becoming a painter. Instead, he became everything else. His weak eyesight, moreover, taught him to draw rapidly, and evolve the system of doodling that became his hallmark. We may be glad, too, that he stayed in Geneva. In Paris he could have made a career as a journalist or as a professional illustrator/cartoonist, or both at once, like Cham. In Geneva, he earned his bread in a very respectable and very Genevan occupation: as a schoolmaster, and then university lecturer. He occasionally grumbled about his confinement to an academic "galley," chained to two iron balls (*boulets*). His complaints at being locked into teaching or supervising classes of boys in his school for seven hours a day should not deceive us into thinking that this constituted an obstacle to his creative work; it may even have encouraged it. The worst was that he often could not get out until 10 p.m. to visit with friends. Assuming, as one may without hard evidence, that his presence in class was more light supervision while the boys got on with their own work than actual teaching, which was probably confined to Greek, one can imagine the imagination, as it burned pen or pencil to paper, seeking far and wide respite and refuge from the humdrum tasks to which the boys were fixed, under his eye, in his sight, but faded from his mind.

Töpffer the academic insists that he never wanted to be a professional writer, much less professional artist. He tried, indeed, to make a virtue out of his amateur status, and to carve out for himself the role of one who was precipitated, willy-nilly, into the public sphere, while retaining all the virtues of the amateur: modesty, lack of ambition, simplicity, improvisation, hobbyism, exercise of talent to amuse oneself and an inner circle of family and friends, rather than quest for the market of a big, paying public. In this context, his oeuvre as strip cartoonist is exemplary, as if he had invented the genre in order to prove the merits of amateurism. Caricature had always been something of the province of the gifted amateur.

There is a key passage here, from the autobiographical statement he wrote for his patron and launch-pad the French critic Sainte-Beuve: he was "a sort of author without knowing and above all without wanting it; without knowing it because for a long time I wrote just for the pleasure I took in this hobby and to conjure up a poetic world [as an escape from] the real world where all is prose, obliged by my profession of schoolmaster to spend seven hours a day in a class peopled with thirty to forty boys. It is there I wrote all I wrote, consecrating to this amusing work all the hours when I was not giving the class; [I became an author] unwittingly, because I feared by publishing books my identity as an author would jeopardize my status and interests as a schoolmaster. That is why I published some of my opuscules only long after they were composed, and without any preface and anonymously."[1]

It is curious here to see how the writer subsumes under the term "opuscules," without naming them in particular, that particular category of *histoires en estampes* or graphic novels for which he had by this date gained immediate notoriety, as if he intuited a certain critical resistance to them. Yet it was they, together with the early *Voyages*, that had to wait years to be published, not the novels or art criticism, and it was they above all, rather than any other work, that were capable of jeopardizing his status as an academic. No one could object to a professor of literature publishing works of fiction, especially those of a didactic and moralistic turn. But caricatures? Already his father, a genre painter ipso facto related to caricature, had suffered from the association, which prevented him, the "Hogarth of Geneva," from becoming its David Wilkie.[2]

An English aesthetician damned caricature with characteristic vigor, and venom: caricaturists

> Like maggots hatch'd in summer's noontide hour,
> The filth, which gives them being, they devour . . .
> Crawl out like bugs, conceal'd in shades of night.
> Unknown to all, but when they stink or bite . . .[3]

On the eve of Töpffer's death in 1846 the *Revue de Genève* was vituperating against his comic strips as a corruption of taste, for they were puerile, needed no work, fatigued by the constant repetition of the same figures, and constituted in fine a prostitution of undoubted literary talent.[4] Some years before, with his reputation as caricaturist newly established, the *Journal de Genève* used a review of the prose *Festus* as a stick to beat Professor Töpffer for his unbecoming behavior. The anonymous reviewer reveals a prudish, narrow-minded stance that would have been shared by many influential Genevans, and is worth some attention. Caricature may be innocent as long as it is not personal—Geneva is happy to be without its attendant vulgarity, in art as in the theater. Töpffer has been ruined by his success; while *Vieux Bois*, *Jabot*, and *Pencil* were funny, *Crépin* was not. "It is disgraceful to drag in the mud illustrious names well worth that of M. Bonnefoi, without tainting as low

charlatans all those devoted to perfecting the noble science of education." It is particularly improper for one who occupies an official position in society and has a duty to offer a model to youth. "It is sad to see talent spoiled by success and the flattery of a narrow circle of fanatical friends; it is sad to see a man of wit take the wrong turning, strive to please only by his faults, exaggerate them daily the more, and end up by cultivating the least elevated of his faculties. An ingenious and witty author might thus turn into a tasteless joker . . . We would be truly embarrassed if we had to cite the relevant pages [of *Festus*], whereby the French language is dragged in the mud . . . It is an incredible witless accumulation of vulgar, worthless jokes . . . May the author, who counts among our modest national celebrities, stop on this slippery slope. May this unfortunate experiment deter him from an unfortunate continuation."[5]

This complaint, by 1840, left the artist amused, but gave him pause to reflect on whether maybe the *Festus* type of offending opuscule was not more the true Töpffer than all his more "respectable" literary efforts. Had he perhaps been led astray by a rival muse? "She had me do deathly maudlin books, while the other made me do Festus that the Journal de Genève disliked."[6] Addressing Sainte-Beuve the cosmopolitan Parisian critic, Töpffer pretends that Geneva is too narrow-minded to honor the modest literary pretensions of a schoolmaster, especially when they "descend" to the frivolous and comic. The term *descend* is interesting. The idea of descent into a (more) creative unconscious is attractive. From the start, a decade earlier, he confessed to a friend that he "hid himself" in a "cellar" (*cave*) to draw his picture stories. "Pedagogue by profession, draughtsman on occasion, actor so to speak. I hide in order to draw. I hide myself in my cellar to compose my drolleries (*drôleries*), for fear that I be accused of being cold towards Poland, insensible to the great social movement, frigid towards Belgium,"[7] referring to revolutionary movements in those countries, the topics of the day.

Ironically, shortly before he is to be launched in Paris as a writer by the critic Sainte-Beuve and publisher Dubochet with all the attendant publicity, he tries, in a letter to a correspondent in Russia (Xavier de Maistre, his contact with Sainte-Beuve), to uphold the pretense that he is content to write in obscurity: "The further I go, the more I am content to have no relationship with critics, editor/publishers, journals etc., to write in obscurity for my recreation, without any idea of speculation, without any pretension to celebrity, to be a schoolmaster who writes and not an author who is a schoolmaster." Then, after revealing the plans for a Parisian edition of his works, he recognizes the contradiction, admitting he is "horribly afraid that you are absolutely right," he is a professional.[8] And he is beginning to become greedy for the praise, and the money, that the albums are bringing him, "greedy until that time that I become miserly." "I publish silently, and I love the praise and the reactions that come to me silently."[9]

He includes the comic albums here, and by 1840, when most were published, he confesses "to be more pleased at having made two crazy stories, than another would be to have made three sensible and better ones."[10] By now (1840) he glories in being the author of *Jabot* and company, and even savors the prospect of scandalizing the pedants with *Pencil* and *Festus*. In the Joanne guidebook to Switzerland he is singled out as the one named head of the numerous boarding schools in Geneva, and as the author not of any prose writing at all, but only of the "charming and witty satires of *Vieux Bois*, *Crépin* and *Jabot*."[11]

The artist in prose was praised after his death for a natural modesty that abhorred self-promotion, for having achieved fame without any effort on his part. There is some truth to this, but the self-published picture stories demanded more personal and continuous attention. The quite disproportionate amount of space occupied in his correspondence by the albums reveals a man who is tirelessly peddling his invention all over the place, cajoling friends to pass on copies to their friends, packing up the books himself, pushing distribution internationally, watching production with an eagle eye, and chafing over a missing or misprinted page. He did all this not least because they made him a tidy profit, and as if he wanted to avoid the booksellers' tiny cut, 10–20 percent. On the large volume of *Voyages* he earned a royalty of only one franc per copy; on the albums he grossed eight or nine francs a copy—the price of a good pair of shoes. For six years the "milch cow" has brought him a "charming" and "considerable" income. He tells us that the comic albums brought him "a very tidy haul" (*une très jolie pêchette*) and twice as much as the rest of his writings put together. Money was coming in from the albums "twice a day."[12] The voluminous letters to and from Dubochet (240 pages of manuscript!), much of it over *Cryptogame*, although exceptional and written in exceptional circumstances, is symptomatic of a greater devotion to the production and fate of his comic albums than to any of his prose works.

Revealing to Dubochet the disquieting state of his health, and the prospect of being sent for a "cure" to Lavey, which he suspects will do him no good at all, is occasion for a touching expression of gratitude for "twenty of the most completely happy, radiant, colour-of-a-fine-sun-on-flowery-pastures years, that have ever been vouchsafed to a man of this century." This follows an evocation of the greatest pleasure of them all, the comic albums: "the heavenly pleasures of sketching, scribbling, exuding right and left, and when I am already more than rewarded by the pleasure this has given me, what I consider as a bonus, the big absolutely gratis prize, the deliciously roasted quail, the luck that my rubbish should be engraved, run off this way and that, reach Jack and Jill!"[13]

"What scrawl is this? This is what Goethe praised?" exclaims Professor Vischer, to open his wholly admiring and penetrating Introduction to the 1846 Kessmann collected edition of the picture stories (see Appendix B). "Scrawl" is one of the author's own terms for his invention. When he is not making formal introductions as *histoires en estampes*, he dips at random into a thesaurus of deprecation.

7-1. Grandville: Literature is wound and cut off the spool ready-made, like a silk or cotton fabric (*Un Autre Monde*, 1844).

The albums are (little) *folies, gribouillis, barbouillages,* and *griffonnages* (these last three meaning scrawls, scribbles, and scratchings), *âneries* (literally asininities, silly stuff), *drôleries, fichaises* (rubbish), *bluettes* (trifles), *pochades* (rough sketches), *bonhommes* (mannikins), *fariboles* (nonsense), or *bagatelles*.[14] Subsequent references to them, when not using Töpffer's "official" terms, run the gamut from the dignified *petite comédie dessinée* (which Hogarth would have recognized) to the ignorant and amorphous "series of drawings with explanatory text" of the British Museum Library catalog, which suggests they were not even scanned for the purpose.

The first modern comic strip was a kind of foundling, laid by a whimsical muse at a schoolmaster's doorstep. The foster father loved the babe the better for having no real parentage beyond a distant, noble ancestor he gave it in William Hog-

arth. The foster father, he of the City of Refugees, harbored and nurtured tenderly this refugee from the powerful monarchies of visual art and literature, of which it was a bastard child. The famous preface to all the picture stories, "Va petit livre, et choisis ton monde . . . ," seen in this light, is the anxious farewell of the parent seeing his child off to make his way in an uncertain and possibly hostile world for the first time.

The very idiosyncratic, casual-looking but intensive private distribution system for the comic albums was a way of avoiding the publicity techniques used of necessity for the prose works. These the writer abhorred, especially when the publicity was prolonged over the many months of an installment publication: in 1843 we find him writing his publisher Dubochet (who, being a second cousin, helped no doubt to maintain the illusion that it was

7-2. Grandville: The heavens and criticism protect an innocent pencil traveling alone for the first time (*Un Autre Monde*, 1844). The pen, i.e., literature cocks a snook at the departing pencil, i.e., illustration.

all in the family), "Advertisements strike me like certificates of morality, used only by the bogus." Nothing so much annoys, bothers, and hurts him, "professor, schoolmaster, petit bourgeois, family father, cherishing his dignity, liberty, private obscurity, as to see myself squandered, postered, in three, four thousand covers, once a week, in all the drawing rooms, shops, at every meeting place when already in opening the installment I can be found, in person, with my family." If he were a professional writer, or wanted to be, this sort of thing might delight him, "but I am a man of letters, author, writer only accessorily, as a pastime, surreptitiously."[15]

Töpffer's admirer and spiritual brother in Paris, the caricaturist Grandville, had much to say—or visualize—about the foolishness of publicity, the commercialization of arts and letters, the overproduction endemic to the Parisian scene, and the quest for fame (fig. 7-1). Töpffer dreaded the

installment system, and the posterizing it induced. Putting up posters, as the hapless Craniose does in *Monsieur Crépin* (86) for his phrenological lectures, is a confession of his waning popularity, his charlatanism, and his desperation. Young Albert too tries and fails with a poster campaign to bolster a precocious volume of poetry. The very idea of writing a book as a moneymaking project is anathema to the self-defined Genevan dilettante.

The great French artist Grandville himself suffered from what he felt to be a perpetual amateur or subordinate status as writer, envying Töpffer his capacity to be both writer and artist, to tell stories with pictures and text (fig. 7-2). The Parisian's late work *Un Autre Monde* is rich testimony to the ambitions of one whose fantasies soared visually, and who argued strenuously for the rights of the pencil to tell the story (such as it is), but had to resign himself to a domination by the pen (probably that of

TÖPFFER THE PROFESSIONAL DILETTANTE

7-3. *Histoire de Mr. Vieux Bois*, title page, 1837 edition.

7-4. *Les Amours de Mr. Vieux Bois*, title page, 1839 edition.

Taxile Delord). His sense of being oppressed by writers and publishers, which led to angry quarrels, is well documented in recent studies by Philippe Kaenel.[16] Töpffer, by contrast, writing, drawing, and publishing for himself could claim, as William Blake did before him, to have freed himself from the tyranny of the marketplace, found a liberation. Grandville openly admired this "remarkably privileged man . . . I have often envied this double faculty of translating thought by drawing and [literary] style; I have sometimes tried, but in vain; the pen rebelled under my fingers . . . It is annoying to have collaborators putting themselves forward instead of enhancing the scenes as drawn. M. Toepffer [*sic*] is very lucky to produce both text and engraving . . . his talent is complete."[17]

Töpffer's ambivalent attitude toward a public he felt to be both necessary and dispensable (since he wrote only to please himself) is crystallized in the title pages to *M. Vieux Bois*. In 1839 Töpffer redesigned the title page to his second edition of *Vieux Bois*, combining the two he had used before into one. The first (fig. 7-3) shows Vieux Bois seated in a woodland on a rock looking lovingly upon the back of his Beloved Object. A monk creeps threateningly from the left. The second shows a banner marked "Preface." This second only (also kept by pirate Aubert) is retained in the 1839 edition, but the anonymous figure holding the "Preface" banner, with its succinct description of the plot, and Töpffer's signature *envoi* to the reader ("Va, petit livre . . ."), is now surrounded with a crowd of figures, some seated and looking with astonishment and pleasure as it were at a magic lantern being projected, others emerge from the shadows in a spooky fashion (fig. 7-4). None of the figures, as one might expect, is a character in the album; they are audience, the "monde" the book seeks, nervously. Only one is demonstrably a child, and too small to be present of his own volition. Töpffer, like Busch, sought a mixed, primarily adult audience, and it was not merely a traditional rhetorical device but real ambivalence that made him use the same farewell epigraph on every comic album

(and nowhere else): "Go little book, and choose your world, whoever does not laugh at crazy things, yawns; whoever does not surrender, resists, whoever reasons is mistaken, and whoever wants to keep a straight face, can please himself."

Who indeed, was the audience? Not, officially, children, certainly not younger children, the audience for Lear and Carroll. Töpffer appealed to older children, sophisticated adolescents, adults with the heart of children, adults who like to laugh—children still, of a kind. "Genius is nothing but childhood voluntarily recaptured," said Baudelaire.[18] We must imagine not just schoolboys but whole families gathered round albums of caricatures. We who read in isolation cannot imagine these shared pleasures, Dickens read aloud, Töpffer crowded over, the ricochet of laughter.

Genesis in the schoolroom

By his own and much repeated accounts, Töpffer's invention was made in the schoolroom. "I conjugated [verbs] with one hand and drew with the other."[19] Writing (and drawing) in the presence of thirty to forty boys, even if they are all quiet and industrious and not demanding any personal attention, is not at all like writing in isolation, in a room of one's own, as one imagines most creative writing is done. Having myself written (or tried to) while supervising exams, I know the psychological atmosphere is peculiar: I have to contend with or transcend a pervading aura of tension, of effort, apprehended not only from the scratching of ears and temples (of the mind), the rustling of papers, the occasional stretching of limbs, the rising and fumbling towards me of an unnecessary whispered question, covert resentment (perhaps) at the tasks assigned, and bathroom exits. The numerous presence before Professor Töpffer could not be entirely ignored or escaped; it was best to be engaged in a kind of parallel circumvention, by writing stories that often involved youngsters (in the fiction) and (in the comic strips) mocked excesses of those very intellectual pursuits the boys were engaged in.

The teacher must have found many a boy seeking distraction from his lack of inspiration in the academic task at hand by doodling a face or a figure—and informally indulged him in it. He began to do likewise, and "during long unoccupied hours" scribbling a story which, as it unfolded, he followed with an expressive play of his features that attracted the boys' attention, "so the surveillor became surveilled."[20] Töpffer would also have been cajoled into continuing some nonsense, composed and drawn "under their eyes" as he put in the biographical résumé sent to Sainte-Beuve, at the boys' instance and under their inspiration. If a pupil left early he must, as he handed in his papers, have glanced in wonder at the master's fluttering hand as he drew. At the end of prep time, one imagines the boys crowding round the comic album in progress, to chuckle over the flights and fancies of the man supervising their labors and their pursuit of knowledge which, in so many different forms, he turned to fun.

But the author nowhere admits that he acted on suggestions for continuations from the audience: "they saw the birth with great pleasure, and as indulgent judges."[21] At the same time, one wonders whether the boys' participation was not sometimes more active. Some even came to know details of the stories and characters better than the author himself, as he himself noted.[22] A very intelligent ten-year-old in the Dubochet family, ecstatic over the albums, knew the captions by heart (letter of 9 November, 1843). A pupil who began wandering around the classroom for no good reason, excused himself with the sanctioned excuse that like Festus, "je voyage pour mon instruction."[23] Laughter all round.

With the story complete or far enough along, a moment surely hastened by repeated urgings, the boys were allowed to hold the album in their own hands. As they did so, one can see them in the careless abandon of the stories themselves, grabbing and turning the pages with dirty fingers and dog-earing them; seeing the marks of which, the author would add a sharp little written reprimand and warning on the first page. On one *carnet* he added drawings of funny guards threatening retribution. These albums were precious to the author even if he did not yet know what to do with them other than let them pass from the schoolboys to the family and friends. But they should not, in principle, pass out of the house. *Trictrac* disappeared that way.

Nothing in the above contradicts the author's own accounts of the genesis of his "little follies." The masterpieces of children's literature have often been made in direct intercourse with the intended audience. To be sure, the interaction between author and audience in Töpffer's case cannot have been as intimate and direct as we know was the case with Lewis Carroll, or rather Charles Dodgson before he became known under the published name. Oxford University mathematics lecturer Dodgson was clearly stirred to the depths of his being by the physical presence and imaginative participation of the Liddell girls in the rowing boat on the Isis on that famous Sunday afternoon in 1863. They encouraged him, as he spoke, with their voices, their eyes, their movements. They begged for more, and Alice, who became the favored one, "pestered" him to write the magical stories down—which he did, gradually and carefully improving written drafts, as did Töpffer, for publication. Unlike Carroll, Töpffer left his drafts dormant for many years, for he could not at first share Carroll's confidence in a wider, appreciative audience out there.

For all the differences in audience—Töpffer's obviously older—we pursue in the *Voyages* chapter the parallel between the two men in terms of linguistic invention and as purveyors of nonsense. Both writers, deeply attuned to the youthful imagination, opened up to the future, and not just to children and adolescents, autonomous worlds of fantasy. In one respect at least, Töpffer's achievement exceeds Carroll's: for the *Alice* books depended much for their success on the art of another hand, that of the foremost professional illustrator of the day, John Tenniel.

Chapter Eight

VOYAGES EN ZIGZAG:
HUMOR OF THE UNEXPECTED

This chapter is dedicated to my hiking
companion in the Swiss Alps, cousin Brita.

With the enthusiasms of the Genevan Jean-Jacques Rousseau for his native countryside, with the first ascent of Mont Blanc in 1786 by the naturalist Horace-Bénédict de Saussure who thereby sparked awareness of the natural-scientific treasures of the Alps, and especially with the reopening of Europe to travel after the Napoleonic wars, Switzerland and notably Geneva became a prime tourist destination of Europe. Guide and travel books, dioramas and panoramas, poetry, engravings, and paintings proliferated. The wild Swiss Alps were the essence of the Romantic, with its essential components of picturesque and sublime. After Byron and his friends sojourned on the banks of lake Geneva, and Mary Shelley wrote *Frankenstein* there, Alpine Geneva was magic, mystery, and terror. Switzerland responded in a practical way, with high-quality roads and inns.

Töpffer, like Ruskin after him, stimulated the social process of mass tourism, the effects of which on the Swiss landscape and character both writers abhorred. The *Voyages en Zigzag* of the Swiss, which became a popular classic especially among youth, extolled the educational, spiritual, and physical benefits of tourism, a word invented by the British at the beginning of the century. Töpffer insisted it be pedestrian, and savored like a good meal, against a prevailing trend for ever faster, ever more vehicular travel that continues madly. Töpffer did not live to see the accelerating developments which caused Ruskin to explode in disgust at Cook's invasion of Switzerland: "You have made race-courses of the cathedrals of the earth . . . all tourist destinations are covered by 'a consuming leprosy of new hotels.'"[1] We are all tourists now, with Dr Festus. We see more than he, and imagine less. Tourism is now the world's largest single industry, representing 12 percent of the world GNP and an environmental disaster. Töpffer intuited this, although he could never have imagined the scale it would take.

It was something of a tradition in Swiss boarding schools for the boys to be taken on summer excursions and for some kind of diary to be kept. Such that survive tend to be didactic, scientific, academic: impersonal exercises in geology, botany, and zoology. The trips were often organized in a militaristic manner, with disciplines and punishments,[2] and with the obligatory keeping of notes, which were collected, perhaps edited and reworked by the master, and occasionally printed up. The Pension Töpffer went about things in a very different way. The master did all the writing (and final sketching) himself, and left the boys to hunter-gather on their own, to draw for themselves, collect insects, plants, and minerals, and put clouds in bottles along the zigzag (not Linnaear) way (*NVZZ* 64).[3] He himself averred that twenty days of life on the trails was educationally worth twenty months of classroom. In the evening there were self-organized games, music, and occasionally dancing. It was all meant to be fun.

8-1. Grandville: Aerial locomotions, Zigzag travel (*Un Autre Monde*, 1844). A concept combining the idea of Töpffer's *Voyages en Zigzag* and the aerial travel of his characters.

The *Voyages en Zigzag*, which Töpffer wrote all on his own but on which he imprinted the boys' idiosyncrasies, are conceived somewhat in the spirit of the picture stories, which are also travel tales in their way, as are many of his short stories collected under the title *Nouvelles Genevoises*. Both picture stories and *Voyages* were improvised from day to day or episode to episode, and enlivened by moments of crazy hilarity and absurd inconsequence, although even the silliest bits of the *Voyages* are meant to be credible. No doubt the fun and good moments were enhanced over the embarrassing and painful, and the fun of writing would blot out painful memory. But the *Voyages* stand as a kind of model of permissive, happy Alpine adventure (the term tourism is

not really appropriate), and in its informal way was intended to be, and was viewed as, a how-to-do-it manual. It was written against a prevailing type of (English) tourism, expedited in a hurry, slave to the guidebook, seeing all and enjoying nothing. In the nostalgic account of his last trip the diarist recollects exactly how *not* to do it, thinking back to his first hike as assistant master in the Pension Heyer: up at 1 a.m., horrible suffering, total demoralization (*NVZZ* 61)—and certainly no laughter. Heyer himself did not participate.

Although obviously more serious in intent, digressively moralistic and didactic at times, text-rather than illustration-driven, the *Voyages* bear a closer relation to the comic strips, the protagonists

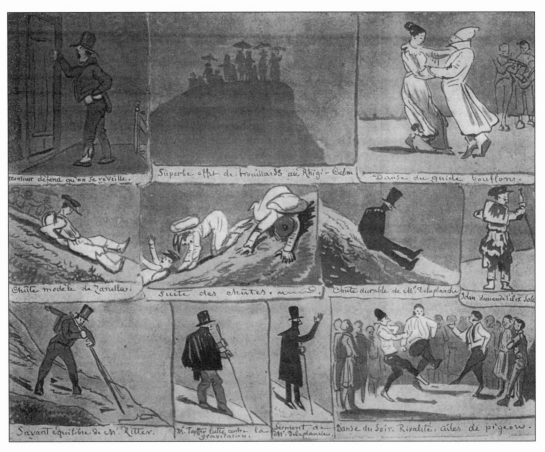

8-2. Monsieur (Töpffer) orders that no one be awakened. Superb mist effect on the Righi-Culm. Dance of the comic guide. Exemplary fall of Zanella. Consequence of the falls. Lasting fall of Mr. Delaplanche. John asks if he is dirty. Clever balancing of Mr. Ritter. Mr. Töpffer struggles against gravity. Oath of Mr. Delaplanche. Evening dance. Rivalry, pigeon wings (drawing for *Voyage entre deux eaux*, 1829, *VZZ* vol. 3).

from which they often cite, than has been realized. We can imagine Dr. Festus, awakening from his truly crazy dream, relaunched on his "educational tour" but on actual Alpine trails, which could be crazy enough in reality. On the 1829–30 trips, a time when Töpffer was in full flood of composing his *histoires en images*, he occasionally composed his illustrations to the *Voyages* in strips (fig. 8-2).

If an analogy be drawn with humorous travel-writing today, it might be with Bill Bryson, with his mildly caricatural style, like Töpffer enchanted with the magic of the commonplace, and riding constantly astride a see-saw between delight and dismay. Both are sensitive to slight changes of mood

in persons, nature, and weather, both deplore the depredation of the ugly modern over the traditional and historic. Both engage in an impenetrable degree of embroidery of actual experience, and manage to render the absurd credible.

Töpffer's accounts of his annual excursions into and beyond the Alps surrounding Geneva, written at first (like his comic strips) to amuse himself and his cohort of boys, became a substantial publishing enterprise. At first (1825–31) left in manuscript, encouraged by Goethe (as with the comic strips), from 1832 he was autographing them with their numerous illustrations for private circulation. He then polished and expanded them considerably for a general audience, and found a wide and appreciative readership in the last years of his life and posthumously. They were first published, much to the author's distaste, in sixty installments, a method he found vulgar. Filling seven volumes of the *Oeuvres Complètes*, their extent is such that few today can have read them all (there is no recent re-edition), and the quality is uneven. In the later volumes the narrative becomes diffuse and tediously inflated with the author's conservative social rhetoric. At their best, and a little everywhere, they sparkle with gaiety, fun, laughter, and astute social comment.

The two- to four-week-long excursions, conducted in summer and early autumn to occupy the boarders who could not return home for the holiday, were annual affairs from 1825 until 1842, when the author's health began to give out. The number of boys involved varied between thirteen and a maximum of twenty-five, spanning in age from early to upper teens, although in this respect (ages are never given) they are treated as homogeneous. The higher number of participants must have been a real headache for the organizer, who treads lightly over all the numerous if transitory anguishes, usually involving money, of his multiple roles: "head cashier, general banker, universally responsible, undersigned editor-writer" (*VZZ* 7). Occasionally a friend or two, an assistant master, Töpffer's wife (before family responsibilities took over), and the school servant, the majordomo called David, a much appreciated practical help, would go along too.

As printed, most of the excursions start with a list of the dramatis personae. These constitute in themselves brilliant cameos of contrasting character, costume, motivation, and walking style. If this level of amused observation extended to classroom interaction, Rodolphe must have been a very amusing teacher; one may suspect, however, that in the classroom Töpffer adopted more conventional methods, and used the excursions to vent the joys of freedom from them. The cameos of the *Voyages* are like jocose

school reports. To take just one example at random: G. Pourtalès: ". . . Frolicsome type. Gait inconstant, ferruginous, mystical, noisy and silent and generally good.—hikes in order to escape work, and to melt his shirt. Hat now bucolic, now Henri Quatre style, now three-cornered.—Always strapped of cash. . . ."[4] All the boys had nicknames, of course, some several; there were on one occasion sixty different names for eighteen individuals.

In the company of these youngsters, in the age of "careless gaiety, elastic vigor, frolicsome laughter, artless flowering of feeling," Töpffer learned that most precious of human attributes and pleasures: the *fou rire*, crazy or hysterical laughter. *Fourire* became a verb. "Broad, true laughter, laughter to die for, is ordinarily crazy laughter, that is, without object, for its adorable stupidity, or no object." It is of course infectious. "One laughs simultaneously at the thing, and at oneself, and at the other, at everything and nothing." All this is said in nostalgia, as the master redacted his last trip.[5]

"Once the stimulus was given, and the diaphragm set in motion, it goes of its own accord. A nothing, less than nothing, the most miserable of puns, makes you and the lot of you shake with laughter." Laughter is "gigantic and foams" like champagne. Sometimes it is childish, a matter of tickling, with no parts of the body immune: "an epic amalgam of ticklers which gets all tangled up in a hotchpotch of tickled who counter-tickle each other." If it was not tickling, it was snowball and mud fights in which the master joined, and likened to epic battles of history. Töpffer was always tickled, if not literally, by the behavior of his charges; without sentimentalizing, he clearly loved them, in part simply because they made him feel young. So young, that he shows himself about their own age, tall and slim, when in reality he was as an adult always bald (or balding), short and quite plump and even fat as he described himself in his letters (fig. 8-3). It was said, then and since, that he remained an adolescent in his literary work all his life.[6]

8-3. Töpffer falling, self-portrait as a youngster (*VZZ* vol. 2, p. 130).

What has remained his single most popular work in prose, and what launched him onto the local literary scene in 1832, *La Bibliothèque de mon oncle*, is clearly autobiographical and contains a satirical portrait of one of his teachers in the guise of the narrator's tutor M. Ratin, the very type of humorless, repressive, sexophobic prudery. The wart on his nose was an invitation to laughter. "Crazy laughter is one of the sweet things of life—a forbidden therefore exquisite fruit. . . . To delight in crazy laughter, you must be a schoolboy, and if possible have a master with a wart on his nose adorned with three sprightly hairs."[7] *M. Crépin* is Töpffer's *fou rire* at the expense of all pedants and educational fanatics. It is also touched by the satanic and a real madness that Baudelaire—perhaps consciously following Töpffer—saw in the comic: "true laughter, violent laughter, a crazy, excessive mirth expressed in paroxysms and endless collapses."[8]

The structure of the *Voyages* is strictly that of a diary, with an entry, varying greatly in length, for each day, and the progress of the itinerary precisely marked. In organizing the trip, Töpffer, unlike some of his predecessors, left much to chance and leeway to his philosophy of expecting the unexpected. Unlike today, when the hiker in the Alps can expect similar, practical distances between pre-bookable, regularly spaced huts, where the standard accommodation in terms of food and bunk beds is of invariably high quality, and prices regularized, Töpffer and his company never knew what was coming at them. It was a bit like wondering what could possibly happen next to Messieurs Vieux Bois or Cryptogame, liable to be cast unawares into a haybarn for the night, or the belly of a whale, and always vulnerable to the caprice of outrageous circumstance.

The really wrong kind of accident, the serious physical kind, happened only once: a death by drowning, from the imprudence of a young man accompanying them (a twenty-two-year-old Greek, not of his school); the trip (1831), and the account of it, was forthwith aborted. Otherwise Töpffer counts his blessings: the roads and trails were remarkably

8-4. The mobile tree for resting under (*Voyage à Gènes*, 1834, *VZZ* vol. 6, p. 41).

safe, and highway brigands, that species in which romantic literature abounds, which his own short story *Lac de Gers* features, and which adds spice to Töpffer's picture stories, no longer infested the Alpine passes, despite the self-interested attempts of guides to create fears of such. There were faces and characters ugly enough to give pause, but the only real brigands were the customs officers, guides, hoteliers, coachmen and mule-drivers.

Töpffer disliked traveling by water, and feared the steamboat, epitome of a civilization addicted to speed and subject to exploding on a lake, as he shows happening in *Festus*. Without having seen, much less experienced any accident, he conjured up the horrors of being "thrown up boiling into the sky, multiplied by the three hundred and fifty heater tubes of a low or high pressure machine."⁹ He took steamers of necessity, regarding them as an inferior

form of locomotion. Not all travel was on foot, and the occasional segment by coach or cart, which usually followed the troop with baggage and which was otherwise reserved for the sick and infirm, was gratefully accepted.

In the spirit of the picture-story heroes, Töpffer codes the idea of losing the way and getting nightmarishly stuck as part of the fun of life itself. All travel is potentially a part of, synecdoche, or metaphor for the Voyage of Life itself. Surprisingly, the boys were left on a long leash; they were free to engage in their own *spéculations* (experimental shortcuts), and the dispersal of the group over miles would, I suspect, horrify any Boy Scout leader or such today. Strays, somnolents, narcoleptics were casually abandoned, and always showed up eventually. The master himself sometimes "speculated," and came tumbling down the hill; to the merriment of his young charges (fig. 8-3), he too got lost and stuck: "M. Töpffer and the rear-guard having lost the way, set off into a bog from which they escape by climbing up a dung-heap, from which they descend so as to enter a dead-end, from which they turn back to resort to a by-path, from which they exit to meet a cretin who puts them on the right track." (This, be it said in passing, is one of the many references to the lamentably common cretinism and its accompanying goitrism among the Alpine populations, which would decline as the remoter valleys were exposed to the outside world.) The Alpine excursions were a kind of that *flânerie* (mooching, sauntering about) much prized and practiced imaginatively if not physically by writers of the period, notably Baudelaire. Life and art should be a flânerie, not work, "for the man who knows not flânerie is an automaton traveling from life to death, like a steam engine from Liverpool to Manchester."[10] True *flânerie* connotes the effortless and restful; the hiker's utopia would be to lie dreamily under the shade of a tree on wheels that carries you to your destination (fig. 8-4). Yet was there a life lived with more restless, set purpose than Töpffer's?

Nature seemed to oblige with more variety and extremes of weather, mood, and drama than I myself have ever encountered in the Alps, where I have been walking annually for ten years. It seems that the Alps at this time, at the end of the so-called Little Ice Age, was still subject to extreme conditions that have warmed away. There were dangerous thunderstorms, impenetrable rain, whirlwinds, dense fog, rockslides, and avalanches—the latter, however, often provoked by gunshots as a tourist spectacle (and paid for). Natural phenomena such as these occasionally retarded progress, sometimes for the whole or much of a day.

Romantic-era writing on the sublime and picturesque of nature in the wild was inevitably anthropomorphic; it still is. Töpffer's anthropomorphism

has moments of high melodrama; his sense of the sublime and the picturesque undergoes not only the usual literary enhancement, but is also colored by his frustrated ambitions as a landscape artist, and his actual practice as critic of landscape painting. He tries to paint the ever-changing scenic effects with words (ekphrasis), to realize in the other medium the cherished dream denied him as a youth by his eyesight; and he compensates for that poor eyesight by evoking, one suspects, not only what he can actually see through his green-tinted spectacles, which was always limited, but also what he imagines and sees in landscape painting: delicacy, mystery, and grandeur in the atmospheric variations of hue and light, in the effects of mist, and cloud and sun, which he conjures up with such finesse. He sees nature through the prism of the dramatic landscapes of his favorite painter (and engraver of his landscape drawings) Alexandre Calame, whom he was promoting against Parisian criticism that thought them virtually kitsch.[11] The Swissness of all this is also Töpffer's form of patriotism, which is poetic rather than historical, and speaks to his desire to be midwife to a Genevan school of landscape painting.

Food

Unlike so many nineteenth-century writers, in his sketching and writing Töpffer does not seem to have been much interested in food—except on his Alpine excursions. Then the topic became obsessive. The immediate rewards of these trips were primarily of three kinds: the spectacle of nature, good food, and a good bed. All three, in their different ways, epitomized the unexpected, the capricious, and the principle of infinite variation. Nature was expected to improvise, to spring surprises on you; and in their catering the Alpine innkeepers seemed to take their cue from nature. As wet weather was followed by dry, so abundance of food was followed by scarcity, feast by famine, and honesty by cheating. Above all, the variation in the kind and quality of the food never ceased to astonish, sometimes with disbelief. "Crazy laughter" was damped in the rumbling belly.

History should record the unique pleasure of a banquet composed of soup improvised from radishes (rape), potatoes, rice, milk and bread, salt and cheese. "These banquets won by walking, seasoned with fatigue, and flowering with expansive gaiety!" Fatigue and hunger are indeed the great spices, but food, the expected reward for hard work on the trails, sometimes turned out to be a punishment. Hunger, like snow in Inuit language, has in Töpffer a hundred names. It comes "screaming" (*hurlant*) from "crevassed" bellies "bleeding with pain" (*saignant de douleur*) and fit to make one devour one's backpack straps, and even stones. It can be excruciating, outrageous, when expectations are cheated: when a miserable dozen eggs, for instance, are presented for twenty-five people. "When this first sighting lends their jaws their usual masticatory energy, the Caravan resembles a machine set to work by an irresistible force and on the point of exploding on failing to encounter any resistance." The famine at Misocco leaves a hole in the belly it will take a week of good dinners to fill.[12]

Insufficient quantities, the *omeletticule transparente*, proportions "horrible to contemplate" cause first anxiety, then alarm and terror and reflections on the direct relationship between a hostess's charm and her avarice. Decent and ample food, especially in the remoter regions, is generously praised, especially when improvised by the collective effort of the whole village, but bad food, for lack of resources or, too often, avarice and extortionism, is all too common, and the occasion of some bitterly funny analogies: The coffee is a decoction of hay in color, and of quartzish schist in taste, elsewhere, greenish and rustic; it resembles cowshit (the author's euphemism: *conclusions bovines*). There is bread tasting like conifer bark, only harder on the teeth; the lo-

cal black product is kept as a mineral sample by the "learned" of the troop. The pheasant tastes of fish, and the pork of mattress. As for the jam at Lauterbach: it deserves conjugating thus: it is of "the resinous kind, of the resinaceous species, of the family of the resiniferous and of the consistence of resins."[13]

The popularity of Alpine tourism has caused the cheats and rip-off artists (*écorcheurs*) to multiply. The tourists themselves are partly to blame: they, especially the rich, and the rich and arrogant English, with their airs of superiority and exigence, set themselves up to be overcharged, which others then suffer from. Ever mindful of his tight budget, of his responsibility to protect the health of the "common purse" (*bourse commune*), a personification apt to groan, complain, become faint and emaciated, the troop leader makes a dramatic demonstration of his righteous anger against an innkeeper in Misocco presenting an outrageous bill: "Sir, when you flay people alive, you have to listen to the cries of the victims. First you starve us, then you steal from us."[14] Töpffer says this, laying the money on the table, in public, loud and clear, "like Simon de Nantua" (the pedlar-philosopher to whom he ascribes the *Histoire d'Albert*), to the shame of the innkeeper and the great diversion of all around. Not surprisingly, the famished and thirsty boys tended to "rob" orchards of overhanging fruit, a peccadillo the schoolmaster has to halfheartedly reprove and repress.

Like the food, beds, humorously called *moyens couchatoires* (sleeping apparatus), could vary enormously. They were shared: on one occasion, seven among seventeen, with bedtime "hilarified" by the discovery of their properties and perfections. The collapsing bed elicited laughter prolonged until sleep took over. It was a challenge to sleep with the head touching the floor and the feet the ceiling. Beds offered their own acoustic appeal: the camp-beds (*grabats*) when they collapsed were apt to squeal like pigs taken to the butchers'; there were

NOTE D

NOTE E

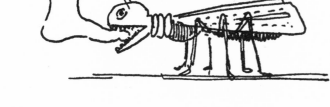

NOTE F

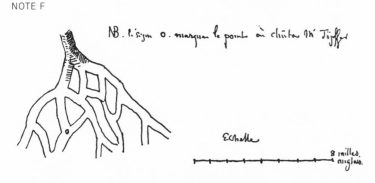

8-5. Note D. Resting on a rock as hard as a diamond. Note E. Musca pedivora, probably as seen through a microscope. The best way to get rid of it is to tread on the insect, but be careful to do so before it has eaten your foot. Note F. Very precise topographic diagram of the passages. NB: the symbol "o" marks the point where Mr. Töpffer fell (*Voyage à Chamonix*, 1828, *VZZ* vol. 2, p. 101).

beds that made "noises lateral, vertical, horizontal, augmented by a dull rumbling in all directions at once, and sustained by mysterious sounds, oblique, immobilized, inadmissible and imprescriptible." Occasionally, the troop had to sleep in the hay, even the master, whose orders "one, two, three: let's sleep!" only increased the hilarity and disorder.[15]

The scorpion in the bed was imagined, but the fleas were not: their infestation was called *kangourisme*, and, like beggars, guides, and innkeepers, they hopped from one body to another in search of blood. Worse were the pedivorous insects (fig. 8-5).

Guides, the bane of tourism

One of the worst diseases of tourism was the plague of guides. Only in Chamonix, with its serious, intelligent, trained teams, were they useful and reliable. The Cicerones, as guides were traditionally called, especially in Italy and Savoy, are generally the "scourge of travelers, vermin of towns, tourist sites and museums, always ready to jump on their prey, and throw boredom and discomfort into the most precious moments . . . a calamity. First, they are of stupendous ignorance: 'This is where Hannibal, seeing the English, pushed their artillery down the rocks.' They seek to overwhelm you with information." It was part of Töpffer's plan to avoid the reflex of the guides, be they human or paper, by not describing sites and monuments, by not naming trees and flowers. Such recitations paralyzed expectation and inhibited the personal response. He wanted no "chattering Linnaeus." As for guidebooks, they should be hanged: "read them, and you are lost! They spoil everything in advance." To the grand historical association of a place, he preferred the chance encounter with a laundry maid. All this tallies with his anti-systemic philosophy, and the kind of pedagogy he had satirized in *M. Crépin*, the joker Farcet from which he cites there and then, drawing and caption, in a tiny vignette (fig. 8-6). He (and no doubt his boys) liked to cite this story: The previous year (1838), soon after the publication, he saw in Glaris a family on their evening walk "like the Crépin family," and he refers to it again twice in 1842. There are "Jabots" too, officious, self-important types who give useless and contradictory advice, who hang out at the best cafés and in Milan preen themselves on horseback. In Novara he takes on the shape of a fat abbé; Jabots here, there, everywhere. By contrast, Töpffer imitates his own M. Vieux Bois, adopting the name of Tircis in a bucolic area of the Valais.[16]

Considering subsequent development, it is difficult to imagine Switzerland in the 1830s and 1840s as perceived to be already corrupted. Rodolphe saw his homeland as a virgin violated, or (although he cannot of course use the word) a willing prostitute, a harpy, at best "a great, barefoot beggar-woman with unkempt hair. . . . Poor Switzerland, what have they done to you!" Everything is bought and sold. The Alps have become a commodity, from the mountain views to the local demonstrations of songs, wrestling, and the echoes, all for sale, and not just the carved wooden souvenir trinkets and cheap scenic engravings. Tilling the soil and related rural virtues are abandoned in pursuit of the tourist franc.

M Crépin visite l'institution Farcet, où la méthode est d'instruire en amusant. Dans ce moment c'est la leçon d'histoire, où le maître fait danser la pyrrhique à deux petits Macédoniens en carton.

8-6. M. Crépin visits the Farcet School, where the method is to teach by having fun. At this moment it is the history lesson, where the master makes two little cardboard Macedonians dance the pyrrhic (*VZZ*, 236. Taken from *Crépin* 75).

8-7. "Bon Logis." One of the worst among all the "wild beasts of hoteliers, this one calculates precisely how and how much he will cheat you. His rough dress indicates a poor mountain shepherd, but he has a thieving mouth, a rapacious nose, and under the long stiff hair shadowing his face, one can glimpse a wild eye gleaming with something insatiable, greed . . . / To which he adds all the forms of the most creeping humility . . . the honeyed tone, the gesture of the lowest servility, the salutatory back . . . He brings for 18 of us, two small loaves, a fragment of cheese and a transparent omeletticule. / A quarrel over the monstrous bill. M. T. outraged, ends up paying. The lamb is at the mercy of the foxes up there, and if he cries for help, it only brings on more foxes. The best is to leave your fleece, and shut up. "Excursion dans l'Oberland bernois en 1835" (*OC* vol. 7, p. 92–94).

The hospitable local farmer and pastor is replaced by the gouging innkeeper. Töpffer touches on this lamentable situation, to which he knew he was himself contributing, lightly, and turns the various tricks of the trade to humor. He challenges, when he can, overcharging and cheating, wins with an air of triumph and loses with good grace; he learns to suspect the ulterior motives of the pretty and charming hostess; and he delights in the trusting vagueness or ignorance, the "pay what you want" of the innumerate peasant host who just watches him lay down coins, and says stop when he thinks the pile is high enough.

Nonsense and logic: Verbal fantasy in the *Voyages*

Töpffer doodles ideas and words as he doodles faces. The *Voyages* are a verbal feast. With his precise sense of genre and audience, Töpffer avoided the grosser and more extreme forms of verbal humor in his novels and short stories. The nearest parallel lies in his (then unpublished) comic plays, which indulge, predictably, in some silliness and comic quid pro quos. The *Voyages* turn out, perhaps unexpectedly, to be rife with a form and degree of wordplay that only those familiar with his (hitherto largely unpublished) correspondence could have imagined. The ostensibly factual chronicles are interlaced with all kinds of absurdities, verbal inventions, and logical illogicalities. He is a forerunner of Edward Lear (whose first book of limericks was published the year Töpffer died—and in the same medium, auto-lithography, as the comic albums) and, I dare to claim, of Lewis Carroll.

The comparison with Carroll overreaches, no doubt. Allowing for the lesser development of nonsense in the French tradition, Töpffer should rank as a master denied, perhaps, the proper environment such as England might have provided for the flowering of his instinct for verbal frolics. I would not claim that he reaches the impeccably simple arith-

metical logic of the Mad Hatter's famous response to Alice's complaint that she cannot take any more tea, since she has not had any yet: "It's very easy to take *more* than nothing." Töpffer's is a bit more complicated, and thus less striking, but claims veracity: the master counters a boy's complaint about an increase in loss of strength, that this must represents a minus times a minus, and ends therefore in a plus. There are paradoxes and reversals of the norm Carroll would have enjoyed: The pleasure of walking is resting; one can be tired not from exertions of yesterday, but of the day before; tiredness can come from fear of being tired.[17] Walking backward (which a couple of boys undertake in order to relieve the tedium of two leagues of "ribbon," i.e., boring straight road), can be more interesting than walking forward; Jolibois, instead of falling suicidally downwards into the water, is swept upwards by the wind. Many actions of Töpffer's comic-strip characters result in the diametric opposite of what is intended or normal. Töpffer even anticipates Carroll's famous mirror law, by which running forward takes you backward, and left and right switch places, in his unfinished draft of *Sébastien Brodbec*, where physical laws work back to front (see Appendix A). And I think Carroll would have appreciated the arithmetical finesse of Töpffer's maniacal doctor in *Claudius Berlu*, who figures he had saved an average of five patients in nineteen.[18]

Töpffer's nonsense in the *Voyages* differs from Carroll's above all in that it is not supposedly invented. Ever on the prowl for peculiar customs, he matches an absurd superstition to an impossible hypothesis: in Chablais one can get married only on a Tuesday, all other days being unlucky. But what if there were no Tuesday? he asks; you could not get married at all. He encounters the logic of literalism, endemic to the rural mentality (and folktale): asked to wake everyone at 4 a.m. in order to experience the sunrise, the guide informs the master at that hour that the sun is obscured by mist, what to do? Since there is nothing to see, let everyone sleep, says he. So the guide goes around knocking loudly on all the doors, to announce that Mr. Töpffer says not to wake up, the sun is not rising. Laughter all round. One, two, three back to sleep.[19]

There are classic farcical quid pro quos with natives, where answers bear no relation to questions: the head guide, "a beardless youth of the greatest promise," is asked how far to Trento. "Yes, Sir, you will find bread there." "But what is the distance?" "There are five beds." The guide, who does not know the way, is paid twelve francs for his trouble in being led to Chamonix, where he has never been before.[20]

Some of the nonsense is in the form of jokes traditional to rural areas. How to catch hares: at midnight, they run along a specially constructed balustrade (*garde-fou*), see their own shadow down a ravine, and, trying to reach it, fall into the gravel, where we pick them up at dawn. There are places where time is measured by ninety-minute hours, and distance by leagues that are longer than wide. Then there are always different systems of arithmetic when it comes to totaling the bill. A peasant asks them to say hello to his son, a chimney sweep in Vezouille. But where is Vezouille? Oh, in "that place where they say Monsieur le Marquis, do you want *caudes*?"[21]

Words, like people, have their own physiognomies and personalities. They can be changed at will. "The question is," said Humpty Dumpty, "which is to be master—that's all." Many of Töpffer's new verbal coinages involve adjectiving of nouns, sometimes as if they were Latin: thus *politique voiturine* (vehicular politics), *propositions navigatoires*, and *poudre sternutatoire* (for snuff). This is a standard comic device: making simple everyday things sound comic, or difficult, or learned. Thus *inventions fermatoires* for non-closing doors and windows, *intraguétral* for under or between gaiters, *enthousiasme grimpatoire* (mounting enthusiasm, to give the translator here a chance to pun), and *déjeuner absyptiforme*—for what kind of dinner, pray?[22]

One would expect Töpffer to put the brakes on neologomania and logorrhea for publication. He did so, allowing publisher Dubochet (letter of 18 January 1843) to prune some neologisms, and excessive "stylistic exuberance, too local or familiar locations." But they show up even more in his correspondence, to a degree that must have left some recipients *archikadrupedisé* (apparently meaning stupefied). The author, himself submerged under his own "archisuperoccupations," fears his publisher is likewise at the mercy of "occupations tant gazeuses qu'editojournalipittorillustrfricassées" (26 June 1844). He splits long words: "cet atten qui pourrait faire du mal drissement" (this tender which could cause harm ness). His childishness with august colleagues: "Cher bullullullulivilliez . . ." surprises more than the virtually infantile blabberings to his small children: to daughter Adèle he sends presents "très turlururuficotibiolustrumandicoticolabrimirondilli fistibulés."[23]

Wordplay in French, although never as developed as in English, has a noble ancestor: Rabelais. In a typical Rabelaisian list, Töpffer has suffixes existing in one word infect the next in a nonexistent form: thus an inn is "crevassée, échafaudée, rapetassée, pierracée et charpentacée" (crevassed, scaffolded, patched up, stonified, and framified). He shortcuts from noun to verb, as in "embriocher" (serving brioches to all), and makes Carrollian portmanteaus by packing together two French words as in *suaviloquence* or a foreign and French word such as in *gentlemanie*. He conjugates a German word as if it were French: *Gewaschenfié* (laundered). His *beefsteakement malin* (beefsteakenly cunning) merely adjectivizes the stereotypical food of an English John Bull. *Tapâtes* (you hit, preterite), for all its normality, is discovered to sound funny, and by dint of repetition becomes absurd, pure rejoiceable, mesmerizingly percussive sound. One could make a learned lexicon of Töpfferisms, and determine the mix of Genevese dialect, ancient Greek, archaic French, Rabelais—and pure linguistic invention. I chased down, or tried to, two favorites that recur in Töpffer like "runcible" in Lear: *embraminé*, which seems to mean misty (from *embrumé*?), but neither the *Glossaire Genevois* nor any dictionary of French old or new has the form, and *matagrabolisé*, no longer current in the nineteenth century but coined by Rabelais, and referring to the imagining of crazy things. If I had dared (or UPM had let me), I might have called this book *Töpffer: Matagraboliser of the Comic Strip*.[24]

Töpffer loved bizarre and evocative place names, which have their own graphic physiognomy, as he says, ever adept at overlapping verbal and visual. The writer-artist demands a Lavater of place names, which can be "as solemn as a schoolmaster, vulgar as the paraph of a counter-jumper, or bloated as the greeting of a cretin."[25]

Töpffer liked the idea of circular and self-devouring logic, and the logic that exhausts itself to the point of nonsense in the enumeration of hypotheses. In the theater in Milan, "most of the songs get lost, either because the theater is too vast or because the actors' voices are too weak, either the one and the other, or the one or the other, or for another reason, or, finally, for no reason at all, because one shouldn't commit oneself." The Mayor in the prose version of *Festus* goes one better, in his inventory of "objects stolen, objects left behind, objects neither stolen nor left behind, then those which were both stolen and left behind." Exhaustive enumeration of possibilities, surely derived from Rabelais, and aspiring to a kind of mathematical finality, escalates from the commonsensical to the fantastic and nonsensical: like the famous hypochondriacs, the boy Vernon has recourse to every combination of drugs, prescriptions, and recipes, trying his rucksack every conceivable way, straps above arms, below arms, short straps, long straps, cold, lukewarm, hot, with sugar and without, balanced, suspended, homeopathically, allopathically, "morévesimacbéficassippocondrilliquement."[26] There was certainly more of

this sort of thing that did not survive the revision for the big French audience.

Generally, the master of a delicate, purified prose style had no time for the vulgarity of puns; even as part of captions to the picture stories, puns are a rarity—unlike Cham, who piles them on. In real life, and on the Alpine hikes, they spiced up any conversation. Puns were of two kinds: deliberate and unintentional. The boys let them rip, explain the master's unintentional ones, and egg him on until, "fit to scare his friends" "he falls into puns as into a muddy-hole."[27]

The classics master was not good at learning living languages. He started on English as a youth in Paris and got nowhere; his German and Italian were very rudimentary, and hardly up to the needs of his travels. He even dedicated a book to his admirer and translator, the well-known German-Swiss writer Heinrich Zschokke: "A Monsieur Henry Szcokke." His spoken German got little further than a bizarre *Gewaschenkeitsfrau* (laundry-woman), and his description of a picturesque inn as "archifabolo et aceto que je vous dico" about sums up his Italian. To a professionally polylingual Pictet de Rochemont (22 February 1845) he assembles a mosaic of seven languages in one sentence, here verbatim: "Toutefois ελπιζομαι, φιλε, dass Sie n'êtes pas fait per [Arab word for "to remain"] in those dispositions, and that when you shall have un poco recuperato votre moi veritable quem nunc quassant et labefaciunt." (However, as I hope, friend, that you are not made to remain in those dispositions, and that when you shall have recovered a little your true self which right now they shatter and shake.)

On his Alpine excursions he found failures to communicate amusing. His own failure with respect to foreign languages is cast back chiefly on Englishmen who, like Americans today, expected everyone to speak their language, or at any rate understand it. Töpffer's Milords (as they always are) make up for their lack of language by violence and obtuseness. Helplessly and arrogantly they haunt the Alps, his plays, the *Voyages*, other prose works, and the picture stories, totally and tiresomely stereotypical, capable only of monosyllabic grunts in French and the usual imperfect tense chosen by the French, one suspects (wordplay aside), to encapsulate the imperfectness of their linguistic capacities. The taciturnity of the Nono is proverbial and invariable. The English tourist is known as the Nono because things are never right for him. In his "cuirasse" of reserve, his ideal is never to have to communicate outside the family and group he travels with. His daughter, the odd Miss, is better, has some French, and is the object of romantic speculations; but there should be no social or amorous shortcuts in the Alps. The garrulous and gregarious Frenchman is the opposite of the Englishman.[28]

The local guide is a sort of "confidential fool who passes for French without daring to speak it, speaking German without being able to make himself understood, but fluent in Iroquois that none of us knew." The Genevese nationalist vents enthusiastic insults upon Romansch (or Romonsch), spoken at the other end of Switzerland, now and long since the fourth national language but then hardly considered civilized, it seems: "a strange language, originally unintelligible, which, when written resembles the swearing of an angry Spaniard and when spoken, the gibberish of a throat obstructed by an onion . . . but interesting" (he adds) "for its energetic roughness, with those picturesque turns, vigorous, compact, with vivid, somewhat harshly scented flowers of diction." Knowing no other language, unused to tourists, the Romansch-only speakers of eastern Switzerland used sign language with them.[29]

Provençal, spoken then in the south of France, "we reduce to a clicking of *d*'s and *z*'s artistically amalgamated. M. Töpffer makes in this new language frightening progress" by adding *–az* or *–iz* to the end of every other word. Actually, Töpffer always had a weakness for the curiosity of rustic dialects that reminded him of the archaic French

he liked to flourish in his writing, and of which vestiges survived in the Genevan dialect he also appropriated, especially in his correspondence. Like the artless, naïve style of drawing he promoted and claimed to practice, and so brilliantly systematized in his picture stories, the peasant linguistic style was "lively, eloquent, picturesque, expressive, audacious." It was the original French (*français de souche*), so unlike the bastard French of the new novels and press. Sometimes, however, the natives' dialect or failure to articulate is annoying, if amusing, as when "the intelligible part of their language is swallowed up in nasal crevasses." As in landscape painting, Töpffer prizes in language expressiveness and feeling before accuracy and clarity. Likewise, the local mystery play and street music encountered en route may be preferable to the sophisticated, urban kind. Local dialects are a kind of linguistic graffiti, spontaneous, rough, and idiosyncratic.[30]

The laughter grows thinner in the 1840s, and the social philosophizing, which for our purposes culminates in *Histoire d'Albert*, thicker. No doubt, Töpffer gets boring, prim, long-winded, clutching at every excuse to sound off politically, tiresome even if you sympathize with his conservatism. His pose is that of many a conservative who pretends just to dislike politics, that is, any kind of agitation for change, period. What good does politics do in the Alps? Or economic change. Modernization means corruption. The artist is, however, not without a social conscience, blaming the corruption of rustic mores on the tourists as much as the peasants, noting sardonically that the abbés in Austrian Italy are florid and fat while the peasants are thin and bony (see fig. 1-19), and expressing sympathetic shock at the sight of young, handsome, intelligent-looking convicts in chains, condemned to hard labor. The working conditions in the mines and furnaces are as bad or worse: watching the furnaces operating at Saint Martin near Aosta, Töpffer describes how they ruin the workers' health, killing and maiming them in the flower of their age; none live long, and no wonder they develop immoral habits.[31]

This in 1838. There is real social compassion here. A few years later, with the political temperature rising throughout Switzerland and especially the Valais, the whole *Voyage* to Venice (1841, his next to last) is haunted by his fear of signs of democracy and "progress." His animus against all politics as "a sad assemblage of doubtful principles substituted by [political] parties for the healthy rules of common sense" dilates into the cultural sphere: "instead of fine books you have literary products, a fabrication and a consumption, of the Balzacs and Sands; your model society . . . counts neither on you, nor even on God, but on chance, on riots, revolutions, on wars, on dreadful and bloody disasters. . . . And then, go cure it with your utopias that are not even innocent and moral, with your foolish and impossible systems, with your shameless press, with your mendacious egalitarianism, with your hideous materialism!!!" Then he adds, "Here we are, for no reason, really angry. Sorry, reader."[32] Then, suddenly, back to the hotel, and on to the Corso. For the reader, none too soon.

Most writers on Töpffer regret his political conservatism, which has a certain vulgarity or at least an obtrusive brashness. Yet it is mitigated by many humane observations, such as those we have cited on exploited mineworkers. His opposition to U.S. slavery is expressed in *L'Heritage*. His resistance to industrialization, in the economy in general and in culture in particular, is prescient. So are his diatribes in the essay *On Progress and its relations to the petty bourgeois and schoolmasters* (1835) against useless inventions, the "fury of producing, manufacturing, perfecting, capital creating proletarians, production for its own sake," progress as an end in itself, not a means to happiness. Today, in the twenty-first century, we are in a better position to judge the idea of "progress" and bourgeois "democracy" that became the shibboleths of nineteenth- and twentieth-century progressives: they have brought us "hideous materialism," environmental disaster, increased to intolerable levels the gap between rich and poor they were supposed to bridge, corrupted political and electoral processes, and, on the technological level, made war unimaginably destructive. Currently, the world's self-appointed democratic leader flouts international law, kills en masse, and tortures at will. If this is "progress," I am with Töpffer, even if for different reasons.

VOYAGES EN ZIGZAG: HUMOR OF THE UNEXPECTED

Chapter Nine

THE LEGACY

France after Töpffer: Cham, Nadar, Petit

In an early assessment of Töpffer's picture stories, the cleric Jean Gaberel predicted that the genre he invented could have no future without him.[1] How wrong he was. The impact of Töpffer's new invention was immediate, long-lasting, European wide, and even reached the United States. It was first felt, logically, in France. The first true and consistent disciple of Töpffer in the appealing but difficult genre he created was a déclassé aristocrat from the illustrious house of the counts of Noé, whose title he inherited and never assumed. Charles Amédée de Noé took the acro-pseudonym Cham as the son of Noé (French for Shem, son of Noah), and created in his long and productive life an unceasing flood of imagery of immeasurable dimensions. It started with Töpffer. As an aspiring artist in his late teens Cham was given copies of *Jabot*, *Vieux Bois*, and *Crépin* by his cousin the Duc de Feltre. In 1839 the leading Parisian publisher of caricature, Gabriel Aubert, ever alert to the commercial advantages of series (those of Daumier and Gavarni became instant successes) and having plagiarized the three Geneva-published Töpffer albums mentioned, decided to launch an original album series, small, oblong, lithographed, and at six francs cheaper than Töpffer's ten-franc originals. He called them Albums Jabot after Töpffer's initiating work.

The first Cham album was titled *M. Lajaunisse*, published on 3 August 1839, very soon after the first Aubert plagiary, and followed in quick succession with six or seven more, all more or less Töpfferian but fresh and original: they are less absurdist, more realistic, eschewing real impossibilities like aerial travel but also lacking the cogent intellectual satire of Töpffer (fig. 9-1). Apolitical, addicted to crude puns, Cham aimed surely for a lower market, and indeed used typically a lower class of hero: instead of Töpffer's upper-bourgeois wealthy man of letters or *rentier*, the typical Cham hero is a grocer, a *Monsieur Lamélasse* (Mr. Molasses), or a poor, frustrated artist like *M. Barnabé Gogo*. This latter is, in a way, self-persiflage, although, unlike so many other caricaturists and illustrators, Cham never aspired to painting and being shown in the Salon. It was a condition of the métier to envy the "real artist." Cham owed his considerable celebrity, which eventually surpassed on the popular level that of Daumier (to whose style, miniaturized, he deserted after his youthful Töpfferian frolics), entirely to his tremendously prolific output on every conceivable topic of the day. He could also show a turn of verbal phrase, not as well as Töpffer but better than Daumier. He is also credited with operettas and vaudeville. His line initially favors, like Töpffer, the contour, but is less quavering, less flighty; it invited color, which Cham wanted but could not get from the publisher.

Cham's albums of this type were not and have not been reissued, but he soon broke into the big commercial market through the various popular magazines of which he became a mainstay. He stuck to the topics being mined by the other cartoonists

9-1. Cham: Mr. Lajaunisse realizes he has got into the drawer on top of the letter. / At which he laughs gracefully. / Since he has lain down on the sealing wax, the letter sticks to him. / How to get rid of it? / The ingenious Mr. Lajaunisse raises the chest-of-drawers and shoves the letter beneath. / Delighted with the procedure, he pulls with all his might. / To such good effect that the chest-of-drawers falls on top of him. / The noise of which brings up the neighbors. / He is picked up / and water thrown over him. / Furious, he chases off the neighbors (*Mr. Lajaunisse*, 1839, 9–14).

and even, amusingly, to the objects and services advertised. Cham himself was the perfect consumer, afflicted with a typically lower-middle-class hypochondria that he satirizes in *The Story of Monsieur Jobard*. The big-city obsession with hygiene, by which this class tried to set itself off from the adjacent, sweaty working class, is expressed in the recurrent theme of bathing, which we see in Töpffer only as an accident and punishment. Changing one's linen, as Monsieur Vieux Bois does constantly between

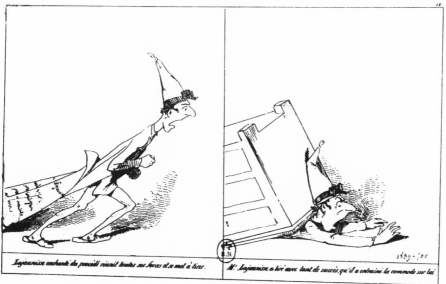

episodes, has less to do with bodily hygiene than his need to restore his nerves for the next twist of fate. Töpffer's characters get beaten up, but are not really hurt physically (precursors here, too, of animated cartoon); no one in Töpffer suffers anything so gruesome as having all his teeth drawn, a symbolic castration, like Cham's poor M. Jobard.[2] The whirlwind cudgeling inflicted by Töpffer's Milord is not permanently damaging, like the flogging suffered by Cham's Boniface when he is caught up in the British army.

But by 1840, after his first three Albums Jabot, Cham was already drawing away from the nonsensicality and absurdism of his Swiss model toward more conventional social satire, in a cryptically realistic style. In the years 1845–52 he made a speciality of parodies of travel and tourism, featuring himself and other reluctant adventurers in

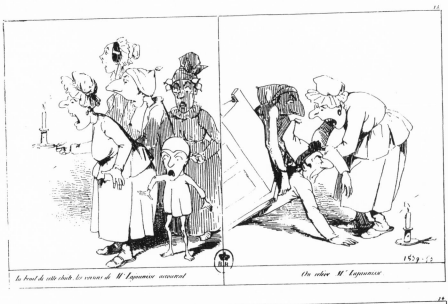

geographical locales all over Europe and as far as French Algeria and Russia. This was an excuse for mockery of national types, customs, and conditions, to which *Cryptogame* of 1845, by far Töpffer's most popular and best distributed picture story, with its Algerian episode, surely gave the signal. The comic strip thenceforth became mock-adventurous and exotic, in parody of incipient mass tourism and, perhaps, Euro-American imperialism in Africa. Cham, who redrew Töpffer's designs for *Crypto-game* in *L'Illustration* in 1845 (see p. 97f.), surely had not forgotten it when he set his own exotic *Episodes from the History of a Savage Nation* (*L'Illustration*, July 1846) among American Indians, who become totally corrupted by "civilization" (fig. 9-2).

The sheer length of Töpffer's stories, which were more suited to separate albums than to serial magazine publication, inspired Cham to some extended efforts: *Lithographic Impressions of a Journey by Messieurs Trottman and Cham* occupied twenty

Le Nuage-Blanc arrache de désespoir tous les poils de son bonnet, en reconnaissant l'affreuse boulette qu'il vient de commettre en répandant les bienfaits de l'instruction.

Cependant, une partie de la nation i-o-way s'étant révoltée, le Nuage-Blanc assemble son armée, et décore tous ses soldats sans exception, par manière d'encouragement.

De son côté, le chef des insurgés assemble sa troupe, et termine sa harangue, s'engageant, avant le coucher du soleil, à boire grog dans le crâne de son ennemi le Nuage-Blanc.

Arrivée en présence l'une de l'autre, les deux armées se couchent en joue.

Et tirent toutes deux à la fois avec une si admirable précision, que tous les soldats tombent blessés à mort.

Les femmes, qui ignoraient la nouvelle, ne voulant pas se mettre à table avant le retour de leurs maris, moururent toutes de faim. Ainsi finit la nation des I-o-Ways, victime de la civilisation.

9-2. Cham: In despair, White Cloud tears every hair from his busby, seeing what a blunder he has committed in spreading the benefits of civilization. / When a segment of the I-o-Way nation rebels, White Cloud assembles his army and gives decorations to his soldiers. / The rebel chief gathers his troops and swears he will be drinking grog from the skull of his enemy White Cloud before sunset. / The two armies fire at each other simultaneously / and all fall dead. / The wives, unaware of this and unwilling to sit down to eat ahead of their husbands, all die of hunger. Thus ended the I-o-Way nation, victim of civilization (*Episodes from the History of a Savage Nation, or the benefits of Civilization, L'Illustration*, 1846).

pages in two months of the *Charivari* (November–December 1846). But the typical post-Töpffer French comic strip, in these early days, always excepting the feverishly productive Cham, was short, spasmodic, incoherent, and unimaginative. A quick look at the very vehicle of *Cryptogame*, *L'Illustration*, reveals how hard artists, no doubt urged on by editors, tried and failed to come up to scratch. Benjamin Roubaud's awkward *Les Aventures de Scipion l'Africain*, published in 1845 soon after *Cryptogame*, obviously capitalizes on Töpffer's Algerian episode and is interesting only for its au-

dacious indications of sexual promiscuity (Paris or Muslim style?). Cham, dominant in the magazine 1845–49, alternates between Töpfferian narratives and Cruikshankian "scraps and sketches," called by the French *études* or *macédoines*, on contemporary topics. Some of the stories have an imaginative flourish: the Munchausenesque Baron de Crac (September 1845), trapped in and precipitated from a bell with the bell-ringer, reminds one a little of Töpffer's astronomers in the airborne telescope.

All this anarchic flurry of woodcut graphic jokes and tales does not survive the advent of Na-

9-3. Cham: In the tunnel M. Clopinet has his watch pinched, and sees a train headed toward him on the same track. Indescribable travel impression (*Journey from Paris to America Pursued to Le Havre inclusive, Le Charivari*, 1844–1845).

poleon III in 1851, when the censorship hardened and *L'Illustration* began to drop caricature altogether. Nor does it bear comparison to the *Charivari*, with its stately procession of monumental lithographic designs by Daumier, Gavarni, and company. But the mini-cut, Cham-style, does something else signifi-

cant, on the impulse surely of Töpffer and *Cryptogame*, as the latter gentleman embarked on his European and U.S. tour. Whether linked in attempts at narrative or grouped by theme, the caricature pages of *L'Illustration* and the *Charivari* systematically deploy numerous small vignettes, such as Cham

A FEW FRIENDS TO TEA, AND
A LYTTLE MUSYCK.

9-4. Richard Doyle: A few friends to tea, and a lyttle musyck (*Punch*, 1849).

is to make his speciality in different magazines all his life. Twelve cartoons on a page—all scanned in a moment. This is in the logic of railway reading, which allowed for variety, distraction, and interruption, for superficial and momentary attention; for looking, in a shaking carriage, rather than sustained reading.

The railways, in which Töpffer invested heavily (and cynically, since he certainly did not believe in them and had never seen them), fascinated Cham, ever alert to novelty. Railways brought the dangers and discomforts of travel to a new and fearful pitch. While in Daumier these seem more psychological than physical, the all-too-real disaster on the Paris-Versailles line in 1842, when fifty-five people were killed and over one hundred injured, seems to be reflected in the near-collision and explosion in Cham's

Journey from Paris to America (1844–45, fig. 9-3). The comic strip and the magazine containing it became a kind of railway literature sold in magazine or album form at station kiosks, mirroring the anxieties and terrors, the stop-and-start rhythms and hectic movement of the railways. Is it a coincidence that Töpffer drafted his very first picture story at the very moment when the railways were first tried out, in Britain, and that his popularity was established (in the early 1840s) at the very moment when it was apparent they would revolutionize travel—and constitute an entirely new kind of psycho-physical experience?

The promoters and idealists claimed that the railways would be a socially and culturally as well as geographically unifying force. This was much needed in the 1840s, an era of seething social discontent. Töpffer's amalgam of absurdism, nonsense,

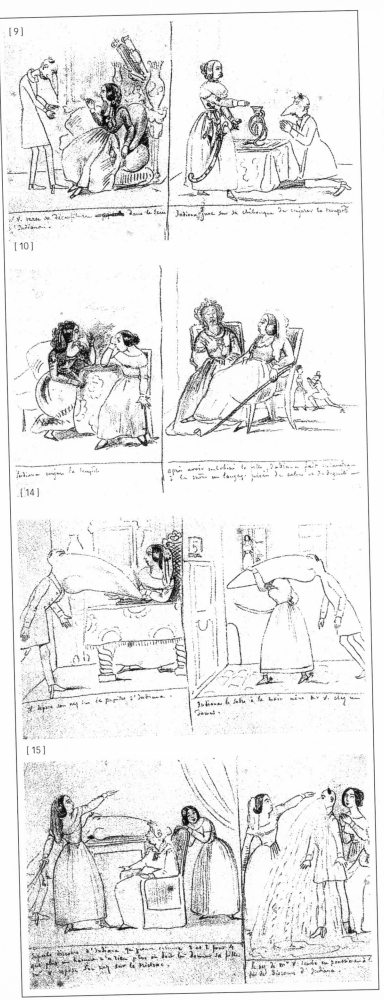

[9]

[10]

[14]

[15]

and arbitrary violence often leading to death—the desperate mixture of the macabre, foolish, and cruel characteristic of caricature in this decade—collide with a burgeoning artistic realism, of which the French (Daumier, Corot, Courbet) are the avatars. Töpffer, absurdist-realist, straddles an era.[3]

Cham may have abandoned the pure outline style of Töpffer, and other artists never attempted it, but its attractions persisted, to be taken up by the young Gustave Doré. The fact that it represented a true, workable alternative graphic style, particularly suited to cartooning because of its brevity, was sensed by *L'Illustration*. We today recognize it as perhaps *the* style with a long future, passing into the twentieth-century cartoon via Wilhelm Busch. In 1849 the French magazine reproduced, with credit to *Punch* but without benefit of the name of the "celebrated unknown" author, a drawing of a musical soirée in that style, taken from the mock-archaic series *Manners and Customs of the Englyshe* by Richard Doyle, which ran in *Punch* 1849–50 (fig. 9-4). The young Doyle, who had no academic training but shared with Tenniel the honors of the big political cartoon in *Punch*, was the primary English exponent of this style that *L'Illustration* explicitly credits to Töpffer, who gave him the secret "in the guise of simple outline of a child-like naïveté."[4] It was a *popular* style, actually rather different from his own, valued by Töpffer as that of the Parisian gamin's graffiti or of

9-5. Alfred de Musset (and/or Auguste Barre): 9. L. V. [Louis Viardot] pours his discomfiture into the bosom of Indiana. Indiana swears on her chiboiuque [Turkish pipe] to avert the storm. 10. Indiana averts the storm. Having got around the girl, Indiana lets her mother know in highly dignified language. 14. He sets his nose down on Indiana's desk. Indiana, saber in hand, takes M. V. to those ladies. 15. Superb speech of Indiana which proves that 2 plus 2 makes four, that the more a man has nothing, the more he should be given one's daughter. M.V. rests his nose on the backgammon table. The M. V. nose dissolves into dust at the end of Indiana's speech ("Marriage of Pauline Garcia and Louis Viardot," Sand, p. 70 no. 47; no location for the drawings given).

According to the biography of his father by Paul de Musset (1877, p. 240), in 1840, after suffering a grave illness, the poet Alfred de Musset occupied the days of his convalescence, feeling again like a seventeen-year-old, "with an album of caricatures in the Toppfer [sic] style"—fifty-one drawings, of which half were by Musset and the other half by his neighbor Auguste Barre, while others did the captions. This excerpt (the rest remain unpublished) recounts the vicissitudes of a marriage between a young singer and a theatre owner. Spirit and style, using an enormously magnified nose, are more Cham than Töpffer.

9-6. Toulouse-Lautrec: then armed with a hammer . . . (drawings from *Submersion*, 1881, *Toulouse-Lautrec*, exhibition catalog, Hayward Gallery, London, 1991, p. 89, Curnonsky, 1938, n.p.; and Schimmel and Murray, p. 149n).

Experts on Henri de Toulouse-Lautrec have detected in an album of forty-nine drawings this artist's acquaintance with Töpffer, confirmed by the title of the Notebook "Cahier en Zigzag," and the reference to *Cryptogame* in a letter to his mother.

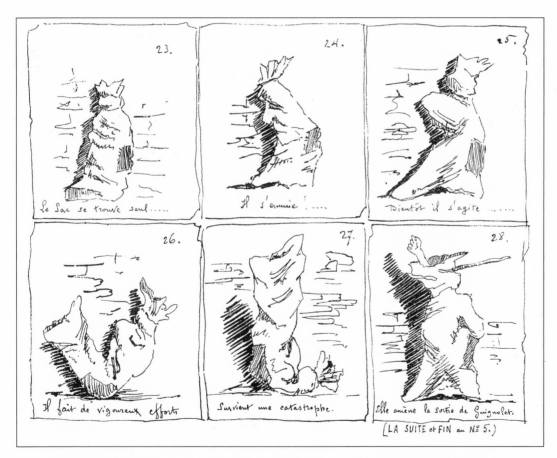

9-7. Henri Hébert ("Phantaz"): The sack is alone. . . It is bored! . . . Soon it shakes . . . It makes great efforts. A catastrophe happens. It results in Guignolet's escape (*Le crime de Châtelaine*, Geneva, 1879–1880, from J.-D. Candaux, *Töpfferiana*).

An "overview" by the Swiss literary authority Jean-Daniel Candaux has found a number of Genevan imitators of Töpffer's *Voyages en Zigzag* and picture stories, some published in small auto-lithographic edition and privately circulated, some remaining in manuscript, none achieving any publicity and generally more curious than truly original. We single out *Le crime de Châtelaine*, thirty-eight pictures published in four installments in the journal *Guguss* in 1879, one page signed "un disciple de Töpffer," by "Phantaz," that is Henri Hébert (1849–1917). Hébert was a professional painter of genre and landscape who enjoyed a brilliant career locally as a caricaturist under the pseudonym Tubal, virtually introducing political cartoon and comic strip into the Genevan press. His style is more French than Töpffer, but our excerpt reveals a memory of Vieux Bois in his corn-sack (76) combined perhaps with Jolibois in his crate (46).

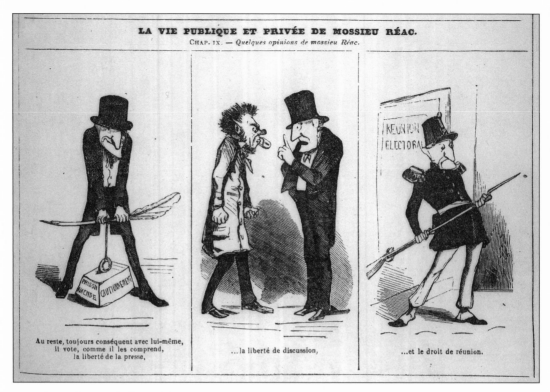

9-8. Nadar: M. Réac votes for liberty of the press as he understands it [i.e., with heavy restrictions and punishments], . . . for freedom of speech, . . . and rights of assembly [by the national guard] ("The Public and Private Life of Mossieu Réac," *Revue Comique*, 1849).

the schoolboy scribbling in his textbooks. By this time (1849) *L'Illustration* was advertising *Cryptogame*, with Cham's *Boniface*, as a *prime* or bonus, at 1.50 instead of 5 francs, to (re)subscribers.

Daumier, meanwhile, had been pushed into a semblance of narrative by Philipon, his publisher, who usually determined the topics and wrote his captions for him. It was in 1839, clearly under the impact of Töpffer's albums, that the Philipon-Daumier *Mésaventures et désappointements de M. Gogo* was used to launch a new magazine, the *Caricature provisoire* (November–December 1838), followed by a *Journée d'un célibataire* (Day in the Life of a Bachelor, June–September 1839), both of which dragged on for a while and were then aborted. Neither scenarist nor artist, nor any French artist save Cham and then Nadar, had the necessary literary gifts to sustain a true narrative, and follow the sug-

gestion of Töpffer himself (written to Sainte-Beuve) that they do so.[5]

Nadar's Réac

The revolutions of 1848 infused new energy into the comic strip, and while Cham continued in his post-Töpfferian mode, Nadar (Gaspard-Félix Tournachon), who became better known as a photographer and balloonist but who started as a gifted caricaturist, created the radical, anti-Bonapartist *Revue Comique* and a continuing character in it called Monsieur Réac. He is a satire on the political reactionary as his name implies, and lasted only as long as the magazine (November 1848–end 1849), before both character and magazine succumbed to censorship; the character, in his role as representative

9-9. Gustave Doré: Hercules, happily, and the hind, unhappily, fall into the river. Hercules, 1,000,000,000 leagues from home, earns his passage back by public performances (*Les Travaux d'Hercule*, 1847).

counterrevolutionary, helped kill himself and the magazine off, as it were Frankenstein destroyed by the monster he had created (fig. 9-8). At 148 drawings, Nadar's invention shows exceptional staying power, and the marks of Töpffer entirely to its advantage: in the framing, in the diminution of background, in the emphasis on contour, in the physical hyperactivity, in the nimble development of incidents and farce, and above all in the maintenance of a distinctive but expressive physiognomy for the protagonist. Réac is a counterpart and political antithesis to Töpffer's revolutionary agitator Albert, and cast in a similar hostile role; both use journalism for their nefarious ends, and both end up marrying aristocrats or money. Nadar's Réac, who tried to censor the rest of his own story, finds his wife in compromising intimacy with a "horrible rebel" who might, one fancies, be Albert himself.

Gustave Doré

Töpffer wrote his picture stories, as he tells us, as an escape from political reality. On the eve of the 1848 revolutions, in December of the preceding year, Philipon launched a new magazine whose overt purpose was entertainment, "to amuse a bored century." This was the *Journal pour Rire*, in which the boy prodigy Gustave Doré made his debut. Doré's inspiration was certainly Töpffer, although he seems to have learned from the childish-looking outline style of Richard Doyle as well. His *Travaux d'Hercule* was published in 1847 and promoted by Philipon's brother-in-law Aubert as the work of a fifteen-year-old and the twelfth in the Albums Jabot series. Doré's is an astonishing, mature performance by any standard, and the disappearance of the album, now impossible to find, from the market and its absence

Cependant le cocher croyant nous être agréable distribue aux crétins maints coups de fouets. L'un d'eux est enlevé de terre par l'instrument,

ce qui les irrite violemment. Animés par l'esprit de corps, il font pleuvoir sur nous une grêle de pierres

tant il y eut qui fallut transporter ma femme essorée au plus voisin châlet, tandis que moi je châtiai cruellement un de ces crétins que j'avais pris sous ma casquette.

— "Voulá vous adopta nious infans" Refrain des grandes routes en Savoie.

— Voy vous m'sieu, on est honteux d'être Savoyard pays est trop pauv' et trop vilain : on tâchera ben une fois que Mont Blanc sont Terrancé pour qu'on y fasse des bons tunels.

— Cocher, cocher, ou donc nous menez-vous ? — Ah! pardon m'sieu c'est que j'ai été cocher à Paris tout dernièrement et j'croyais encore tourner la rue Belle Chasse.

— As pas peur, madame, as pas peur; ici il est tombé 18 personnes, là il est tombé 3 diligences, là, 30 mulets et leurs dames, as pas peur, madame, as pas peur . . . .

Plus loin, la voiture entre dans le lit d'un torrent . . . as pas peur madame, bouge pas, c'est la route.

Enfin madame déclara qu'elle ne passerait par l'eau qu'on lui eut fait un petit pont et ses frais bien entendu et la transporta au plus voisin châlet

9-10. Gustave Doré: To amuse us, the coachman whips the cretins . . . / who shower the coach with stones. / My wife faints and has to be carried to the nearest chalet, and I cruelly chastise a cretin I caught under my cap. / Roadside refrain in Savoy: 'You wanna adopt our chillun?' / 'Look Sir, we are ashamed of being Savoyard, poor and ugly as the country is; as soon as Mont Blanc is French, we'll try to tunnel through it.' / 'Watch out coachman!' 'Sorry, Sir; fact is, I was just recently a cabbie in Paris . . .' / 'Doan worry, madame, doan worry; 18 people fell here, 3 coaches there, 30 mules with their ladies over there; doan worry Madame, doan worry.' / The coach enters a torrent . . . 'Doan worry madame, it's still the road.' / Finally Madame declares she will not continue through the water without a bridge (to be built at her expense of course) and she is carried to the nearest chalet (*Dis-Pleasures of a Pleasure Trip*, 1851).

today even from national libraries is a great mystery. We cannot begin to summarize here, as we have done in the past, some of its original features, which blend a crazy, Töpfferian narrative form (and some Töpfferian verbal tics) with parody of ancient history and myth, as represented in Daumier's *Histoire Ancienne* cartoon series and Cham's *Aventures de Télémaque*. Hercules becomes a kind of squat, potbellied, boastful Jabotesque upstart finding himself in Munchausenesque situations (fig. 9-9).

In his early years, before he definitively deserted the caricature that gained him instant celeb-

9-11. Gustave Doré, illustration, to *The Adventures of Baron Munchausen*, 1864.

rity (and in which he proved unbelievably prolific) for "straight" illustration of the classics, Doré (like Cham) came to specialize in parodic travel tales. The time was propitious, for around 1851 the postrevolutionary quiescence set in and travel became cheaper, easier, and much commercialized. From his many comic travel tales we may single out his *Dis-pleasures of a Pleasure-trip* (1851), which although closer to Cham than Töpffer in draughtsmanship, exploits the absurdism of the Töpffer comic album tradition and, set as it is in the Genevan Alps, may derive also from the prose *Voyages en Zigzag* of the Swiss (fig. 9-10).

Doré's ultimate travel tale is the ultimate in (historical) travel tales: his ineffable *History of Holy Russia* (1854) takes on the whole history of Russia and is by far the largest narrative comic album of the century. Published in the midst of the Crimean War and unashamedly, indeed excessively (even for French political purposes) anti-Russian, it is a tour de force (or farce) that in a way submerges the Töpffer tradition in Rabelaisian hyperbolism.

Its anti-Russianism has ensured its republication in our own times, unlike the rest of the considerable Doré comic strip oeuvre. Even as he scaled the height of world literature he did not entirely forget Töpffer, and his illustration to *The Adventures of Baron Munchausen* shows the two captured English officers who escape from being hanged dragging the gibbets after them (fig. 9-11), which is not warranted by the text but which echoes both the escape of Vieux Bois and the Beloved Object from the stake and that of the Abbé from Algiers in *Cryptogame*.

Léonce Petit

The *Holy Russia* would seem to signal the end of the immediate Töpffer legacy in France; but then, the era of Napoleon III (for our purposes, c. 1853 to the late 1860s) seems to have put the comic strip in France generally on hold, discounting the amazing comic-strip parody by Cham of Victor Hugo's *Les*

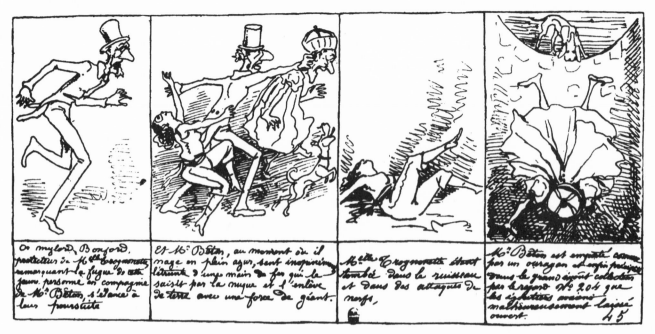

9-12. Léonce Petit: Lord Bonjon, protector [of Mlle. Crognonette] pursues the absconding pair. At the height of his ecstasy, M. Bêton is seized by an iron hand which lifts him up with colossal force. Mlle. Crognonette falls into the gutter and a nervous fit. M. Bêton is flung as by a hurricane down main sewer no. 204 (*The Misadventures of M. Bêton*, 1868).

Misérables (1862). On hold, that is, up to the advent of Léonce Petit, whose beginnings clearly carry the Töpffer stamp, and whose whole impressive (and neglected) oeuvre stands as a tribute to the Swiss master. The hiatus in French comic strip production coincides with a general decline in the quality of caricature (even in Daumier), and may be partly explained by a general social pacification under the Second Empire. It was in Germany, with Wilhelm Busch and others, that the baton of the picture story was picked up, while France (and England) lay relatively fallow.

Léonce Petit was often called the French Töpffer. His *Misadventures of M. Bêton* (Mr. Booby, 1867–68) are interlaced with very funny, Töpfferian emotional and physical frenzies, chases, misapprehensions, coincidences, and arrests. The work is Töpfferian all the way from its transfer-lithographic technique, graphic line, montages, and refrains right down to finer points of format, frame, and handwritten caption (fig. 9-12). One might have

expected an earlier Töpfferian revival prompted by the republication in 1860 of Töpffer's entire comic-strip oeuvre in faithful copies by his son François Töpffer, printed in handsome albums by the big Parisian house of Garnier. But the *Bêton* album, with its companion called *M. Tringle*—which has a motif that might be derived from *Vieux Bois*, the hero disguised as a devil sowing panic and chaos in town and country[6]—were the Töpffer-dependent precursors to the Töpffer-transcendent, enormously successful *Histoires Campagnardes*. These ran over the years 1872–82 in thirty-six complete stories and in ninety-eight issues, to a total of 252 pages of *Le Journal Amusant*.

This extraordinary series constitutes a history of rural and small-town provincial France, notably Normandy and Brittany, whence Petit came, and confronts the simple but avaricious and litigious peasant with the selfish small-town bourgeoisie and its repressive police. It was the era of the Third Republic's attempt to turn "Peasants into

34074

Job Laderouille est toujours prêt...
mon Dieu, oui... toujours prêt... à rendre
service aux amis.

34075

Malgré les désagréments qu'il a eus à ce
sujet... et il en a eu! Dieu le sait!

34076

Sa manie d'obliger prend toujours le des-
sus... mais elle le ruinera... oh oui!...
elle le ruinera!

9-13. Léonce Petit: The patience of rustic usurer Job, who has you mercilessly evicted but is always ready to oblige his friends, even if it ruin him (*The Usurer*, 1875).

Frenchmen," to use the title of the indispensable book by Eugene Weber (1976): educating, cajoling, disciplining. The alienation of urban man from the countryside, and the perplexity of rural folk when confronted with the compulsions of bourgeois "modernization," coded in farcical ways already by Töpffer, Cham, and Daumier, are here writ large, complex, and analytical. We may assume certain similarities between the peasants of the canton Geneva and its foreign neighbors, and those of Normandy and Brittany a generation later, but for the French the problem was immense and is perhaps still not resolved (France of recent years has been noted for its agricultural stoppages). The peasant interludes that in Töpffer are surely significant of a local malaise in Petit seem like the clash of two irreconcilable worlds.

Petit's outline style certainly goes back to Töpffer. So do some expressive variations in at-

titudes (fig. 9-13), and even certain physiognomic types, excellently maintained throughout a story as Töpffer taught. Petit has also learned from Doré and others in the interim, with greater variety in size and shaping of scenes, viewpoint, shading, close-up, montage, and graphic style, which extends to the silhouette and occasional nocturne. At the same time, unlike Töpffer's his long prose captions plod heavily along. Petit seems to wander into the novel and short-story forms that he also practiced, with a notable lack of success. His panoramic scenes of peasant life, with which he also supplied the magazines under the generic title *Bonnes Gens de Province*, and his occasional Salon paintings show the rustics as indeed *bonnes*; in the *Histoires Campagnardes* they are not. Like Töpffer, he was willfully misunderstood by the critics, who preferred to ignore the satirical picture stories, and lauded his naïveté.

England before and with Töpffer

Contemporary England and France offered great models in caricature, but it was a more distant English ancestor alone whom Töpffer explicitly and repeatedly honored. William Hogarth enjoyed a lasting European reputation for his demonstration that not only could visual art tell original, amusing stories all on its own, but that popular, moralizing contemporary subjects could rise to high aesthetic level. Rodolphe inherited a taste for Hogarth from his father Wolfgang-Adam, a genre and landscape painter who was called "the Genevan Hogarth" and who brought Hogarth plates back from his visit to England. In his will, Rodolphe specified that his "inalienable" Hogarths should pass to his son François.

Before Hogarth, European graphic narrative, or the ancestors of the picture story or "comic strip" as I define it,[7] starting more or less with the invention of printing, was confined, mostly, to single broadsheets telling religious, moral, and polemical stories, dividing in the seventeenth century between humorous-satirical and heavily political. In the seventeenth century the compartmentalized, narrative engraved broadsheet got into its stride, with stories of rakes and harlots in Italy, the horrors of married life in Germany, and Dutch denunciations of French and Catholic military atrocities, the latter crystallized best in Callot's exquisitely painful *Miseries and Misfortunes of War* (1633).

Hogarth seems to subsume all the earlier social, if not political targets of graphic (together with much literary) satire in work that is not strictly (by his own terms) caricatural at all (see fig. 6-16). With their relatively few (six to twelve) intricate, relatively large, rich, dense, and highly allusive compositions (the first three series first painted, then engraved), they seem very remote from what we conceive as mainstream comic-strip art of the twentieth century. But I would call Hogarth the grandfather, if Töpffer is the father, of the modern comic strip.

Working a full century apart, these two seem to represent antipodean approaches to narrative. One can hardly imagine anything more different from the overflowing, richly painted-engraved compositions of Hogarth than the spare, casually doodled pen sketches of Töpffer that spin in spidery lines a spidery narrative web.

What Töpffer admired in Hogarth was not only the literary (narrative) side, but also his capacity to be thoroughly moralizing even as he made you laugh. Hogarth was as serious a satirist as Fielding or Swift. But when I first came to Töpffer from Hogarth (with no sense of what happened in between), I was struck and enchanted by a contrast: Töpffer embodied a lack of seriousness, a pure love of mayhem and silliness, as opposed to the often sinister-scary implications, brilliantly masked in humor and satire, of Hogarth. Hogarth requires a bit of work, hard looking and some figuring out; Töpffer was all there at once, a jovial companion with no moral axe to grind and only funny, impossible tales to tell. There is of course much more to him than that, as this book hopes to show. Yet his genius lay in an escape from conventional moralizing—as represented, for example, in his own prose fiction and aesthetic writings. Ironically, Töpffer always wanted popular art to recover its earnest, moralizing mission, and for that mission, insofar as it was fulfilled in the crude popular imagery of his day, to be validated by the critics. His own experiments in popular art, the graphic novels, consciously retaining as they did a *grain de sérieux*, quickly outreached their initial audience, the boys of his school; but they can never have reached the masses beyond, just once, the middle-class subscribers to *L'Illustration*.

The long interlude between Hogarth and Töpffer, who was born a generation after Hogarth died, was full of pious imitations, aborted efforts, and semi-successful experiments, mostly in England but also in Germany (Chodowiecki) and even a glimmering in France (Greuze), too classicist to be otherwise hospitable to the low-class and contemporary. I have laid out all of this in some detail in my *Early Comic Strip*. The first English imitator of Hogarth, John Collet, tried to maintain his humor. But subsequent admirers, painters of history and genre John Mortimer, John Northcote, and George Morland, simply substituted sentimental pathos, and none struck a chord in the popular market. Broadsheet caricature of the "Golden Age of Caricature," which from around 1780 competed so successfully in that market (and created a new, politically curious one), with the gigantic and ruthless energies of a Gillray, looked nostalgically and gingerly back to the mighty Hogarth and produced a number of "progresses" (the very term now more Hogarthian than Bunyanesque), on single sheets, of individual politicians and social types. Some of the best were by a prolific youth named Richard Newton, who died at the age of twenty-one. The term "progress" as with Hogarth is used ironically, for there is usually a moral and professional regression.

Vis-à-vis Hogarth, the golden age of caricature (that is, the generation around 1800), especially in its compartmentalized, narrative comic-strip form, introduced important innovations that were to become standardized and that stand halfway between Hogarth and Töpffer: simplification of contour, isolation of essentials, use of rhetorical (or "telegraphic") poses, reduction of background and accessory, and no Hogarthian subplots. They were personally allusive, and often scurrilous and rude. Töpffer would generally sublimate the personal into the generically social, *Crépin* and *Albert* being the exceptions. The acceptance of more text as such, outside the picture frame rather than in the Hogarthian form of naturalistic inscriptions on objects such as notices and letters, placed below the vignettes, and often enough in speech balloons also represented a step toward the strictly hybrid form the nineteenth-century comic strip, via Töpffer, was to adopt: concisely sketched pictures with short captions beneath helpful or essential to the understanding of the story. Hogarth, meanwhile, had

undergone extensive wordy commentary, which seemed irresistible, but his picture stories stand as pictures alone.

Töpffer enjoyed a great advantage, which was not to be repeated until Wilhelm Busch, that he was both skilled artist and writer. Much of the history of the illustrated novel in the nineteenth century can be read in terms of a struggle and a relationship, often conflictive and at any rate actively collaborative between writer and artist. Grandville wanted to be a writer; writers liked to dictate illustrations. Dickens, often at odds with his illustrators and riding herd on them, aimed to absorb the visual antics of the illustrators (and Hogarth) into his very literary style. The English Victorian novel represents in some sense a triumph of writer over artist, but this was not at all a given. Dickens himself, never exactly lacking in self-confidence, started out granting George Cruikshank equal billing (at least on the title page). He did so in recognition of the pulling power of a well-established caricaturist and illustrator like Cruikshank, and the proven capacity of good graphics to sell mediocre literary texts.

It may be argued that the immediate precursors of the Töpffer comic strip are not the (very) sub-Hogarthian "progresses" by mostly lesser caricaturists that the Swiss would not even have known. It is common for scholars to adduce here the immensely successful *Tour of Dr. Syntax in Search of the Picturesque*, published first as installments 1809–11 and available to Töpffer in French translation (figs. 9-14, 9-15). He himself is even compared in a letter as another schoolmaster Dr. Syntax.[8] For *Syntax* the polymath writer William Combe wrote his jog-along verses "up to" (as the phrase went) preexistent designs supplied to him (then in jail, for debt) by Thomas Rowlandson. With a full-page illustration to every episode of eight to ten pages of verse, this is formally still quite distant from a comic strip. Nor are the episodes really linked. As the title implies, the Combe-Rowlandson collaboration was a parody of the "search for the picturesque" that engaged so

9-14. Thomas Rowlandson: Dr. Syntax setting out on his tour to the lakes (aquatint from *Tour of Dr. Syntax in search of the Picturesque*, 1809–1811).

Ayant attendu quatre ans, pour laisser grandir le mulet, le Docteur Festus part pour son grand voyage d'instruction.

2.

9-15. Töpffer: Having waited four years for his mule to grow up, Doctor Festus leaves on his great educational voyage (*Festus* 2; comparison from Kaenel, 1990.)

many hopefuls and amateurs of the Romantic eras. But insofar as Dr. Festus bears a vague resemblance to Dr. Syntax by undertaking a rural *voyage d'instruction* or educational voyage, it is characteristic of the different cultures in London and Geneva that, from the start, the ambition of Syntax is to write what in effect Combe writes for him, a series of amusing adventures that when published will put the cash-strapped pedagogue and cleric on easy street; whereas Festus is embarked, obscurely, dreamlike, on a quest for pure if unspecified knowledge. As Syntax says, in the first canto: "I'll ride and write, and sketch and print / And thus create a real mint,/ I'll prose it here, I'll verse it there, / And picturesque it ev'ry where." This is the professional cynicism of Syntax's author, too, from his debtor's jail, a pole from the attitude of Festus and his creator.

Dr. Syntax and the sequels in which he figured were followed by a sort of urban equivalent, the raffish search for excitement in the city, the *Life in London* where the writer Pierce Egan wrote "up to" the designs of George and Robert Cruikshank. *Pierce Egan's Life in London* became in 1824 the name of a magazine, and it was henceforth the illustrated magazine that would, with books, absorb the energies of the caricaturists and illustrators, and move the former into the latter category. The range of George Cruikshank caricature and illustration in this period alone is enormous and includes much nonsensical stuff. It would no doubt be possible to point back (and contemporaneously with Töpffer) to some example or another in the incomparable oeuvre of the Englishman, for many of Töpffer's satirical motifs. This is not to suggest that Töpffer consciously used any particular Cruikshank etching, admired as the "inimitable George" was, generally speaking, on the continent. Cruikshank offered another kind of model, however, which reflected a state of malaise with respect to caricature generally, as well as a new market psychology: the taste for "Scraps and Sketches" (1828–32), which is the title Cruikshank gave to "Cruikshankiana"—miscellaneous small vignettes either disconnected or loosely connected by a theme, united on a single page and series of pages, inviting readers to connect the dots. The Frenchman Cham, a little later, would do something similar, as we have seen. Here the satirical barb mixed with the plain silly. Töpffer's method is, in a way, to take scraps and sketches of satirical and silly ideas that occurred to him pell-mell, in an alchemy singular with him, and connect them into the kind of narrative that was the envy of Cruikshank as well as Grandville and many another artist.

Dickens's first independent effort *Sketches by Boz and Cuts by Cruikshank* tells us by the title alone not to expect a coherent narrative. Thematic linkage is to be found in his next work *The Pickwick Papers* (1836–37, but set in 1827, the year Töpffer sketched his first picture story), while it still adhered essentially to the "Scraps and Sketches" format and was written as a kind of verbal caricature, and in acute awareness of the role of the forty-three illustrations: "What a study for an artist did that exciting scene present!" (ch. I). The overlap with Töpfferian characters and episodes testifies to the coincidence of comic repertoire in two distinct languages—visual and verbal—and two distinct cultures. In both writers events manipulate people, especially the hero, and run on coincidences galore. To start with the lead character and prime structural agent: Mr. Pickwick is a kind of Dr. Festus, bent on voyages of discovery, although of a sociological rather than scientific kind. There are absurd quarrels between men of learning, and satires of learned societies (ch. XI). Changes of clothes bespeak changes of identity. There are duels on the absurdest of pretexts, and blind sexual jealousies. The law, judicial procedures, and jail are subject to the roundest excoriation. The hero's erroneous invasion of a lady's bedroom leads to disastrous consequences. There are plans to pack up Pickwick inside a piano, as Festus is carried off inside a trunk. Finally, we may add that Dickens's Mr. Jingle speaks in breathless, staccato, abbreviated captions, and that old-fashioned Mr. Pickwick, like Töpffer's middle-aged protagonists, wears breeches and gaiters or stockings. We know that Töpffer owned and treasured a copy of a *Pickwick* translation.[9]

The late 1820s, when Töpffer first discovered how to do picture stories, and the 1830s, when he first published them, was in Britain a period of restless searching for new formats for caricature and illustration that lasted into the 1840s, overlapping what appears in retrospect the inevitable and definitive "victory" early in that decade of the illustrated magazine in two kinds: satirical (*Punch* 1841) and newsy (*Illustrated London News* 1842). France had, since the 1830s, a satirical, illustrated magazine: the weekly *La Caricature* followed by the daily *Le Charivari* (*Punch* was subtitled *The London Charivari*), which Töpffer certainly knew. The incorporation of woodcut vignettes into lower-class, often radical newspapers in Britain gave them a working-class and political allure that had later to be shed; and Hogarth, ever concerned with lower-class virtue and vice, presided here too: a miniaturized (to 2 x 3 inches per scene!) version of his *Harlot's Progress* may claim to be technically the first newspaper strip, published in *Bell's Life in London and Sporting Guide* in 1828. Hogarth might keep his harlot, but marriage was the topic of the day. The suppression of overt sexual vice, of casual acceptance in Hogarth's day, has been deemed responsible not only for the well-known sentimentality and idealizations shared by Töpffer in his prose work but also, and more interestingly, for the extreme flights of fancy, the escapism, the morbidity, the grotesque and the horrific, in the novel and down to the nonsense of Lear and Carroll, which is deemed by some to be not without its darker, erotic side.

The European comic strip after Töpffer found its permanent and primary home in the illustrated, usually comic magazine. The English "restless searching for new formats" referred to should, logically, have included Töpffer's invention. That this was made in Geneva, not London (or Paris), must seem anomalous, especially since Geneva had no il-

lustrated magazines at all and no tradition of public caricature, beyond what Rodolphe's father Wolfgang-Adam had risked and prudently restricted to private circles. Art lithography was quite undeveloped in Geneva, and engraving on metal was taught for the benefit of watchmakers. But Geneva, as we insist here, tapped into the intellectual climate of both Paris and London, and it may be that its relative smallness and provinciality, its immunity to metropolitan market pressures, allowed a new, noncommercial form of art to germinate whose eventual success in the bigger market surprised the inventor himself.

England after Töpffer

Three Töpffer albums were soon plagiarized and copied in England: *Vieux Bois* as *Adventures of Mr. Obadiah Oldbuck*,[10] published by Tilt and Bogue in 1841 and again 1849(?), cofinanced by George Cruikshank;[11] *Jabot* as *The Comical Adventures of Beau Ogleby*, from the same publisher about 1845, with a frontispiece by Robert Cruikshank; and *Cryptogame* as *The Strange Adventures of Bachelor Butterfly*, a volume so rare that it escaped the British Library.[12] This appeared as an album in 1845 even before the much-delayed original French one of Dubochet, from whom Bogue bought copies (*clichés*) of the woodblocks (thus not technically a plagiary).

Despite these editions Töpffer never caught on in England compared with France. Thackeray, who was certainly smitten by Töpffer as a youth, as we shall see, was a curious case of a might-have-been who never went public with his several series of sketches for picture stories, perhaps because he was simply too closely identified among the main line of major novelists of his day to risk getting sidetracked. We deal with him in more detail below, with his encouragement of Cruikshank's weak attempt at the new genre. Was Töpffer somehow seen as somehow un-English? This is hard to imagine,

9-16. Albert Smith and H. G. Hine, "Mr. Crindle's Rapid Career upon Town:—Part the Second" (*Man in the Moon*, 1847).

given the breadth and eclecticism of the English comic art tradition, but a hint of incompatibility is given in a review of *Oldbuck*, which found it too "continental" and too Munchausenesque.[13]

The overall pattern of comic strip development from mid-century presents a curious, desultory patchwork to begin with, with some originality revealing itself over the last third of the century. Major *Punch* artists such as Leech, Tenniel, and Du Maurier generally avoided the narrative form, preferring always single cartoons, although Du Maurier had a brief quasi-narrative, Darwinian fling. In the search for new formats in mid-century it is the cheaper magazines, as long as they lasted, that carried the comic strips. *Man in the Moon* (from January 1847) was a peculiar sixpenny monthly in tiny size (5 x 4

inches, 64 pages) boasting a special attraction in its huge fold-out plate, folded five times horizontally and vertically into the magazine, a vehicle expressly created for the narrative strips. The magazine started out with a *Life and Death of Don Guzzles of Carrara*, a romantic parody mistakenly attributed to Cham, just arrived in London, followed by *The Foreign Gentleman in London; or, The English Adventures of M. Vanille*, an uninspired sequence by Cham cut short by his departure back to Paris. *Mr. Crindle's Rapid Career upon Town* (also 1847) improved on these and ran for nine installments and 140 drawings (fig. 9-16). This remarkable performance, a collaboration of the writer Albert Smith and the artist H. G. Hine, went unremarked, although it transcends Töpffer and Cham in its montage and use of pictography,

9-17. Richard Doyle, "Italian Lakes" (*The Foreign Tour of Messrs. Brown, Jones and Robinson*, 1854).

pars pro toto, hyperbole, variable framing and viewpoint, and breakneck speed of narrative. Such inventiveness seems less to look back to Töpffer, or even Cruikshank, whose graphic style it emulates, than forward to Doré, who was asked to copy it in the *Journal pour Rire*, and surely learned much from it for his stupendous *History of Holy Russia*.

Crindle's successor by the same team, *The Surprising Adventures of Mr. Touchango Jones, an Emigrant*, though running to only five parts, is little inferior. The motivation for Mr. Jones's flight, wife trouble, harks back to that of M. Cryptogame, but the few years that had passed since, culminating in the 1848 revolutions, gave reason for more permanent emigration, and in the case of Mr. Jones, offering imperialist success among the natives of Quashybungo which suddenly becomes France, with duplication of major events of the revolution there. The third Smith-Hine story, *How My Rich Uncle Came to Dine at Our Villa*, features police repression, with Töpfferian mistaken jailings and switching of clothes and identity.

Press reviews of the magazine, thinking surely more of this fold-out plate rather than the magazine as a whole, call it "inimitably ludicrous" and "grotesquely comic." Unfortunately, the critical but expensive and awkward folding plate proved impractical; it was abandoned, and the magazine proved unable to survive without it. Another alternative format, the tiny (4 x 5 inches) self-lithographed pocket album, was tried out by the artist John Leighton (using the pseudonym Luke Limner), whose flaccid account of the dangers, unpleasantness, and boredom of travel to and life at the seaside is given in *London Out of Town or the Adventures of the Browns at the Sea Side* (1847). The feat of cramming 154 tiny vignettes and self-scripted captions into sixteen pages is aided by Leighton's use of Töpffer's autolithographic method, which earned its rescue from deserved obscurity by a historian of lithography.[14]

After the stimulus of 1848 the comic strip lost much of its energy, and the major effort at pictorial narrative, Richard Doyle's *The Pleasure Trip of Messrs. Brown, Jones and Robinson*, which started in *Punch* 1850 and appeared in expanded form as their *Foreign Tour* in 1854, is a lackluster affair that seems to strive in terms of graphic and plot for the mediocrity of experience familiar to an already blasé public. The only excitement develops at frontiers, where there is the familiar official harassment (fig. 9-17).

In this case, the shift in the 1850s toward greater realism of experience, which we noted also in France, had a deadening effect in the hands of an artist like Doyle, whose forte was whimsical fairytale illustrations. Realism becomes a more positive factor in *The Adventures of Mr. Wilderspin on His Journey Through Life* by William McConnell in *Town Talk* (1858–59), with 184 drawings, a record for the age, leaving the *Russia* of Doré *hors de concours*. The life of Wilderspin, "a railway clerk with ideas above his station," is social documentary mixing Pierce Egan with Henry Mayhew, plus a parliamentary interlude reminiscent of the German *Piepmeyer* (p. 178).

Was there not in England imagination and skill enough to sustain a comic-strip tradition; did publishers not quite trust the public with this new-fangled format? Only in the 1870s did artists settle in with characters they felt to be rich enough in possibilities to carry through the years. The first was Charles Ross with Ally Sloper, a lower-middle-class cheat developed by Europe's only professional woman caricaturist, Ross's wife Marie Duval, who signed her innumerable narrative squibs that are the true ancestors of the three- or four-panel gag-strip today. Duval's aggressively amateurish, childlike style is hardly Töpfferian, but her resolute silliness perhaps is. At the very least, the principle defended by Töpffer of the merits of being childlike and silly must be recognized as alive and well in the England of Lear, Carroll, and Marie Duval.

Thackeray (and Cruikshank's *Lambkin*)

Among the many artists affected by the Töpffer picture story, the great English novelist and amusing draughtsman William Makepeace Thackeray must be the least known in this respect, and he is also the earliest. He must have seen the *Cryptogame* and *Festus* received in the Goethe circle De-

cember 1830–January 1831, and very possibly was aware, Germanist as he was, of the imprimatur that Goethe gave to Töpffer albums in *Kunst und Alterthum* in 1832. The circumstances are not conclusive and Thackeray does not, unfortunately, in his correspondence or otherwise mention Töpffer by name at any time, although he does refer in a letter to *Vieux Bois* as a model, and a character in *Vanity Fair* has a Töpfferian name (Jabotière). Thackeray's own early essays in pictorial narratives were all published posthumously. This is not surprising, and perhaps deserved: they are fragmentary and inconsequential, and were not taken seriously by the writer, who obviously preferred that his graphic skills support his verbal narratives. These little experiments do however command our interest, and that of literary history, as a record of a writer's intermittently exercised gifts in an as yet (in England) underdeveloped genre he denied himself, overtaken as he soon was by his quickly unfolding literary success. The twinned ambition to be an illustrator as well as writer, to be indeed a writer-artist, murmured on, and he ended up, uniquely in England which was brimming with talented graphic artists, and at the risk of invidious comparison, illustrating four of his major novels, and doing much graphic work beside, for *Punch* (anonymously).

Like Töpffer, Thackeray compensated for his failure to realize a youthful ambition to be a real artist by illustrating his own writing; like Töpffer his facility for doing funny sketches was first honed among and to the applause of children; and like Töpffer he was reluctant to publish his experiments in picture stories. How far his sense that pictures could tell longer stories, à la Töpffer, really made their way into his novels, which are richly illustrated and written in an illustration-conscious way, is an interesting question, and has elicited from one Thackeray scholar the theory that the (unillustrated) *Henry Esmond* is a kind of picture story told in words, and that "the fractured syntax of the comic strip predominates in Thackeray's works."[15]

The Fatal effects of the Robbers gun

The Destruction of the Bandit by Rivaldi —

9-18. William Makepeace Thackeray, "The Bandit's Revenge" (*The Picture Magazine* vol. III, 1894).

Thackeray revealed his gifts for improvising comic sketches as a schoolboy, where he regaled his fellows with caricature in quantity,[16] taking his cue for subject matter from an enthusiastic audience. In 1830, at age nineteen, on an unauthorized break from Cambridge University, he went to Paris, where he considered becoming a painter, and from there made a prolonged side-trip to Weimar. In that tiny dukedom he found himself spending many months, entranced by the philo-English culture and Ottilie van Goethe. The poet's daughter-in-law reigned over an informal salon, giving the occasional, highly selective and much prized access to the great man himself, then aged eighty-three and in his last years. Young Thackeray was admitted to a short conversation with him just once. The witty, sprightly Ottilie, who jokingly titled herself the British Consul in Weimar, liked gifted young Englishmen, as did

the young ladies of Weimar. Thackeray soon found himself in demand sketching caricatures that appealed particularly of course to the children, including Goethe's own grandchildren. They, like Töpffer's (older) schoolboys, participated and egged him on in what was recognized as a social game. It served to while away the long winter evenings, which Goethe himself lightened by scanning the comic albums Töpffer had sent to him, as we know, and also Thackeray's sketches, as we may presume. Some of these were carefully preserved and bound into a Weimar sketchbook (Berg collection, New York Public Library). Thackeray seems to have remembered his stay in Weimar for the Pumpernickel chapters in *Vanity Fair*.

Two picture stories by the Englishman in Weimar testify to his quick reaction to Töpffer. Both stories are more gruesome than Töpffer would have allowed, and are essentially parodies of a kind of Grimm fairy tale, very popular in England. Count Otto van Blumenbach, newly married to Ottilia, Melanie, Jenny von Rosenthal (*sic*—one person) is not allowed beefsteaks for breakfast, which causes him to grow thinner while she grows fatter. The wife turns out to be a necrophagous cannibal who devours churchyard corpses at night. The second story features a mother who kills and eats her own son.[17] This gruesomeness was sketched out for a small girl called Caroline Vavasour.

It may be that Thackeray was predisposed, like Töpffer himself, to pictorial narrative by William Hogarth, with whose *Idle Apprentice* the writer empathized during these years of apparent, guilty idleness, and whose *Marriage A la Mode* he declared "to be more moral and more beautiful than West's biggest heroic piece, or Angelica Kaufmann's most elegant allegory."[18] Around 1832 he executed a scenario called "The Bandit's Revenge or the Fatal Sword. A Romantic Drama," that features a hero called Vivaldi who is put in a frightful jail by a bandit.[19] He escapes on a mule, which causes a terrified rustic to take him for "Death on the pale horse" (this is very Töpfferian). Thus mounted he leaps through the window of his beloved, Bertha, grown fat on the victuals prepared for his marriage; they are ambushed en route to the church, and Vivaldi pierces the whole bandit group right through into a tree-trunk with a single stroke of an immense sword (fig. 9-18). Connubial bliss provides the happy ending. *The Picture Magazine* also printed with this some five illustrated limericks headed "Simple Melodies." The date 1832 on this sheet (which gives us the presumed date for the bandit story) puts Thackeray's illustrated limericks well ahead of those famous avatars of nonsense verse printed by Lear in his first *Book of Nonsense* (1846).

Another early picture story by Thackeray, said to date from just before his marriage in Paris in August 1836, was not printed until 1946 in an edition of his *Letters and Private Papers*[20] and survives incomplete. "The Count's Adventures" now totals twenty drawings and is based on the character of a friend Thackeray was staying with, an eccentric Scottish artist named John Grant Brine. The drawings were made to amuse the children of Thackeray's friend Eyre Evans Crowe. The count is a kind of Don Quixote, of the type who would enter Thackeray's novels. Captured by the Spanish, he refuses to abjure his religion, even on the rack; at the stake, he cuts off the heads of his executioners. The parallel with Töpffer's *Vieux Bois* (first edition 1837), where the hero barely escapes the monastic stake, is fortuitous, if the date 1836 is correctly inferred for Thackeray's venture. More violence or the threat of it, mistaken identity, a serenade, invasion of the queen's bedroom, the magical effects of a portrait the count paints of a Dulcinea called Ximena, are all in the vein of Thackeray's early parodies of the romantic cliché in which Töpffer also engages. The long flowing outlines and shading are not Töpfferian, but the vivacity is.[21]

Thackeray's trip to Paris 1836–37 allowed him to collect material for an article on French caricature, but it was not until his visit of 1840 that he had a chance to see Töpffer's three picture stories, in the originals or as plagiarized in the French capital: *Jabot*, *Crépin*, and *Vieux Bois*. Thackeray mentions *Vieux Bois* by title in letters to his mother of April 1840, as the inspiration for *The Adventures of Dionysius Diddler* (fig. 9-19), "all in pictures like M. Vieuxbois—quite fabulous," and "something in the style of Vieuxbois," which was supposed to guarantee the launch of a new magazine he planned called *Foolscap Library*.[22] Diddler was based on a miscellaneous writer and scientist called Dr. Dionysius Lardner. The proposed weekly never materialized, partly because Thackeray joined the staff of *Punch*, which started up the following year, and gave ample outlet to Thackeray's genius for the sketch, graphic and verbal, as well as financial stability. *Punch* was, oddly, never very receptive to the concept of the picture story, which throughout the century evolved

This is Dionysius Diddler! young, innocent, and with a fine head of hair,—when he was a student in the University of Ballybunion.— That is Ballybunion University, in the hedge.

He goes to call on Mr. Shortman, the publisher of the 'Closet Cyclopædia,' and, sure an ouns! Mr. Shortman gives him three sovereigns and three £5 notes

The first thing he does is to take his wig out of pawn.

"Faix!" says Diddler; "the what-d'ye-call-ems fit me like a glove!"

"And upon me honour and conshience, now I'm dhiressed, but I look intirely gintee!"

"And now," says he, "I'll go, take a sthroll to the Wist Ind, and call on me frind, Sir Hinry Pelham."

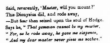

In Pelham's coat, hat, boots, and pantaloons,
Forth issues Diddler from the Baronet's house,
In famed Red Lion's fashionable square.
And 'twas it strange that Hodge, Sir Henry's groom,
Mistook the dandy doctor for his master?
And while he for his foot the stirrup held,

Said, reverently, 'Master, will you mount?'
This Dionysius did, and rode away,
—But fear than seized upon the soul of Hodge.
Says he, " That gemman cannot be my master.
" For, as he rode away, he gave me sixpence,
" And my dear master never gives me nothen."

Here he is, after forty years of fame, and he thinks upon dear Ballybunion. " I'm famous," says he, " all the world over : but what's the use of riputation? Look at me with all me luggage at the end of me stick—all me money in me left-hand breeches pocket—and it's oh! but I'd give all me celebrity for a bowl of butther-milk and potaties."

9-19. Thackeray, *Dionysus Diddler* (*The Autographic Mirror*, 1864).

in England independently of this relatively elite vehicle of graphic humor. If it judged the genre by Thackeray's *Diddler*, an uninteresting sort of Irish Jabot, *Punch*'s attitude is understandable.

But Thackeray may have suggested the idea of the picture story to his friend and etching teacher George Cruikshank, whose hitherto brilliant career was faltering in the early 1840s and who was looking for new formats. Cruikshank must have known something of Töpffer's work, for the frontispiece of *The Adventures of Obadiah Oldbuck* (i.e., Töpffer's *Vieux Bois*), published by Cruikshank's publisher in 1841, was designed and engraved (with, possibly, copies of the whole work beyond) by George's brother and collaborator Robert.[23] French plagiaries after Töpffer must have been available from Delaporte in the Burlington Arcade, the authorized agent of their publisher Aubert in Paris.

George Cruikshank's only independent narrative venture in this period—he had done much earlier a few not very distinguished comic strips on scenarios by others, etched on the single broadsheets customary at the time—was a lackluster affair, more Thackeray than either Hogarth or Töpffer. *The Progress of Mr. Lambkin* was, however, twenty-four plates clearly inspired by the social climber Jabot, the eponymous hero of the first picture story published by Töpffer in Geneva 1835 and plagiarized in Paris.[24] The name was remembered by Thackeray in *Vanity Fair* (1847–48) in that of the Duc de la Jabotière, an old roué and ambassador who is mentioned in passing. We too may mention in passing that the orientalist charade that featured the heroine of that novel, Becky Sharp as Clytemnestra, in a sensational role murdering her husband Agamemnon with a dagger, paired in the same charade with an odious pasha seducing a white slave,[25] may well—who knows?—derive from some memory of the comparable incident in Töpffer's *Cryptogame*. But such scenes were no doubt commonplace, as was the idea of a clumsy dancer bringing his partner and others down in the ballroom, as do both Jabot (see fig. 3-1)

and Thackeray's Fitzboodle in *Fitzboodle's Confessions*, and in *Pendennis*. The social climber was of course a favorite type in novels by Thackeray.

Despite the relative failure of *Lambkin*, Cruikshank went on to attempt other, more promising forms of sequential graphics: *The Bottle* (1847), followed by *The Drunkard's Children*, works of a passionate temperance reformer that spoke eloquently to a major concern of the age, in very large, most uncomic compositions; and *The Tooth-Ache* (1849), pure comedy as painful as the subject, a true comic strip that pulled out like a paper concertina.

In 1848 Thackeray met Töpffer's principal imitator Cham in London, where he, Cham, became an instant familiar and favorite of the *Punch* circle. Dickens and Thackeray gave a "hurricane welcome to this devil of a Frenchman,"[26] and courted him for a permanent presence in England. Graphic narrative may have been in the air, but it was not freshened much by Thackeray's colleagues on *Punch*, Doyle's tepid *Foreign Tour of Messrs. Smith, Brown and Robinson*, or Tenniel's "Adventures of Mr. Peter Piper," a short-lived series in *Punch* in 1853.[27]

Even in the midst of writing his most famous and successful novel, *Vanity Fair (*1848–49), which he illustrated, profusely, himself, Thackeray seems not to have forgotten the charms of the independent picture story. A twelve-part tale with captions in French called "The Heroic Adventures of M. Boudin" (not published until 1980 and then in a limited edition), can be dated, on the basis of a (gratuitous) passing allusion to Count Alfred d'Orsay, to 1848–49, and was done perhaps for a soirée of which he was an ornament.[28] Crudely violent, as his previous essays in the genre had been, its historical basis is the Napoleonic wars, and shows (and mocks?) stereotypes of English cruelty and inferiority held by the French (fig. 9-20).

Thackeray's final (as far as we know) and most ambitious undertaking in the picture story was titled "Specimen-Extracts from the New Novel The Orphan of Pimlico. A moral tale of Belgravian Life by

9-20 Thackeray: 1. Boudin, fisherman of Boulogne, with three compatriots seizes an English frigate, kills the ship's captain, 83 sailors, soldiers etc. (1797). 2. Boudin appears before the Directory, which gives him a [paltry] reward. 3. Boudin joins battle with the English fleet, sinks 33 warships, but is captured by the 34th (under Lord Nelson), all aboard being massacred except Boudin. Note. The battle is invisible because of the smoke. 4. Riddled with wounds, loaded with chains, Boudin appears before Lord Nelson. The victor trembles before the vanquished. 5. In the infernal dungeons of Portsmouth where so many other Frenchmen have already perished, Boudin expiates his ill-fated courage. He is given only half a pint of water and a twopenny loaf each week. 6. Miss Fanny, the prison governor's daughter, comes to console him. 7. A tender and romantic scene. Boudin and his faithful Fanny escape in a seventy-four. 8. After landing at Calais with his adored wife, Boudin sets off for Paris. (Chaste and legitimate caresses enliven the tedium of the journey.) 9. In Paris Boudin presents himself to Emperor and King. The puny Portsmouth Miss is no longer recognizable in the sprightly Fanny, embellished by Parisian art. The Grenadiers admire her with many oaths. 10. Delighted to see his faithful Boudin again, His Majesty tweaks his right ear, and has Talleyrand decorate him. 11. All the court ladies burst with envy seeing the celestial beauty of Boudin's wife, who kisses the hands of Her Majesty. 12. [His widow and child mourning Boudin, killed at Waterloo] (*The Heroic Adventures of M. Boudin*).

Dans les cachots intérieurs de Portsmoot
où tant d'autres Français ont déjà succombés
Boudin expie sa funeste valeur.
On ne lui donne qu'une demi pinte d'eau avec une pénirole
par semaine.
(pénirole – petit pain de deux sols.)

Miss Fanny fille du gouverneur vient
le consoler

Scène tendre et romantique. Boudin avec
sa fidèle Fanny s'échappe sauve dans un
seventhifore

Pic nique à Calais avec son épouse adorée. Boudin se rend à Paris
(Les caresses chastes et légitimes égayent les longueurs de la Route.)

Miss M. T. Wiggleworth . . . London 1851," and first published by Thackeray's daughter Anne Isabelle in 1876.[29] In her preface Anne Isabelle reminds us that her father never set much store by such things, drawing them only for his amusement and finding the activity rested him when tired, while drawing on wood or etching on steel demanded unwelcome effort. The "new novel" never got past its prologue, thirteen drawings on seven numbered pages, and suffers from an excess of text, which puts it midway between a picture-dominant Töpfferian graphic novel and a romance illustrated with vignettes, in which some of captions embrace the drawing on two sides, as in Thackeray's woodcut illustrations to his own novels. The story is again parodic, one of passion, rivals, and a duel in aristocratic circles.

Was Thackeray deterred from going further by two factors: the lack of evident demand for the genre in England compared with the continent; and the very success he enjoyed with the novels he himself so richly illustrated? Caricature, in the continental sense, was in decline in Britain, and graph-

ics tended to be swallowed up in the great maw of literature, as Cruikshank had reason to complain. Whether Thackeray the writer might have found in Töpffer a "graphic realization of [his] pervasive sense of character as multiple fragments," is food for thought.[30]

Edward Lear

Like Töpffer, Lear invented (or popularized) a genre that would have an unimaginable future: the limerick. This and his other nonsense verse occupied a minor, recreational place in a life otherwise rigorously dedicated to landscapes, watercolors and topographical illustration, comparable to the place of the comic album for Töpffer, drawn in relief from his multifarious other activities. It has been said Lear "frittered away his life earning a living," a fear shared by schoolmaster Töpffer. Using in his *Book of Nonsense* (1846) an auto-lithographic technique for both text and drawing similar to Töpffer's, he established the viability, almost the respectability of the truly childish crudity of drawing; Töpffer's

9-21. Edward Lear: 1. Lear sets out from the house of Captain Hornby. 2. L. rushes unconsciously into the sentinel's box, to the extreme surprise of a sentinel. 3. L. is ignominiously dragged out of the sentry box by the exasperated sentinel. 4. L. enquires of an intelligent policeman as to the office of Capt. Hornby, R.N. 5. L. is instructed by the intelligent policeman that it is necessary to sign his name. 6. L. pursues his investigations in an earnest and judicious manner. 7. L. discovers Capt. Hornby's office—but learns from several official persons that Capt. H is gone to a basin [dockyard]. 8 L. searches in a basin for Capt. Hornby, R.N. but without success (*Visit to Capt. Hornby*, from Liebert, 1975, much reduced).

only looked naïve, and was never truly childlike. We have commented on Töpffer's Lear-like verbal inventiveness, both writers remaining imaginatively adolescents, or boys all their lives. Lear's nonsense, like Töpffer's, was the "safety valve of his consciousness,"[31] emotional relief from everyday stress.

Lear also dabbled a little in the picture story, and if the dating into the mid-1830s of his drafts, unprinted at the time, is correct, he predates both Töpffer and Thackeray. The first is an inconsequential fragment of eight drawings with short captions relating a visit to a naval friend of Lear's, one Captain Hornby, with some reference, prescient of the comic strip of the future, to tiresome bureaucracy and tyrannical cops (fig. 9-21). His crude, deliberately childish style is similar to the one he used for his limericks, and reminds us how to his own exasperation he never mastered articulation of the human figure in action, in the way that Töpffer did.

Lear's "Adventures of Daniel O'Rourke" is a dream sequence in thirteen drawings about a drunken Irishman who falls into a bog, is marooned on an island, and carried by an eagle to the moon, from which he falls onto a whale. This is executed with a somewhat greater but not successful attempt at realism. The six drawings of the "Adventures of Mick" are disconnected fragments about the evils of the bottle. These two are said to be reactions to Lear's trip to Ireland in 1835,[32] and may have been done in the summer of that year to amuse the small children at Knowsley, where the artist had been engaged to draw the Earl of Derby's zoo. If, however, they date from 1841, as has also been suggested,[33] some acquaintance with Töpffer becomes chronologically possible.

It was for these same children, the grandchildren of the Earl of Derby and friends, that Lear first produced the immortal nonsense limericks. The success of this and subsequent *Books of Nonsense*, and of the limerick verse form that became his trademark, seems to have discouraged further experiments in pictorial narrative.

John Ruskin and George Eliot

The most famous English art critic of his day was several times in Geneva (first 1841–42) and the Alps, and would have had ample opportunity to obtain copies of Töpffer's albums. Without being particularly attentive to French caricature, much of which he found degraded by the "search for the grotesque, ludicrous or loathesome subject," Ruskin felt compelled to insert, mal à propos one would have thought, some unexpected lines on Töpffer into his *Art of England, Lectures Given in Oxford*, written 1869–72. In lecture V, on John Leech and Tenniel, Ruskin expounds on the cartoonist's habit of seizing on comic incidents always associated with some ugliness, and his exultation in disaster, which was true even with "so wise and benevolent a man as the Swiss schoolmaster, Töpffer, whose death a few years since [sic], left none to succeed him in perfection of pure linear caricature. He can do more with fewer lines than any draughtsman known to me, and in several plates of his 'Histoire d'Albert,' has succeeded entirely in representing the tenor of conversation with no more than half the profile and one eye of the speaker."[34]

Ruskin had also been reading Töpffer's *Voyages en Zigzag*, and admires his capacity to switch abruptly from the beautiful and sublime of the landscape to the "the rascalities of the inn . . . the roguish guides, shameless beggars, and hopeless cretins." It could also be that Ruskin sensed an affinity with Töpffer as a writer on aesthetics, in the diffuse, meandering "zigzag" style of his argument.

Töpffer was known also to George Eliot, who lived in Geneva for several months 1849–50, as a plaque near the rue Jean Calvin reminds us. In her journals, a Recollection of Weimar prompts thoughts of Goethe, and passes from Goethe to Töpffer. Amused at the sight of her companion and life partner George Henry Lewes's losing his hat in the wind, she watches him as "He ran in pursuit of it and so entirely lost the sense of annoyance in that of the comic, that he began to run with squared legs and arms, making a perfect Töpffer sketch of himself."

The United States

The English plagiary of *Vieux Bois* by Tilt and Bogue 1841 was taken over in the U.S. under the same title *The Adventures of Obadiah Oldbuck* by two different publishers in New York.[35] They stand at the beginning of a breakthrough in cheap publishing, relying on plagiary of popular English novelists, notably Dickens. Original responses to Töpffer, most of them in oblong format, seem to have been set off by a real-life craze: the discovery of gold in California. The earliest I have found is *Journey to the Gold Diggins*, illustrated by J. A. and D. F. Read, with the story attributed to the hero himself, Jeremiah Saddlebags.[36] Many features of this long story (sixty-three pages, fig. 9-22) in oblong format hark back directly to Töpffer: violent emotions culminating in a *tapage diurne*, a pars pro toto scene of kicking out from *Albert*, escape from jail enabled by extreme emaciation, a comic dog perched on a mast, a ship taken by pirates, whom the hero is forced to join, before being retaken. The facsimile edition of this extremely rare booklet, obviously designed for youngish children, relates the narrative to the Davy Crockett tradition of exaggerated adventures, and accounts of the California Gold Rush, which the authors may have witnessed firsthand.

The Adventures of Mr. Tom Plump (Huestin and Cozans, New York, after 1849), with its tiny (6 x 4 inch, 15 x 10 cm) six pages, carrying mostly six minute woodcuts each with a short single caption below, narrativizes the picture-driven children's book. The hero wins his dream of getting Californian gold, loses it, quits, gets married, but becomes so fat that he falls through a bridge and drowns. The whale episode in the terminally crude *The Wonderful and Amusing Doings by Sea and Land of Oscar*

9-22. J. A. and D. F. Read: The discovery of 500 tons (of gold) tests Mr. Saddlebags' credulity. Being a man not to be deceived, he called on a banker who had received a specimen. Hearing that cradles were used for washing gold, he buys one. The landlady, whose daughter Mr. Saddlebags was engaged to marry, seeing a cradle in his room, demands an explanation. Mr. Saddlebags attends a meeting of a gold mine association, and makes a speech (*Journey to the Gold Diggins, by Jeremiah Saddlebags*, Cincinnati, 1849, from Wheeler).

9-23. Angelo Agostini: Sufferings of minister Sr. Ze Bento, captured by Brazilian savages, in jail ("As Aventuras de Um Ministro," *Revista Illustrada*, no. 18, Rio de Janeiro, 13 April 1876).

Shanghai (1852–53, and 1870s–88) obviously derives from *Cryptogame*.

John McClellan's *Sad Tale of the Courtship of Chevalier Slyfox-Wikof, Showing his Heart-rending Astounding most Wonderful Love Adventures with Fanny Elssler and Miss Gambol* (New York, Dick and Fitzgerald, c. 1850? "with near 200 comic engravings," forty-eight pages), datable to around 1850 for its references to contemporary celebrities,[37] includes some Töpfferish elements: a rough outline style, an attempted suicide after rejected courtship, repair to Switzerland, an episode with the monks of St. Bernard.

There will be other works hidden or lost in the notoriously wasteful juvenile market.[38] The evidence so far is that Töpffer did not really "take" in the U.S. as he did in Europe; when Americans did finally adopt the comic strip, over the last third of the century, they did so under the impact of plagiaries of Wilhelm Busch. But we may conclude this insignificant (and elusive) episode in American graphic humor, with *The Fortunes of Ferdinand Flipper, . . . his birth . . . childhood . . . ripe old age . . . and final exit . . . ,*[39] an artefact so hastily produced that even the title page is screwed up, but testifying, curiously, to some sense of helplessness when confronted with the task of,

and demand for, redoing Töpffer. *Ferdinand Flipper* is a bizarre concoction with many themes coinciding with if not taken from Töpffer (plus the Gold Rush), casually discontinuous and inconsequential, executed in sudden changes of style ranging from the penny dreadful crudity to the sophisticated romantic. The whole thing is cobbled together from a miscellany of woodcuts, mostly French, whose chance availability determines the narrative, such as it is, rather as in the parlor game "Consequences."

A very long and enthusiastic article on the Swiss in the serious and prestigious *Atlantic Monthly* of 1865 failed to rescue the artist from oblivion.[40] He was not resurrected until the twentieth century, and then patchily, for some major histories preferred to ignore him, in fear perhaps that he oust U.S. artists from the perch of inventors of the genre.

Töpffer reached as far as Cuba, to judge by a quotation from the end of *Cryptogame* (the Belle Provençale's children climbing all over the hero) in a "protohistorieta" in a Cuban magazine of 1858.[41] In Brazil he was remembered in 1876 by the major local caricaturist of the era, Angelo Agostini, the Italian who introduced the comic strip, and in a pre-Tarzanic form, to Brazil, in an episode from *As Aventuras de Um Ministro* (fig. 9-23).

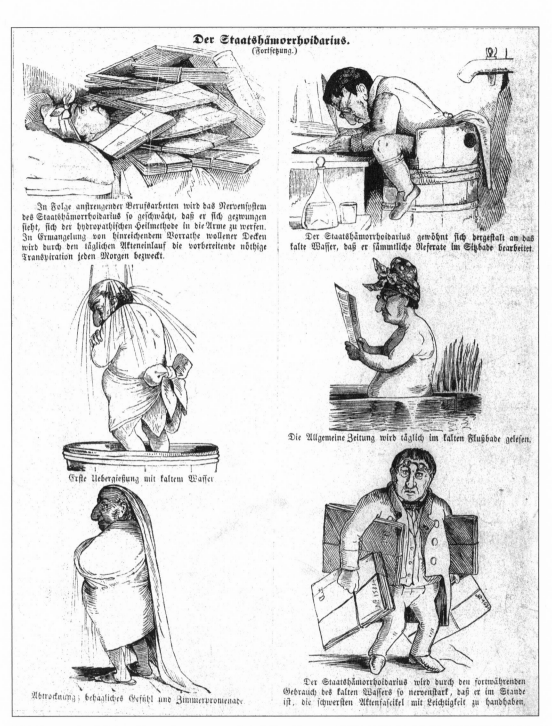

9-24. Franz von Pocci: Hydropathic cure for a nervous system shattered by overwork. The continuing daily flow of dossiers takes the place of woolen blankets and induces the necessary early-morning sweating. Comfortably working on reports in the cold hip bath. Cold shower. Reading the *Allgemeine Zeitung* in the cold river. Drying off; feeling good and a walk round the room. So strengthened by the cold water cure that he is able to carry the heaviest portfolios with ease (*Der Staathämorrhoidarius*, 1845).

In einsamen Stunden übt Piepmeyer sich in mimischen Darstellungen, die namentlich den Fall beziehen, wenn einmal Soldaten in das Sitzungs-Lokal der National-Versammlung eindringen.

In welcher Weise Piepmeyer sich die Statüe denkt, welche ihm das Vaterland einst errichten wird.

9-25. Johann Detmold (text) and Adolf Schrödter (drawings): Piepmeyer spends solitary hours practicing attitudes to conjure up what would happen if soldiers forced their way into the halls of the National Assembly [of the Frankfurt Parliament]. Piepmeyer imagines the statue which the fatherland will erect in his honor (*Deeds and Opinions of Deputy Piepmeyer*, 1849).

Germanic variations: Pocci, the *Staatshämorrhoidarius, Piepmeyer,* and Busch

The nascent sparks of satire and caricature in Germany were largely snuffed out by the repressions of the 1848 revolutions. The primary vehicle of mild humor, the *Fliegende Blätter*, where Busch would later begin his career, after peeking out its head over the barricades, allowed for some safe comedy. An early contributor was Franz von Pocci, a nobleman who functioned as a kind of minister of culture, director of entertainments, and general court jester at the royal court in Munich. His very earliest sketches shows signs of Töpffer, and the graphic achievement for which he may be remembered, *Der Staatshämor-*

rhoidarius, who actually constitutes the earliest continuing comic strip character (an honor he scarcely deserves) discounting *Cryptogame*, is a satire on bureaucracy with perhaps a glance at Töpffer's frustrated bureaucrat, the Mayor in *Festus*. The opening of the series seems to coincide with Töpffer's *Cryptogame* in early 1845.[42] In that year the *Fliegende* initiated the diary, as it were, of this "true" *German* bureaucrat, a most un-Töpfferian type insofar as his only idea of adventure is that of a paperwork worm. He is, deliberately and tediously, graphically nondescript with ponderous body and obtuse features, and psychically torpid: an emanation of the bureaucratic slime, or shit (fig. 9-24). This unappealing character lasted, surprisingly, in self-contained episodes that

Der Meister läuft nach seinem Hause,

wo seine Frau in Ohnmacht fällt, als sie ihn erblickt.

Wie er hierauf zu Pips in die Werkstätte kömmt,

springt dieser vor Schreck mit allen Gesellen in den Brunnen.

Als sich Meister Lapp im Spiegel sieht, springt er vor Entsetzen gleichfalls

in den Brunnen, da dieser aber ganz voll Schneider steckt, hat er keinen Platz mehr darin.

Der Meister sieht seinen Advokaten und fragt ihn, was da zu thun sei. Dieser fällt vor Schreck um.

Darauf läuft der Meister auf das Gericht, um sich zu beklagen, daß Alles vor ihm davon läuft. Das Gericht ergreift aber bei seinem Anblick ebenfalls die Flucht.

9-26. Carl Reinhardt: Master Lapp rushes home, where his wife faints at the sight of him. When he arrives in the workshop, Pips and all the other apprentices, terrified, jump into the well. When Master Lapp catches sight of himself in the mirror, he also leaps in horror into the well, which being already full of tailors, has no room for him. Seeing his lawyer, Lapp asks for his advice. The lawyer falls over in shock (*Tailor Lapp and his Apprentice Pips*, 1848/1851).

3. welches auf die mannigfaltigste Art geschehen kann.

4. Beim Engagiren treten Sie der Dame gerade gegenüber, machen mit geschlossenen Beinen eine Verbeugung und erwarten leicht gebückt die Entscheidung.

Les jeunes Crépins en se subordonnant avec convenance à Madame leur mère lui causent une admiration mélangée d'un doux attendrissement.

(33)

9-27. "The well-bred toady in a nutshell" (*Fliegende Blätter*, 3–4, 1861, vol. 34 no. 283).
The young Crépins, making proper obeisance to Madame their mother, inspire admiration mingled with tender emotion.
Monsieur Crépin having inadvertently made a pun, all the young Crépins rise with a great burst of laughter (*Crépin* 33–34).

maintained his essential character and appearance, intermittently until 1856.

Meanwhile a more promising character showed up, in the disillusion following the failed 1848 Revolutions in Germany, this time in Töpffer's transfer lithographic, album form (the *Staatshämorrhoidarius* was woodcut, of necessity, in the journal). This was the *Deeds and Opinions of Deputy Piepmeyer* by Johann Detmold (text) and Adolf Schrödter (drawings, 1849), clearly inspired by Töpffer's *Albert*, with formal touches of *Jabot* and *Pencil* (fig. 9-25). *Piepmeyer* is a satire on the aspiring lower-class politician, meeting in Frankfurt 1849 who hoped to reform Germany, and who, we know, bought Töpffer's albums a the time. He is hypocritical and boastful, a cynical self-persiflage of the author who moved to the right with the political winds. The artist uses more internal shading than Töpffer, but the political thrust, against reform, revolution and demagoguery, is similar to *Albot*.

The future of the comic strip in Germany lay less with politically inspired stuff, and rather with travel misadventures as in France and England. The *Pleasure Trip of Herr Blaumeier and his Wife Nanni* (1852) has much about the discomforts of tourism in Germany, and police harassment at the militarized frontiers of the numerous petty states into which Germany was still divided. The *Travel Memoirs of Baron Blitz-Blitz-Hasenstein auf Rittwitz*, by Carl Stauber, mocks the Prussian tourist who wants to take over and build railways all over Germany, while the countryside resists. These are realistic satires, and for the last resurgence of Töpfferian fantasy one must pass to Carl Reinhardt's *Tailor Lapp and his Apprentice Pips* (*Fliegende Blätter* 1848/51), a breakneck, crazy-quilt, super-absurdist adventure story totaling a Töpfferian length of 133 drawings, obviously intended for children (album 1851). This is Töpffer miniaturized and imaginatively equaled, in a world of small shopkeepers (fig. 9-26).

There has been much debate whether the mighty Wilhelm Busch owed anything to Töpffer. Busch himself claimed to know the Swiss "until now only by hearsay," and it is true that he was not too accessible in Germany: the Franco-German

Monsieur Crépin ayant fait par mégarde un calembourg, tous les jeunes Crépin se lèvent en partant d'un grand éclat de rire.

(34)

Kessler edition of the graphic novels was out of print by 1852, and the Nef German-only edition did not appear until 1887, following a collected edition of Busch (1884) "of astonishing physical similarity," itself first suggested by Nef.[43] Friedrich Vischer, in 1881, made a full comparison of Wilhelm Busch and Rodolphe Töpffer, concluding that there was no substantial debt of the former to the latter. My own view is that whether or not Busch could have seen Töpffer in the original or in the Kessmann edition (and forgotten about it later), it is unlikely if not impossible that the more or less Töpfferian variations listed above did not pass through his consciousness. Some of them appeared, after all, in a magazine that he must have read as a youngster and where he made his debut in 1859. Beyond the earlier ex-amples cited, we may catch, somewhat at random, also in the *Fliegende*, a satire of 1861 on exaggerated urbanity of manner, clearly infected by the Crépin children (fig. 9-27).

This is not the place for a comparison of the two giants of the nineteenth-century comic strip, except to say that while it may be that Busch's line, wound as tight as a Genevan watch-spring, as tight as Töpffer's looks loose, owes little to Töpffer, the very idea of the picture story, a type of *Bilderge-schichte* and *Bilderbogen* combining physical farce with a certain satirical realism, surely does. And Töpffer would have presented a model of the need to develop both physiognomic clarity and consis-tency (in the recurring character) and maximum physiognomic variation.

Envoi

"Go, little book, and choose your world . . ."

Considering that the comic strip, and the audience for it, barely existed in his own time, and that he had virtually to invent both medium and market, it is not surprising that Rodolphe Töpffer—in utterances both public and private—adopted towards them a casually deprecatory, throwaway stance. There are other examples in history of an author misreading the nature and future of an achievement: Geoffrey Chaucer, for instance, who wrote his title to immortality, *The Canterbury Tales*, in a hybrid Anglo-French vernacular rather than the fashionable court French, and apologized for the frivolity of its content. Töpffer, too, apologized, less sincerely, for the frivolity and the "vulgar" hybridity of his graphic novels—a hybridity that initiated a new, universal language mixing verbal and visual, correct and incorrect.

It is not clear why one kind of art crosses national and language boundaries and another does not. Wilhelm Busch, a name better known than Töpffer's (and an icon in Germany), has not caught on as he deserves with the Anglophone public, despite a brilliant translation by Walter Arndt that has not been reissued in the twenty-five years since it was first published and has never been rivaled. It is sometimes said, in explanation, that Busch is "too German" (that very German casual cruelty, as if U.S. popular culture

were lacking in cruelty). Is the historic sidelining of Töpffer due to his being seen as "too Swiss" or "too Genevan" (whatever that may mean) or even too French? A little, maybe, but I would rather attribute the neglect of Töpffer, as of Busch, to a narrowness of vision, a chauvinism that cannot bear to see the invention of so fertile, popular, and *American* a genre conceded to a European master. It is also true that tastes in humor, as in food and customs of all kinds, vary from one culture and language to another.

"Go little book, and choose your world . . ." starts the *envoi* prefacing Töpffer's picture stories and braving an audience of uncertain temper. This world, now, has potentially no earthly limits, and we hope that we have enlarged them here.

Appendix A

HISTOIRE DE SÉBASTIEN BRODBEC

This unfinished story (BPU Mss Suppl. 1256a, 12 pp.) responds to Töpffer's unfulfilled ambition to write in prose alone within what he elsewhere (Mss Suppl. 1257c) calls an underexploited literary field, "ce vaste et riche domaine du fantastique, du surnaturel, de l'invisible." I summarize this curious fable, which moves from the jocose to the sinister, is little known, and was not published until recently, for its relation to the fantasy in the comic strips. The story begins as a halting, ramshackle, and fantastical narrative and reveals some similarities with the style of a Töpffer picture story, containing elements of Trictrac *and* Vieux Bois *(descent down chimney, substitution of sick man in bed). The name Cavagne occurs in the "Histoire de Claudius Berlu." The text is perhaps most curious for its daring to approach otherwise taboo topics (for Töpffer and his audience) of sexual lust and attempted rape.*

Sébastien Brodbec is a homunculus child born to and created, without female intervention, by the most famous alchemist of the age, Athanase Brodbec. The child spoke only Algonquin, the original language on earth. He revolted and created chaos in the laboratory, where everything worked and went back to front and upside down. The more the father pursued his son, the more he found himself going in the opposite direction—a paranormal state in alchemy. The father got used, after a month, to putting forth his right foot in order to place his left slipper on it.

The son was a perfect amoral, emotionally and physically insensitive rebel. His voice was dry and bony, like the sound of castagnettes, and he hissed like a snake. His movements were agile but acute-angled, and his body was immune to shocks, which foretold that he could not be raised by the favored methods of the time, consisting of coercive and preventive thrashings. He was a bi-sexed male, and ageless, a child of maybe twenty-five or fifty. His body-surface was a scalene triangle, which circumscribed three unknown cabbalistic characters as in a cartouche, and changed in color according to the phases of the moon, so that in one lunar month it ran through all the colors of the rainbow and back again; but this was invisible only as long as he was seated.

Sébastien's mental world was structured by a fusion of self and non-self, and time was reduced to the present. He used no complication of [grammatical] mood or person, which conduced to very bare and laconic conversation, with more ideas fixed in his head than words to explain them. The father, Athanase climbed a ladder to seize his son hidden behind a spider's web, but caught only the spider—a tarantula which bit him and caused him to dance the tarantella, from which he was rescued by neighbors who tried to cure him by means of a barrel organ turned endlessly by a stream of water over the paddles of a waterwheel.

After some escapades in the alchemist's lair, including shedding his skin three times, Sébastien escaped into the countryside, where his ghostly somnambulist presence alerted the police. Despair of the father who had the three skins stuffed. His violent joy on thinking this succeeded in resuscitating his son turned to despair again when it proved to have failed. A complex alchemical procedure led to an explosion, but by copying the three cabbalistic signs in a cartouche, he sought to reestablish contact with his son.

Sébastien meanwhile nestled himself in the chimney of the Cavagne family, and a chimney sweep, Claude, destroyed half the house trying to fix the smoke problem. The Chimney-sweep-cum-joker [*fumiste*—a pun] trying to dislodge the obstacle, hit the cartouche, which shot at him a mortal bullet. The horrified Cavagne family fled, but the daughter Rachel returned to find the child Claude abandoned and bleeding, which aroused her compassion. He died, grateful, in her arms.[There follows a romantic, erotic description of the lovely, virginal, modest Rachel.]

* * *

In another version of the story, Sébastien was carried off by a spirit—or was it Satan? This creature, who looked like a black scorpion against the white cloth of the clouds, pleased him and in twenty-three days he learned mysteries, conceived and felt desires and love dawn in him to complete his being. The Spirit [or Being: *L'Être*] gave him knowledge, face, figure, clothing, language, cunning and hardness of heart.

* * *

Sébastien greedily and jealously watched Rachel cradling the child Claude who she believed was still alive. When she brought a medicine for him, the impassioned Sébastien brutally told her the child was stone dead. Rachel burst into tears and gazed at SB, who detested and adored this innocence so pleasing to the eye, but so impenetrable to any evil-minded approach. He seized her hand, crying Angel! She determined to infuse life back into the child with her body, warmth and life. "At this moment Sébastien, in a climax of jealousy, passion and desire . . ." [sentence breaks off, the text evidently suspended].

* * *

The Cavagne couple returned home. Rachel, troubled, tells how a "young man" seemed to share her pity for Claude, but suddenly cast eyes of fire upon her and seized her in his arms, then disappeared at her cries. Rachel had just escaped the talons of the hawk, but the Cavagne couple were worried only that there might have been a burglary, and thought only of getting rid of Claude's corpse.

* * *

[There follow some suggestions RT made to himself for pursuing the story.]

A continuation device would be to have each time Sébastien presses on his cartouche, a new adventure start with a change of character (and profession), becoming physician, lawyer, politician, prince, bell-ringer, critic, academician, mayor, soldier. Athanase gives by the accidental blood from a nose-bleed life to six stuffed skins, from which seven sons arise. Mutual destruction attempted among the sons, police called. Athanase to prison. Crimes and pranks of six sons—scare tricks, vandalism. The third son descends by the chimney into the bedroom, takes place of a sick man. Doctor business. The fifth son attacks the guard taking Athanase to jail. The six sons evaporate after 48 hours. Gazette announces crimes, attacks against government; police. SB arrested at moment of trying to enter Rachel's apartment. Trial. There is no evidence against SB, but he is condemned to hang anyway. Execution in public—at the moment the executioner gives the signal, SB disappears. Crowd disappointed, makes threats. The most hangable man sent for from prison, and hanged instead, to satisfaction of crowd.

Athanase (with help of the other six sons) have saved SB from hanging by operating on the cartouche. To protect him from being arrested again, Athanase gives him the look of a schoolboy Nicolaüs who died at Béziers in the year 1112. His education by several tutors—no good, replaced by one . . .

APPENDIX A. HISTOIRE DE SÉBASTIEN BRODBEC

Appendix B

TÖPFFER'S COMIC PICTURE-NOVELS

by Professor Fr. Vischer

This long (about 6,000-word) essay, in German, repeated in Jahrbücher der Gegenwart *June 1846, and the collection of Vischer essays* Altes und Neues *(1882, 534–42) introduces and was bound into the Franco-German Kessmann edition (Geneva and Leipzig, [March f.] 1846) of Töpffer's picture stories. I give much of it here in translation because it is the first extensive evaluation of the artist's picture stories, done in his dying months and entirely without reference to his biography and other achievements, aside from a comment on his skill in landscape. The essay attempts to give Töpffer as caricaturist a theoretical grounding in the context of French and German humor. It is picturesque, witty, keenly analytical, and recognizes the picture story as a new invention sui generis, by means of a comparison with the decidedly nonnarrative French graphic satirist Gavarni. This comparison, drawn out more fully in the* Jahrbücher *version of the essay, elevates the Swiss to the stature of one who was regarded as second only if not superior to Daumier.*

Vischer's critique has been very little used by the modern Töpffer literature, never translated and never reprinted, and yet the insights into the essential nature of Töpffer's invention, which the nineteenth century could barely comprehend, are still fresh and surprising, and they are delivered with panache. Friedrich Theodor Vischer (1807–1887), then a relatively young and unknown professor of aesthetics and literature, would later become known for his theory of literary realism. His essay, intended of course for a German audience, ends with a discursive, admiring look (omitted here) at the idea Töpffer incarnates of a kind of free satirist of folly, an ideal frustrated in censorship-bound Germany at the time, but to be striven for there as "pure, unmixed, serious, noble beauty."

In the interests of brevity, and modern impatience with German academic thoroughness, I have made many cuts, major ones in the last pages. I have paraphrased and summarized a point on occasion, and omitted purely descriptive passages, some repetitions, and parts where the author wanders off too far into Gavarni.

What sort of scrawl is this? This is what Goethe praised? I can hardly believe my eyes, this is how our own childish scribbles looked, when we turned boyish fantasies into silly caricatures. But on closer inspection these capricious, lawless networks of lines coalesce into the most decided characterization, this quite crazy, slovenly drawing becomes a well-considered and systematic instrument in the hand of a man who makes sense of nonsense, is wise in delirium, and steers his mad steed to its certain destination, following the rules of a secret calculation. You think it leaps forward on its own, but no, there is a coachman on the box-seat, you just can't see him.

Our eye is accustomed to French bravura in drawing. Töpffer is French Swiss, by name of German origin. His fantastic style is decidedly German, so is his capricious, silly drawing; but he is also French. Compare him with the French caricaturist Gavarni, for example. While Gavarni captures as it were in flight single moments with epigrammatic intensity, while the piquant glimpses we are allowed through the keyhole give us a synthetic view of society today in compilations arranged loosely around various themes and going from point to point, Töpffer by contrast is quite continuous, he never lets go of his topic in order to switch to another. Rather he develops the same topic, lets one scene grow organically out of another, and does not stop until he has spun it out fully, exhausted all the motifs he has seeded there and brought to fruition; he narrates, he draws novels.

For each album he picks a subject, some kind of fool, an individual destined one way or another to be the object of a comic fate; he is the provincial dandy hoping to emulate the metropolitan lion; the well-meaning but narrow-minded family father who has a thousand troubles and tribulations with the education of his children; the complacent artist, the passionate lover, the jealous man, the learned man determined at all costs to pursue his educational journey; the good-for-nothing, who passes through all the forms of and phases of rascality.

The first person on stage is not always the principal. Mr. Pencil for example disappears into the background behind Jolibois and the Professor, and becomes a mere intermediary. The action evolves like a whirlpool that starts with a slight eddy, extends irresistibly, and engulfs half the world into its funnel. Here the satire which was at first directed only at some subjective weakness or caprice becomes more general, drawing in various spheres of life: civic administration, courtroom procedures, jury behavior, military abuses, popular riots and demagogy, oratorical blather, diplomacy, learned stupidity, rage for hypotheses and discovery, academic and private pseudoscientific quarreling, the state of medicine and the humbuggery of abstract educational methods etc.

Social evils in the narrower sense, marital disturbances and suchlike occupy incomparably less space than with the libertine French; in point of sensuality [i.e., sex] Töpffer's heroes are very innocent; they are too foolish to have time for it. With such a Don Quixote ladies can safely disport themselves in forest and mountain. So while French society is undermined by sexual corruption, the extravagance of Töpffer's fools leapfrogs over sexuality, and his comic is never imbued with that eerie prickle we experience with Gavarni.

A comic character thus constitutes a plot pivot in each of the albums. This character is inescapably prisoner to some inexorable caprice, passion, or weakness. No experience, no obstacle, no humiliation can teach him better. These fools are like the weighted dolls that whenever tipped over, bounce back to an upright position. Monsieur Jabot is the perfect example of this. For all his social ambition, he immediately betrays himself as the cousin of a haberdasher by the exaggerated puffiness of his sleeves, the threatening projection of his collar points, and even more by the inordinate affectation of every movement. He commits endless stupidities, but none of this disturbs his self-composure; after every rebuff he stands again there, in his pose, refrain-like: *après quoi M. Jabot se remet en position*. It is to be understood moreover that the delusions of this character are never of a vicious or dangerous kind. These are harmless fools, complete, whole, all-of-a-piece fools, each his own world.

Here is more than satire. Since these fools are a world unto themselves, it follows that the whole world is itself such a fool, a madhouse: this is universal, total comic, this is humor. That there is a world of fools beyond and contingent upon the first fool, that the others whom he impacts with his folly are not in the right just because they are reasonable, that they too have something wrong with their upper storey, all this follows too.

The currently famous French cartoonists are much less in command of the genuine, free, benign comic. In Gavarni malice and moral pain are dubiously veiled in elegant form. There is cynicism, but not that anger that Töpffer admired in Hogarth. Töpffer rises vastly above his English model: Hogarth is strictly prosaic, moralistic, didactic. Töpffer carries true moral justice clear into the purely aesthetic realm of total comedy. Not being seriously condemned, his protagonists cannot suffer serious evil. In the end they find happiness, as does M. Jabot. This, unlike Gavarni, makes you laugh till it hurts—and that is something these days.

Subsidiary characters often end tragically, but this happens so much as the organic result of their behavior and passion, that one can term them happy too, for falling in their profession with grandeur. The Mayor in *Dr. Festus* exercises his troops to death, the astronomers quarrel to death, Fadet in *Crépin* strangles himself in his cravat, and only poor Bonichon in that album goes to a miserable death by the fault of another. *Albert* is the exception to the purity of this comedy. Here reigns a bitter, quite tendentious irony on false education, modern spoiled mommy's boys, Romantic poetry and demagoguery, so that it is the most cutting sarcasm when Albert ends up happy.

The geniality of the comedy and consummate folly that reign in Töpffer with this one exception, are of a quite German type. Drawing style plays its part, for this completely foolish-looking drawing, this witty scrawl, what Töpffer call his silly stuff (*ânerie*) conceals a casualness and virtuosity incompatible with the French sense of elegance, bravura of execution, and perfection of finish. Pigtail and three-master, short trousers, genuinely Swiss philistines and cousins who show up in the course of the action, remind one indeed of phenomena to be found in Switzerland. And Töpffer shows a downright German feeling for animals. In several pieces a mutt shares the fate of his master, who would not abandon him at any price. On the other hand we soon realize on closer inspection that French manner and culture meet here with the

German approach. Those crumpled, curly-wrinkled features, those lips consumed in endless idle gossip, remind one instantly of the decaying, used-up faces that France supplies to its cartoonists. These pinched, hollow, washed-out, corroded faces—those of Fadet and Craniose in *Crépin*, for instance—are possible only in France. The emphatically *theatrical* postures and movements, however clumsily *dégagé*, are likewise French. Thus the inordinate, limitless passions of these fools which spark off the chase, enter the action in an incredible superfluity of activity, wheezing, sweating and thereby necessitating very frequent changes of linen; raging, racing, revolving in a whirlwind on their thorny but happy-ending trajectory; or, for instance, as an orator in his uncontrollably emotional excess, throwing himself over the parapet of the speaker's platform, always desperate and apt to try suicide, which he happily does not manage.

But above all Töpffer gives us *epics*, for he is, as we said, a narrator in pictures, and this more than Gavarni who lets his characters speak for themselves while Töpffer writes his witty texts in his own name. He is epic too in that coincidences, obstacles and challenges of the world of bodies play a much bigger role; indeed an essential part of the comic consists in the fact that unforeseeable consequences, decisive catastrophes result from the smallest causes. Furthermore he follows the main fable with the indulgence of the epicist into subsidiary episodes and spares us nothing; when the astronomers in *Dr. Festus* are saved from the water, we still have to be told what happened to their wigs. Madame Crépin puts on a pitch-plaster and loses it; then it wanders through various hands until it winds up on the skin of Bonichon, former tutor of her children and now customs official. Thus he exhausts the main motifs with epic amplitude. He reels them up unto the last thread.

The whole method of Töpffer is to be characterized as successive, a continuity with refrain-like resting points: Jabot resuming his position, M. Vieux Bois changing his shirt, Pencil always satisfied from whatever angle he considers his drawing, Jolibois' blind passion, the washout son Albert being kicked out by his father, where we see just the foot of the one and the posteriors of the other; or Albert's successively pestering from one floor to the next, in diminishing visibility.

As for the mad play of coincidence, the fantastic suspension of natural laws: the whizzing wheel of a crazy world grabs it by the little finger or its coattails, and swings with it relentlessly away. In several albums much of the story transpires in the sky, into the heights of which a roguish zephyr propels several people. These people are well-nigh indestructible, physically; they must have been ground up and breathed their last a hundred times, were they not comic gods, immortal beings on the Olympus of folly. Gravity is no more, or suspended; there is no more necessity but what may be overcome; human powers know no limits. And human illusions magic us into a free, pure, comic world of their own.

So the bitterness and malice of satire dissolves. This is German too, for Germans easily slip into the fantastic where the least appearance of a motivation and natural law is mocked. In Töpffer's fantastic caprice all bitterness is volatilized in the light champagne foam of humor.

Notes

ABBREVIATIONS

Bouquet   Gautier, Léopold, ed. *Un bouquet de Lettres de Rodolphe Töpffer*. Lausanne: Payout, 1974.

BPU   Bibliothèque publique et universitaire, Geneva

BSET   *Bulletin de la Société des Études Töpffériennes*, Geneva

BU   Bridel, Yves, and Roger Francillon, eds. *La Bibliothèque Universelle (1815–1924)*. Lausanne, Payot 1998.

MAH   Musée d'art et d'histoire, Geneva.

NVZZ   Töpffer, Rodolphe. *Nouveaux Voyages en Zigzag*. Paris, 1854.

OC   Töpffer, Rodolphe. *Oeuvres complètes*. Eds. Pierre Cailler and Henri Darel, Geneva: Skira, 1942–1945.

VZZ   Töpffer, Rodolphe. *Voyages en Zigzag*, Paris, 1844.

PREFACE

1. *BSET*, no. 28, February 1999.

INTRODUCTION

1. Albert Aubert, *L'Illustration*, 20 February 1847, pp. 395–96.
2. Chancellor Christian Müller, *Morgenblatt für gebildete Leser*, 8 August 1846, p. 756; cf. Gallati, p. 39.
3. "Du Beau dans l'Art," *Revue des Deux Mondes*, 1847, p. 887.
4. Review of *Pencil* and *Festus*, *Revue Critique*, August 1840, pp. 250–51.
5. See also his "Gavarni und Töpffer," *[Schweglers] Jahrbücher der Gegenwart*, Tübingen, June 1846, pp. 534–66, which was reworked for (or a reworking of) Vischer's introduction to the Kessmann edition used here in appendix 2.
6. Rosenkranz, p. 415.
7. *Le Fédéral*, 16 June 1846, in a text used for the introduction to RT's novel *Rosa et Gertrude* (Paris 1847), and translated (as here) in the English edition (London, Simons and M'Intyre, 1848).
8. Advertisement in *Le Charivari*, 26 December 1860.
9. Jean-Antoine Petit-Senn, a friend of Töpffer's, was perhaps the best, a poet of popular life, humorous and malicious, but not known outside Geneva.
10. Charles de Bonstetten and Marc-Auguste Pictet, cited in Cassaigneau and Rilliet, p. 19.
11. Cherbuliez, p. 128.
12. Töpffer first attacks Hugo in his "Joseph Homo" essay, *BU*, 1834.
13. Waeber.
14. [R. T.], "La Mission de Jeanne d'Arc," *BU* 97 (1844), p. 59. See also Delattre.

CHAPTER 1.
Töpffer the Satirist: Contexts for Themes

1. See Kunzle, *From Criminal to Courtier*.
2. Boissonnas, *Wolfgang-Adam Töpffer*, p. 138.
3. Ibid., p. 221.
4. Baud-Bovy, p. 36; Boissonnas, *Wolfgang-Adam Töpffer*, p. 218b, fig., p. 219.
5. Boissonnas, *Wolfgang-Adam Töpffer*, p. 240.
6. Ibid., p. 173, pp. 174–75.
7. Walter Zurbuchen, *BSET*, no. 9, February 1981.
8. Töpffer, prose *Festus*, n.d (1840), p. 70.
9. *NVZZ*, p. 413.
10. *VZZ*, p. 436.
11. Letter to Dubochet, 16 February 1845.
12. Ruchon, p. 253f.
13. Blondel and Mirabaud, p. 177.
14. Ibid., p. 133.
15. Letter dated 1 November 1840, Maistre, p. 58.
16. Athanassou-Kallmyer.
17. Lucas-Dubreton, p. 231.

18. Ibid., p. 693.

19. "Barbarie et Choléra," reprinted in Athanassou-Kallmyer, fig. 13, p. 696.

20. Reprinted in Opinel, fig. 2, p. 70.

21. *Du Progrès dans ses rapports avec le petit bourgeois et avec les maîtres d'école*, 1835.

22. Kudlick, pp. 19, 41–42, 47.

23. George, 16823. The first English caricature on the subject had appeared late June that year.

24. Longmate; Kudlick, p. 146.

25. Cf. *VZZ*, p. 83. By 1837, near Lugano, Töpffer no longer needed the armed escort deemed necessary in 1831.

26. Ibid., p. 354.

27. Clinquart, p. 378.

28. Dumas, pp. 45–47.

29. *NVZZ*, p. 5.

30. Cited in Lévy, p. 150.

31. *NVZZ*, p. 349.

32. Ibid., p. 418.

33. *VZZ*, p. 73.

34. Blondel and Mirabaud, p. 179.

35. Boissonnas, *Wolfgang-Adam Töpffer*, p. 361.

36. Ibid., p. 358.

37. Vuilleumier.

38. Ruchon, p. 174f; *Journal de Genève*, 14 April 1831.

39. Boime, p. 110.

40. Roth, p. 265.

41. *VZZ*, p. 77.

42. Ibid., pp. 62, 77, cf. pp. 148, 413, 471.

43. Lescaze, p. 2, surveying the complex question of Töpffer's religious attitudes.

44. Barde, p. 94f.

45. Droin, vol. 1, p. 384.

46. Jeanneney, p. 57.

47. "Au Sabre! . . . A Vingt-cinq pas," reprinted in Kunzle, *The History of the Comic Strip*, vol. 2, p. 170, fig. 7.18.

48. Minois, p. 315f.

49. Chaffiol-Debillemont, p. 41f.

50. Walt, pp. 111–12.

51. Kunzle, *Fashion and Fetishism*, pp. 86–88.

52. Trembley, p. 348. I rely much on this work for this section.

53. Ibid., p. 60f.

54. In 1835 a very successful hoax was carried out by the *New York Sun*, and then much copied, à propos Herschel discoveries, attributing to him the supposed detection of winged, humanoid beings on the moon, fantastically and minutely described.

55. Boissonnas, *Wolfgang-Adam Töpffer*, p. 35a.

56. Letter to Dubochet, 5 January 1842, Gautier, *Bouquet*, p. 208.

57. Letter to Monvert, 20 March 1831, Gautier, *Bouquet*, p. 155.

58. See Kunzle, *Rodolphe Töpffer: The Complete Comic Strips*.

59. A print of this is reproduced in Rendall, p. 11.

60. Description and reproduction in Crown, pp. 123–27 and plates 126–39.

61. Stafford, p. 485.

CHAPTER 2.
Goethe, Töpffer, and a New Kind of Caricature

1. This segment summarizes the first part of chapter 2 (pp. 28–37) of Kunzle, *The History of the Comic Strip*, vol. 2, where more sources may be found, and which is itself drawn from a more extensive treatment in Kunzle, "Goethe and Caricature."

2. Goethe, *Paralipomena*, p. 396.

3. For the magazine as a whole, see Riggert, and pp. 13f for the caricatures.

4. Houben, p. 507.

5. The words "less frivolous" were substituted by Eckermann in his printed report of the conversation.

6. Houben, p. 489.

7. Blondel and Mirabaud, p. 110.

8. Houben, p. 620; Gallati, pp. 91–92.

9. *Kunst und Alterthum* 6 (1832), pp. 552–73.

10. Goethe, *Gespräche mit Goethe*, p. 642.

11. Fischer, p. 110.

CHAPTER 3.
Jabot, Crépin, Vieux Bois

1. Relave, pp. 40, 116f.

2. Sauerländer, Frankfurt-am-Main, 1837, 2 vols., pp. 300–303.

3. Letter to Auguste de la Rive, October 1836. Bornstedt had been circulating in Geneva.

4. As he explains in his self-review of *Jabot* in *BU*, June 1837, p. 334; cf. Blondel and Mirabaud, p. 80.

5. Letter, 7 January 1835, to Mr Sauter, a lawyer.

6. Letter from Freydig to RT, 16 April 1836.

7. Undated letters, both assigned to mid-October 1836, to Guillaume Prévost-Cayla and Frédéric Soret, respectively.

8. Letter from A. Cerclet to RT, 19 November 1836.

9. *VZZ*, pp. 54, 58, 62.

10. I have adapted the translation from Wiese, p. 14.

11. *VZZ*, p. 268.

12. *NVZZ*, p. 283.

13. *VZZ*, p. 43.

14. See Mützenberg, p. 147. This comprehensive work by a Genevan, which gives full credit in various places to

Töpffer's role as an educator in Geneva and reproduces many of his drawings, fails to mention *Crépin* at all, almost as if it was to Töpffer's discredit to have dared to satirize the subject of education.

15. *VZZ*, p. 473.
16. Letter to Auguste de la Rive, Spring 1840, BPU ms. suppl. 1643 f. 61.
17. According to Gaullieur, p. 55.
18. Boissonnas, *Wolfgang-Adam Töpffer*, p. 338; reproductions of caricatures pp. 340–43.
19. *What Fellenberg Has Done for Education*, London 1839, xvi.
20. *Oeuvre célèbre de Gavarni, 559 compositions*, Hetzel, n.d., n.p., caption to plate "Silence du cabinet."
21. Lelut, p. iii.
22. "Our Next-Door Neighbour," *Sketches by Boz*, 1836, p. 47.
23. Pictet de Rochemont, p. xi.
24. *BU*, April 1839, pp. 342–43.
25. Letter to Monvert, 23 January, Gautier, *Bouquet*, no. 95, p. 223.

CHAPTER 4.
Töpffer Launched, Comic Strips Defended, Literary Fame: *Festus*

1. In the officialist *Journal des Débats*, July 1840; in Geneva they were advertised in *Le Fédéral*, 28 July to 8 September.
2. *Revue des deux mondes*: on Töpffer, "M. Rodolphe Töpffer," 15 March 1841, pp. 838–65; on de Maistre, 1 May 1839, pp. 279–315.
3. *Journal des Débats*, 13 June 1846; reproduced in his *Portraits littéraires* and thus his definitive judgment (Sainte-Beuve, vol. 2: p. 935ff), and *L'Artiste*, 1846, p. 244.
4. *Magasin pittoresque* 10, no. 45 (1842), p. 338, an extract from an article originally published in *BU*, April 1836.
5. X, Oct. 1842, p. 338
6. Under the title "Laetitia," paintings and engravings, the latter reprinted in Kunzle, *The History of the Comic Strip*, vol. 1, pp. 343–45.
7. I refer to the two large volumes of *L'Imagerie Populaire Française*. "Robinson Crusoe" is in vol. 1, p. 358, no. 947. See also Renonciat.
8. Feuilleton, no. 49, 2 July 1842.
9. Ibid.
10. Raucourt, pp. 20–22, 41, 103.
11. Droin, vol. 2, p. 414; see Blondel and Mirabaud, pp. 110–11.
12. I consulted the edition of Le Monde en 10–18, n.d., 122 pages, ignorantly credited to Rodolphe Toepffer (*sic*), where the book is assigned a date of 1833. P. Seippel, in *Journal de Genève*, 28 January 1910, notes the rarity of the book, then being reprinted by that journal, and that it

was "probably" written 1829 or 1830 (i.e., before the July Revolution), since the satire on the king of Vireloup and the conspiracy paranoia targets Charles X. In a letter to the same journal (19 February 1910), Lucien Naville confirms the date 1833, and a printing by A-L. Vignier of Geneva, of the one complete copy known to exist, which belonged to the author, with a larger number of corrections and notes for another edition. For the planned second volume RT wanted to render "amour délicat et comique, vie pastorale, vie militaire, vie politique." He printed four hundred copies, with thirty-three on thick paper, and fifteen illustrations. His friends, shocked by the drawings and text, advised at this time against publication. In 1840 he launched the unmarketed copies, redoing parts: changing the preface and first and last chapters, and much of Book 4. The ever cautious Sainte-Beuve, to whom Töpffer had sent a dedicated copy, advised against including the *Festus* text in the 1852 edition of the *Mélanges*, as his friends now wanted. See also Léopold Gautier, *Journal de Genève*, 20 June 1963, à propos another republication, and F. Longchamp, "Rodolphe Töpffer et les éditions originales du Dr Festus," *Bulletin du Bibliophile*, 1923, n.s. 2, pp. 517–23.

CHAPTER 5.
Politics and Absurdity: *Pencil* and *Trictrac*

1. It was advertised (with *Le Docteur Festus*) in the *Journal des Débats*, 14 July 1840, by the French publisher, Abraham Cherbuliez, as the work of the author of *Jabot, Vieux Bois* and *Crépin*.
2. Letter, 20 March 1831, Gautier, *Bouquet*, no. 59, p. 155.
3. Balzer, p. 11.
4. Vincent, p. 52.
5. Lévy, p. 65.
6. Editions du Journal de Genève; the story is reproduced in the hard-to-find Skira (1943) edition, but omitted in subsequent ones, French and German. It has however recently been reproduced and edited by Philippe Kaenel, 1988, when in the possession of M. P.-Y. Gabus of Bevaix. The album was acquired by the MAH in 1996.
7. Indeed, in 1831 Töpffer described the story as "done" (Gautier, *Bouquet*, p. 155).

CHAPTER 6.
The Last Years: *Cryptogame* and *Albert*

1. A complete treatment of *Cryptogame* and its various versions and changes, with sources for some of the

citations in this segment, may be found in Kunzle, "Histoire de Monsieur Cryptogame," 1984, here reworked and updated with newly acquired correspondence. I cannot resist adding a summary of the following modernist fusion which represents a curious homage to Töpffer's invention, in three pages of comic strip by Alfredo Castelli (scenario) and Lucio Filippucci (drawings), under the heading *Martin Mystère* (Castelli 2003 p. 46–49): Töpffer, Ancient Mariner–like, accosts two passers-by in the streets of Florence, to tell his fantastic story, how he escaped from a whale, and so on. One of those accosted, Martin Mystère, thinks he (Martin) must be hallucinating from having eaten too much cheese fondue, and tries to cancel the stranger from the past, though the stranger warns him it could be dangerous to him, Martin. He indeed loses his speech when his speech balloons dissolve, and he begins to question the way he is drawn. RT reappears to ask his way back to the Arno, prior to re-inserting himself into the whale's belly, and then getting home to Geneva. He identifies himself as the inventor of a novel "drôlerie." MM is shocked to realize that if he had indeed cancelled RT as he intended, RT couldn't have invented the comic strip, and thus enabled MM's own graphic existence. MM wakes up and falls out of bed, like Little Nemo, from a cheese-induced nightmare.

2. See Wiese, ch. 5, p. 183.

3. See Kunzle, "Histoire de Monsieur Cryptogame," p. 144a.

4. Groensteen, "Au Commencement était Töpffer," pp. 10–21.

5. Letter to Sainte-Beuve, 29 Dec. 1840, Gautier, *Bouquet*, p. 104; cf. Kunzle, "Histoire de Monsieur Cryptogame," p. 141.

6. Letter to Kity, 11 July 1843; cf. Corleis, p. 174, n. 3.

7. Dubochet to RT, 1 July 1845.

8. Letter of 25/26 May and 22 June 1845.

9. Rodolphe Töpffer, *Théâtre*, introduction by Jacques Buenzod, Bibliographie de Jacques Droin, Geneva, 1981, pp. 179–247.

10. Rotalier, vol. 2, p. 412.

11. Cited in Davis, p. xxvi; horsie: p. 97.

12. Corleis, p. 250–52.

13. "Things to do" list, 1 April 1844, BPU ms. suppl. 1222, p. 63: "poursuivre la révision de Festus."

14. BPU mss. suppl. 1256d.

15. Letters of RT to Dubochet, 17 November 1843, and Dubochet to RT 8 May 1844; cf. Kunzle, "Histoire de Monsieur Cryptogame," p. 141b.

16. Letter to Schmid. BPU ms. suppl. 1256a.

17. It was excluded from Herbig, the most recent major German collected edition, and the most recent French Seuil edition, edited by Thierry Groensteen.

18. Letter from Vinet, 26 January 1845, BPU mss. suppl. 1646, p. 169.

19. Letter of 31 March 1845, BPU mss. suppl. 164, fol. 75–76, cited by Kaenel, "La morale politique de Töpffer."

20. Pichon, p. 206; Daraul, p. 109.

21. Frost, p. 279

22. For a favorable view of Fazy, see Henri Fazy; for an unfavorable view, see *James Fazy*.

23. See Cherbuliez, pp. 128f, 193f.

24. Alamir-Paillard, p. 67.

25. Drost, p. 173, who delves deep into this topic, says that it is not only plausible that Baudelaire knew Töpffer, but "impossible" that he did not. We may add evidence that Baudelaire did intend to write about him, from a letter he wrote to the *Revue des deux mondes* (where Sainte Beuve had earlier praised Töpffer), with notes for a reworking of his essay on caricature, and a list of twenty-one artists' names, including Toppfer [sic], Cham, and Nadar. (See Baudelaire, *Oeuvres Complètes*, vol. 2, p. 1343–44).

26. "Du Beau dans l'art," *Revue des deux mondes*, September 1847, pp. 887–908.

27. Cited by Drost, p. 181.

28. Gombrich, 336–42; Wiese, ch. 5.

29. Töpffer *Reflexions*, p. 288.

30. Ibid., Book 6, chapter 20.

31. Ibid., Book 5, chapter 24.

32. An interesting English edition (the first) is that of E. Wiese, with connections to ancient theories of rhetoric, film theory (of Eisenstein), and modern linguistics. For the latter, see also Junod, pp. 75–84.

33. Tisseron, p. 7.

CHAPTER 7.
Töpffer the Professional Dilettante

1. 29 December 1840, Gautier, *Bouquet*, no. 38, pp. 102–3.

2. Simond, pp. 345f.

3. Richard Payne Knight, cited by Donald, p. 23.

4. 20 June 1846, "M. Töpffer considéré comme écrivain," cited by Corleis, p. 178.

5. *Journal de Genève*, 17 September 1840, noted by RT in letter to Adolphe Pictet, 7 October 1840 (Gautier, *Bouquet*, no. 96, p. 227).

6. Gautier, ibid.

7. To Monvert, 20 March 1831, Gautier, *Bouquet*, no. 59, p. 154.

8. To de Maistre, 21 November 1839, Gautier, *Bouquet*, no. 35, p. 91–92.

9. To Monvert, 6 March 1839. Greedy: to Monvert, 26 December 1837.

10. To Vinet, 20 June 1840.

11. Joanne, pp. 146–47.

12. Letter to Dubochet, 6 January 1841; Gautier, *Bouquet*, no. 34, p. 108.

13. 24 May 1843, Gautier, *Bouquet*, no. 102, p. 243.

14. I add a few terms to the list in Kaenel, "La Muse," p. 27.

15. 1843, cited by Relave, pp. 101–2.

16. Kaenel, *Le Métier d'illustrateur*, p. 299f.

17. Ibid., p. 284

18. Cited by Patten, vol. 2, p. 192.

19. Letter to Zschokke, 4 February 1838.

20. Relave, p. 37.

21. Letter to Vinet, 17 October 1837.

22. Gautier, *Bouquet* no. 83, p. 199.

23. Gautier, *Töpffer en Zigzag*, p. 19.

CHAPTER 8.

Voyages en Zigzag: Humor of the Unexpected

1. Cited by Berghoff et al, *The Making of Modern Tourism*, p. 11.

2. Candaux, in Boissonnas et al, *Töpffer*, p. 190.

3. Citations refer to the seven volumes of *Voyages* in the *Oeuvres Complètes* (*OC*), 1945–1948, which contain all of the *Voyages*. I also refer to the first editions of the *Voyages en Zigzag* (*VZZ*) and *Nouveaux Voyages en Zigzag* (*NVZZ*), which contain chiefly the later *Voyages*, because they may be easier to find than the rare *Oeuvres Complètes*. For convenience I have grouped references at the end of each paragraph. For an excellent, in-depth analysis of the *Voyages* and their illustration, see Kaenel, "Les Voyages Illustrés;" and, further, Candaux, *Töpfferiana*.

4. *OC*, vol. 2, p. 71.

5. *NVZZ*, p. 64.

6. Maggetti, in Buyssens et al, p. 195, and citing contemporaries. Citations: *OC*, vol. 5, pp. 91–92: *NVZZ*, p. 177

7. Cited by Durand, p. 270.

8. Hannoosh, p. 39.

9. *VZZ*, p. 124; *VZZ*, p. 370.

10. Albert Aubert in his obituary of RT, *L'Illustration*, 20 February 1847, pp. 395–96. Cretin citation, *OC*, vol. 4, p. 132.

11. Rambert, p. 350.

12. *VZZ*., p. 96; *OC*, vol. I, p. 84; *OC*, vol. 1, p. 108; *OC*, vol. 2, p. 79; *OC*, vol. 1, p. 123; *VZZ*, p. 172.

13. *OC*, vol. 7, p. 93; *OC*, vol, 4, p. 156; *OC*, vol. 2, p. 79; *VZZ*, p. 9; *VZZ*, p. 387; *OC*, vol. 2, p. 53.

14. *VZZ*, p. 162.

15. *OC*, vol. 1, pp. 104–5; *OC*, vol. 4, p. 24; *OC*, vol. 2, p. 55; *VZZ*, p. 26.

16. *OC*, vol. 5, p. 122; *OC*, vol. 4, p. 116; *OC*, vol. 4, p. 160; *OC*, vol. 4, 162; *VZZ*, p. 385; *VZZ*, p. 527. Crépin: *VZZ*, p. 179; *VZZ*, p. 373; *VZZ*, p. 518. Jabot: *NZZ*, p. 10; *VZZ*, p. 54; *VZZ*, p. 58; *VZZ*, p. 62; *OC*, vol. 4, p. 41. Tircis: *VZZ*, p. 136; *VZZ*, p. 4.

17. *OC*, vol. 3, p. 135.

18. In the unused scenario for a picture story translated in Kunzle, *Töpffer: The Complete Comic Strips*.

19. *VZZ*, p. 354; *OC*, vol. 3, p. 99.

20. *OC*, vol. 3, p. 135.

21. *NVZZ*, p. 8; *NVZZ*, p. 14; *NVZZ*, p. 51. I cannot find *caudes* in any French dictionary. *Caudé* and *cauda* connote tail(-ed).

22. *OC*, vol. 5, p. 123; *OC*, vol. 3, p. 97; *OC*, vol. 4, p. 138; *OC*, vol. 3, p. 66; *OC*, vol. 1, p. 94; *OC*, vol. 3, p. 96.

23. Letters to Monvert, 1 April 1840, 18 May 1837; to de la Rive, 1 February 1837; to Adèle, 24 August 1840.

24. *OC*, vol. 2, p. 56; *VZZ* 297; suaviloquence: to Munier, 5–6 October 1840; gentlemanie: *VZZ*, p. 396; *OC*, vol. 4, p. 137; *VZZ*, p. 297; tapâtes: *OC*, vol. 7, p. 83; matagrabolisé: *OC*, vol. 3, p. 37 (e.g.).

25. *NVZZ*, p. 123.

26. *OC*, vol. 2, p. 152; prose *Festus*, p. 23; *VZZ*, p. 389.

27. *OC*, vol. 3, p. 24; *OC*, vol. 3, p. 131.

28. Archifabolo: *NVZZ*, p. 375; Nono: *VZZ*, p. 304

29. Romansch: *VZZ*, p. 417.

30. *NVZZ*, p. 425; *NVZZ*, p. 166; *NVZZ*, p. 205.

31. *VZZ*, p. 471; *VZZ*, p. 52.

32. *VZZ*, p. 452; *VZZ*, p. 477.

CHAPTER 9.

The Legacy

1. Gaberel, p. 10.

2. Kunzle, *The History of the Comic Strip*, vol. 2, p. 79, fig. 3.4.

3. His example even reached Sweden—see the *Jabot*-influenced *Fritz van Dardels Gubben med skåpet. En svensk serieklassiker från 1849*, preface by Olle Dahllöf and Göran Ribe, Åarp, Sweden: Seriefrämjandet, 2003. Van Dardel was Swiss-Swedish and may have known Töpffer personally. This and his other work (1844–50s) are more episodic than narrative..

4. *L'Illustration* 13 (12 May 1849), p. 172.

5. Gautier, *Bouquet*, no. 38, p. 104.

6. Kunzle, *The History of the Comic Strip*, vol. 2, p. 154, fig 7.5.

7. Kunzle, *The History of the Comic Strip*, vol. 1, pp. 1–4.

8. Letter, Monvert to RT, 24 December 1837. Blondel and Mirabaud, p. 37, say *Festus* was inspired by an "English work."

9. According to a letter to de la Rive of 6 March 1840, Mme. de la Rive had offered her copy of *Pickwick* to help RT place the engravings in his copy.

10. Subtitled *Wherein are duly set forth the crosses, chagrins, calamities, checks, chills, changes and circumnavigations by which his courtship was attended. Showing also, the issue of his suit and his espousal to his ladye-love.*

11. Patten, vol. 2, pp. 198, 203.

12. Subtitled *setting forth how his Passion for natural History wholly eradicated the tender Passion implanted in his breast, and induced him to discard the chosen of his heart—also, detailing his Dire Misfortunes and Hair-breadth Escapes by both sea and Land, and his Singular Marriage to a "beauty from Cork" who proves to be an extremely interesting widow with eight small children—then his domestic Bliss.* Another edition or variant title from Bogue has *The Veritable History of Mr Bachelor Butterfly*, and a quite different subtitle.

13. *Gentleman's Magazine*, January 1842, p. 73.

14. Twyman, pp. 195–96.

15. Robert P. Fletcher, p. 385.

16. Peters, p. 17.

17. Taylor, p. 78.

18. Prawer, *W. M. Thackeray's European Sketch Books*, p. 157.

19. First published in *The Picture Magazine*, vol. 3, 1894, pp. 326–28, as reproduced with fifteen drawings on four pages, the first three of which are labeled Acts 1, 2, and 3, and the last containing the author/manager's address to the audience after curtain falls. Prawer, *Breeches and Metaphysics*, pp. 85–86, has the title "Vivaldi, or the Bandit's Tower," and reproduction of eight drawings of the same subjects, but differently conceived.

20. Ray, p. 509f, appendix 5.

21. Prawer, *Breeches*, p. 84.

22. Ray, nos. 160, 161, pp. 438, 441.

23. Patten, vol. 2, pp. 203–4, says that Tilt and Bogue arranged with George Cruikshank to get *Jabot* and *Vieux Bois* plates copied at eight shillings per page, and went equal partners with Cruikshank on the English adaptation, adding (p. 564, n. 42) that Robert Cruikshank may have done the translation or the illustration.

24. See Kunzle, "Mr. Lambkin," pp. 169–87; Kunzle, *The History of the Comic Strip*, vol. 1, p. 177; and Smolderen, who posits, none too credibly, that Cruikshank used Töpffer for his *The Loving Ballad of Lord Bateman* (1839), and specifically "Man on the Roof" in *Vieux Bois* for his "Last Chance" illustration at the end of *Oliver Twist*.

25. *Vanity Fair*, 1848. Jabotière: p. 450; charade: pp. 457–58.

26. Ribeyre, p. 180; Kunzle, *The History of the Comic Strip*, vol. 2, p. 90.

27. Kunzle, *The History of the Comic Strip*, vol. 2, p. 315.

28. Thackeray, *The Heroic Adventures*. The introduction by Gordon Ray says the sequence was done "conceivably for one of Lady Blessington's soirées at Gore House," where d'Orsay was present. This volume also reprints a comment by Thackeray's daughter Anne Thackeray Ritchie that appeared in *Harper's New Monthly Magazine* 82 (February 1891), pp. 461–71, accompanying redrawn versions of the originals.

29. Thackeray, *The Orphan of Pimlico*, p. 11.

30. Prawer, *W. M. Thackeray's European Sketch Books*, pp. 157–58, citing Robert P. Fletcher, p. 384.

31. Quotations from Jackson.

32. Liebert, pp. 176–85, 200–205.

33. Chitty, p. 60.

34. Ruskin, pp. 184–85.

35. Wilson (as an "Extra" to *Brother Jonathan* magazine, no. 9, 14 September 1842, and again in 1849); and Dick and Fitzgerald (1849, reissued 185–? and 186–?), with a variant subtitle: "Wherein are set forth his unconquerable passion. . . ." *Bachelor Butterfly* (*Monsieur Cryptogame*) was also issued in a plagiarized version by Dick and Fitzgerald.

36. A collotype facsimile of the original edition of 1849, with an introduction by Joseph Henry Jackson, Burlingame, CA: William P. Wreden; and Cincinnati University Press, 1950.

37. The Duke of Wellington (died 1852), Count d'Orsay (died 1852), Count Cavour (very active by 1850), Louis Napoleon before he became emperor in 1851, as well as Fanny Elssler, who made a triumphant tour of the U.S. in 1840–1842 and retired in 1851.

38. My survey coincides with that of Wheeler et al, pp. 44–46, with reproduction of many title pages, and pages from rare colored editions of *Obadiah Oldbuck* and *Bachelor Butterfly* (pp. 30–31). Castelli, p. 45, reproduces a page from a Cham-like strip of 1852 by Frank Bellew.

39. New York, Brother Jonathan, 185–?, 78 pages, 14.5 x 23.5 cm, copy in Yale, Beinecke Library.

40. Henrietta Malan Fletcher; extract in Wheeler et al, p. 34.

41. By Víctor Patricio de Landaluze of Bilbao, in *La Charanga*, 1858; reprinted in Barrero, p. 62.

42. *The Fliegende Blätter* is not dated, so a precise month is hard to come by. See Kunzle, *The History of the Comic Strip*, vol. 2, p. 216.

43. Cf. Kunzle, Review, citing Hans Ries, p. 448, and Ries I, p. 1004–1008, with a detailed account of the debate.

Bibliography

Alamir-Paillard, Marie. "Rodolphe Töpffer: Critique d'art. . . ." In Boissonnas et al, *Töpffer*, p. 67.

Athanassou-Kallmyer, Nina. "Blemished Physiologies: Delacroix, Paganini, and the Cholera Epidemic of 1832." *Art Bulletin* (December 2001): pp. 686–710.

Balzer, Wolfgang. *Der junge Daumier und seine Kampfgefährten*. Dresden: Verlag d. Kunst, 1965.

Barde, Edmond. *La Vie aux Champs. Genève d'autrefois*. Geneva: Journal de Genève, 1947.

Barrero, Manuel. "El Bilbaíno Víctor Patricio de Landaluze, pionero del Cómic Español de Cuba." *Mundaiz* (University of Deusto, San Sebastián), no. 68 (July–December 2004), p. 62.

Baud-Bovy, Daniel. *Les caricatures d'Adam Töpffer et la Restauration genevoise*. Geneva: Boissonas, 1917.

Baudelaire, Charles. *Oeuvres Complètes*. Vol. 2. Edited by Claude Pichois. Paris: Gallimard/Bibliothèque de la Pléiade, 1976.

Berghoff, Hartmut et al, eds. *The Making of Modern Tourism: The Cultural History of the British Experience, 1600–2000*, New York: Palgrave, 2002.

Blondel, Auguste, and Paul Mirabaud. *Rodolphe Töpffer: L'ecrivain, l'artiste, l'homme*. Paris: 1886. Reprint by Geneva: Slatkine, 1976.

Boime, Albert. *Art in an Age of Counter-revolution*. Chicago: University of Chicago Press, 2004.

Boissonnas, Lucien. *Wolfgang-Adam Töpffer*. Lausanne: Bibliothèque des arts, 1996.

Boissonnas, Lucien, et al. *Töpffer*. Geneva: Skira, 1996.

Bridel, Yves, and Roger Francillon, eds. *La Bibliothèque Universelle (1815–1924)*. Lausanne, Payot 1998.

Bulletin de la Société des Études Töpfferiennes. Geneva.

Buyssens, Danielle, et al, eds. *Propos Töpffériens*. Geneva: Société des Études Töpffériennes and Georg, 1998.

Candaux, Jean-Daniel. "Chrono-bibliographie des *VZZ*." In Boissonnas et al, *Töpffer*, pp. 253–58.

———. "Rodolphe Töpffer a-t-il inventé les *VZZ*." In Boissonnas et al, *Töpffer*, pp. 189–97.

———. *Töpfferiana: Un survol des premiers imitateurs genevois de Rodolphe Töpffer*. Geneva: Georg, 1996.

Cassaigneau, Jean, and Jean Rilliet. *Marc-Auguste Pictet, ou, Le Rendez-Vous de L'Europe Universelle 1752–1825*. Geneva: Slatkine, 1995.

Castelli, Alfredo. *Aspettando Yellow Kid: il fumetto prima dell'Industria del fumetto*. Lucca: Museo Italiano del fumetto, 2003.

Chaffiol-Debillemont, F. *Suicides et Misères Romantiques*. Paris: Robert Cayla, 1957.

Cherbuliez, Joël. *Genève: Ses institutions, ses moeurs, son développement*. Geneva, 1867.

Chitty, Susan. *The Singular Person Called Lear*. New York: Atheneum, 1989.

Clinquart, Jean. *L'Administration des Douanes en France sous la Restauration et la Monarchie de Juillet (1815–1848)*. Paris: Association pour l'histoire de l'administration des douanes, 1981.

Corleis, Gisèla. "Die Bildergeschichten des Genfer Zeichners Rodolphe Töpffer (1799–1846)." PhD diss., Munich, 1973, and Munich, Minerva, 1979.

Crown, Patricia. "Edward F. Burney: An Historical Study in English Romantic Art." PhD diss., University of California–Los Angeles, 1977.

Daraul, Arkon. *A History of Secret Societies*. New York: Citadel, 1997.

Davis, Robert C. *Christian Slaves, Muslim Masters: White Slavery in the Mediterranean, the Barbary Coast, and Italy 1500–1800*. New York: Palgrave Macmillan, 2004.

Delattre, Louis. "Les Peintres Étrangers, École Genevoise, Les Paysagistes." *L'Illustration*, 23 November 1844, pp. 184–86, 216–18.

DelPlato, Joan. *Multiple Wives, Multiple Pleasures: Representing the Harem, 1800–1875*. Madison, N.J.: Fairleigh Dickinson University Press, 2002.

Donald, Diana. *The Age of Caricature: Satirical Prints in the Reign of George III*. New Haven: Yale University Press, 1996.

Droin, Jacques, ed. *Correspondance complète de Rodolphe Töpffer*. Geneva: Droz, 2002–.

Drost, Wolfgang. "Rodolphe Töpffer et Charles Baudelaire Esthéticiens—affinités et influences—et le rôle de Théophile Gautier." In Buyssens et al, *Propos Topfifériens*.

Dumas, Alexandre. *Impressions de Voyage en Suisse*. 1837. Paris: Maspéro, 1982.

Durand, Hippolyte. *Le Règne de l'Enfant*. Paris, 1889.

Durand, Roger, ed. *C'est la faute à Voltaire, c'est la faute à Rousseau: Recueil anniversaire pour Jean-Daniel Candaux*. Geneva: Droz, 1997.

Fazy, Henri. *James Fazy, Sa vie et son oeuvre*. Geneva and Basel, 1887.

Fischer, Paul. *Goethes Letztes Lebensjahr*, Weimar, 1931.

Fletcher, Henrietta Malan. "Rodolphe Töpffer: The Genevese Caricaturist." *Atlantic Monthly* 16, no. 97 (November 1865): pp. 556–66.

Fletcher, Robert P. "Visual Thinking and the Picture Story in *The History of Henry Esmond*." *Publications of the Modern Language Association* 113, no. 3 (May 1998): pp. 379–94.

Frost, Thomas. *The Secret Societies of the European Revolution 1776–1876*. London, 1876.

Gaberel, Jean. *Essai sur le caractère artistique et littéraire des oeuvres de R. Toepffer*. Geneva: Gruaz, 1846.

Gallati, Ernst. *Rodolphe Töpffer und die deutschsprachige Kultur*. Bonn: Bouvier, 1976.

Gaullieur, Eusèbe-Henri. "Rodolphe Töpffer." *Album Suisse*, 1856: pp. 1–84.

Gautier, Léopold. *Töpffer en Zigzag*. Geneva: Société des Études Töpfifériennes, 1977.

———, ed. *Un bouquet de Lettres de Rodolphe Töpffer*. Lausanne: Payot, 1974.

George, Dorothy, ed. *Catalogue of Personal and Political Satires in the British Museum*. London: British Museum, 1935–1952.

Goethe, Johann Wolfgang von. *Gespräche mit Goethe in den letzten Jahren seines Lebens*. Ed. H. H. Houben. Frankfurt am Main, 1925.

———. *Paralipomena zu den Annalen*, 1801, *Werke XXX*, Jubiläumsausgabe, Stuttgart, 1902ff, p. 396.

Gombrich, E. H. *Art and Illusion: A Study in the Psychology of Pictorial Representation*. London: Phaidon, 1960.

Groensteen, Thierry. "Au commencement était Töpffer." *Collectionneur de Bandes Dessinées, Histoire et Actualité du 9e. art* 14 (Spring 1990).

———. *Rodolphe Töpffer et l'Invention de la Bande Dessinée*. Paris: Hermann, 1994.

Hannoosh, Michèle. *Baudelaire and Caricature*. University Park: Pennsylvania State University Press, 1992.

Houben, H. H., ed. *Frédéric Soret, Zehn Jahre bei Goethe, Erinnerungen aus Weimars Klassische Ziet, 1822–32*. Leipzig: F. A. Brockhaus, 1929.

Jackson, Holbrook, ed. *The Complete Nonsense of Edward Lear*. New York: Dover, 1951.

James Fazy, sein Leben und Treiben. Offprint of Feuilleton, Zürcher Zeitung, 1865.

Jeanneney, Jean-Noël. *Le Duel: Une Passion Française, 1789–1914*. Paris: Seuil, 2004.

Joanne, Adolphe. *Intinéraire descriptif et historique de la Suisse*. Paris, 1841.

Junod, Philippe. "Actualité de Rodolphe Toepffer: un precurseur de la sémiotique visuelle?" *Études de Lettres* (Université de Lausanne), no. 4 (1983): pp. 75–84.

Kaenel, Philippe. "La morale politique de Töpffer: à propos de *L'Histoire d'Albert*." *Töpffer, pratiques d'écriture et theories esthétiques*. Les Cahiers Robinson, no. 2 (1997).

———. "La Muse des Croquis." In Boissonnas et al, *Töpffer*, 27–66.

———. *Le Métier d'Illustrateur (1830–1880): Rodolphe Töpffer, J. J. Grandville, Gustave Doré*. 2nd edition. Geneva: Droz, 2004. First published Paris: Messène, 1996.

———. "Les Voyages et Aventures du *Docteur Festus* de Rodolphe Töpffer." *L'Illustration: Essais d'Iconographie*. Edited by Maria Teresa Caracciolo and Ségolène Le Men. Paris: Klincksieck, 1999, pp. 39–57.

———. "Les Voyages Illustrés." In Boissonnas et al, *Töpffer*, pp. 201–46.

———. "Mr Crépin: phrenologie et pédagogie." In Buyssens et al, *Propos Töpfifériens*, pp. 79–96.

———, ed. *Mr. Trictrac et autres Dessins, Fac-similé d'un album de dessins originaux*. By Rodolphe Töpffer. Lausanne: Favre, 1988.

———. "Paradoxe sur le comédien: Rodolphe Töpffer, la physiognomonie et le théâtre." *De la rhétorique des passions à l'expression du sentiment*. Paris: Actes du Colloque au Musée de la Musique, 2003, pp. 131–41.

———. "Rodolphe Töpffer et le tourisme dans l'Oberland bernois." *Nos Monuments d'art et d'histoire* (Société d'Histoire de l'Art en Suisse) 40, no. 2 (1989).

Kudlick, Catherine. *Cholera in Post-revolutionary Paris*. Berkeley: University of California Press, 1996.

Kunzle, David. *Fashion and Fetishism: The Corset, Tight-lacing and Other Forms of Body-Sculpture*. Stroud, U.K.: Sutton, 2004.

———. *From Criminal to Courtier: The Soldier in Netherlandish Art, c. 1550–1672*. Leyden: Brill, 1992.

———. "Goethe and Caricature: From Hogarth to Töpffer." *Journal of the Warburg and Courtauld Institutes* 48 (1985): pp. 164–88.

———. "Histoire de Monsieur Cryptogame (1845): une bande dessinée de Rodolphe Töpffer pour le grand public." *Genava*, 32 (1984): pp. 139–69.

———. *The History of the Comic Strip*. Vol. 1: *The Early Comic Strip: Picture Stories and Narrative Strips in the European Broadsheet, c. 1450—1826*. Berkeley: University of California, 1973.

———. *The History of the Comic Strip*. Vol. 2: *The Nineteenth Century*, Berkeley: University of California, 1990.

———. "Mr Lambkin: Cruikshank's Strike for Independence." *Princeton University Library Chronicle* 35, nos. 1–2 (1973): pp. 169–87. Reprinted in *George Cruikshank, A Reevaluation*. Edited by Robert L. Patten. Princeton: Princeton University Library, 1973.

———. Review of Hans Ries, editor of Wilhelm Busch. *International Journal of Comic Art* 5, no. 2 (Fall 2003).

———. *Rodolphe Töpffer: The Complete Comic Strips*. University Press of Mississippi, 2007.

Lelut, F. *Qu'est-ce que la phrénologie*. Paris 1836.

Lescaze, Bernard. "Saints et diableteaux ou la fascination du catholicisme dans l'oeuvre de Rodolphe Töpffer." *Bulletin de la Société des Études Töpfferiennes*, no. 16 (September 1987).

Lévy, Bertrand. *Le Voyage à Genève*. Geneva: Metropolis, 1994.

Liebert, Herman, ed. *Lear in the Original: 110 Drawings for Limericks and Other Nonsense*. New York and London: Kraus and Oxford University Press, 1975.

L'Imagerie Populaire Française. 2 vols. Paris: Musée national des arts et traditions populaires, 1990–1996.

Longmate, Norman. *King Cholera: The Biography of a Disease*. London: Hamish Hamilton, 1966.

Lucas-Dubreton, J. *La Grande Peur de 1832 (Le Choléra et l'émeute)*. Paris: Gallimard, 1932.

Maistre, Xavier de. *Lettres inédites à son ami Töpffer*. Geneva: Pierre Cailler, 1945.

Martin, William. *La Situation du Catholicisme à Genève, 1815–1907*. Paris and Lausanne, 1909.

Maschietto, Manuela. *Trois Histoires en Images*. Paris: Club des Libraires de France, 1962.

Minois, George. *Histoire du suicide: La société occidentale face à la mort volontaire*. Paris: Librairie Arthème Fayard, 1995.

Mützenberg, Gabriel. *Genève 1830: Restauration de l'école*. Lausanne: Editions du Grand-Pont, 1974.

Opinel, Annick. "Du choléra morbus et de ses représentations dans la peinture française du XIXe siècle." *Histoire de l'Art*, no. 46 (June 2000): pp. 67–76.

Patten, Robert. *George Cruikshank's Life, Art, and Times*. 2 vols. New Brunswick: Rutgers University Press, 1992, 1996.

Peters, Catherine. *Thackeray's Universe: Shifting Worlds of Imagination and Reality*. London: Faber & Faber, 1987.

Pichon, Jean-Charles. *Histoire Universelle des Sectes et des Sociétés Secrètes*. 2 vols. Paris: Laffont, 1968–1969.

Pictet de Rochemont, Adolphe. *Une Course à Chamounix, conte fantastique*. Paris, 1838. Geneva: Journal de Genève, 1930.

Prawer, S. S. *Breeches and Metaphysics, Thackeray's German Discourse*. Oxford: European Humanities Research Centre, 1997.

———. *W. M. Thackeray's European Sketch Books*. Bern: Lang, 2000.

Ray, Gordon, ed. *Letters and Private Papers of William Makepeace Thackeray*. 4 vols. Cambridge: Harvard University Press, 1945.

Rambert, Eugène. *Alexandre Calame, sa vie et son oeuvre*, Paris, 1884.

Raucourt, Col. *A Manual of Lithography*. London, 1819, 1832.

Relave, Abbé Pierre-Maxime. *La Vie et les Oeuvres de Töpffer*. Paris, 1886.

Rendall, Ivan. *Reaching for the Skies: The Adventure of Flight*. London: BBC, 1988.

Renonciat, Annie, "Rodolphe Töpffer el l'imagerie populaire," *LeVieux Papier*, Bulletin de la Sociélé Archéologique, Historique el Artistique 326, Oct. 1992.

Ribeyre, Félix. *Cham: Sa vie et son oeuvre*. Paris, 1884.

Riggert, Ellen. *Die Zeitschrift London und Paris als Quelle englischer Zeitverhältnisse um die Wende des 18. und 19. Jahrhunderts*. Göttingen, 1934.

Ries, Hans. *Wilhelm Busch, Die Bildergeschichten*, 3 vol., Hannover 2002.

Roney, John, and Martin Klauber, eds. *The Identity of Geneva: The Christian Commonwealth, 1564–1864*. Westport, CT: Greenwood, 1998.

Rotalier, Charles de. *Histoire d'Alger et de la piraterie des Turcs*. Vol. 2. Paris, 1841.

Roth, Cecil. *The Spanish Inquisition*. London: Norton Library, 1937.

Rosenkranz, Karl. *Aesthetik des Hässlichen*. Königsberg, 1853. Leipzig: Reclam, 1990.

Ruchon, François. *Histoire Politique de la République de Genève 1813–1907*. Geneva: Jullien, 1953.

Ruskin, John. *The Art of England: Lectures Given in Oxford*. Sunnyside, Orpington, Kent, 1884.

Sand, George. *Une Nature d'Artiste*. Exhibition catalog. Paris: Paris Musées, 2004.

Sainte-Beuve, Charles-Augustin. *Oeuvres*. Pléiade edition. Vol. 2. Paris: Gallimard, 1951.

Schimmel, Herbert, and Gale Murray, eds. *The Letters of Henri de Toulouse-Lautrec*. New York: Oxford University Press, 1991.

Simond, Louis. *Voyage en Suisse fait dans les anées 1817, 1818, et 1819*. Paris, 1822.

Smolderen, Thierry. "Thackeray and Töpffer: The Weimar Connection." *International Journal of Comic Art* 7, no. 2 (Fall/Winter 2005): pp. 249–61.

Stafford, Barbara. *Voyage into Substance: Art, Science, Nature, and the Illustrated Travel Account, 1760–1840*. Cambridge: MIT Press, 1984.

Taylor D. J. *Thackeray*. London: Chatto and Windus, 1999.

Thackeray, W. M. *The Heroic Adventures of M. Boudin*. Reproduced in facsimile in honor of William Pearson Tolley. Syracuse, NY: Syracuse University Press, 1980.

———. *The Orphan of Pimlico and other Sketches, Fragments, and Drawings*. With some notes by Anne Isabelle Thackeray. Philadelphia, 1876.

Tisseron, Serge. *Psychanalyse de la bande dessinée*. Paris: Presses Universitaires de France, 1987.

Töpffer, Rodolphe. *Oeuvres complètes*. Centenary edition. Edited by Pierre Cailler and Henri Darel. 17 vols. Geneva: Skira, 1942–1957.

———. *Réflexions et menus-propos d'un peintre genevois*, 1858.

———. *Voyages et Aventures du Docteur Festus*, 1840. Le Monde en 10/18, n.d.

Trembley, Jacques, ed. *Les Savants Genevois dans l'Europe Intellectuelle du XVII au milieu du XIX siècle*. Geneva: Éditions du Journal de Genève, 1987.

Twyman, Michael. *Early Lithographed Books: A Study of the Design and Production of Improper Books in the Age of the Hand Press*. London: Farrand Press and Private Libraries Association, 1990.

Vincent, Howard. *Daumier and His World*. Evanston, IL: Northwestern University Press, 1968.

Vuilleumier, Marc. "Politique et Société à Genève. . . ." In Buyssens, et al, *Propos Töpfflériens*.

Waeber, Paul. "Sismondi et *Le Presbytère*: une convergence," *Bulletin de la Société des Études Töpfflériennes*, no. 17 (September 1988).

Walt, Jeffrey. "Reformed Piety and Suicide in Geneva 1550–1800." In Roney and Klauber, *The Identity of Geneva*.

Wheeler, Doug, Robert Beerbohm, and Leonardo de Sá. "Töpffer in America." *Comic Art* (St. Louis, MO), no. 3 (Summer 2003).

Wiese, Ellen, trans. and ed. *Enter: The Comics: Rodolphe Töpffer's Essay on Physiognomy and the True Story of Monsieur Crépin*, 1845. Lincoln: University of Nebraska Press, 1965.

Index

Boldface page numbers indicate an illustration.

Aargau convents, 16, 32
Abd el-Kadr, 104
Académie, Genevan, 48, 57, 62–63
Adventures of Mr. Obadiah Oldbuck, 162–63, 169, 175
Adventures of Mr. Tom Plump, 175
Affaire des Polonais, 15
Agostini, Angelo, *As Aventuras de Um Ministro*, 176, **176**
Ainsworth, Harrison, 28
Albert, Histoire de, 6, 9, 14, 21, 38, 95, 98, 100, 108–13, **109–10**, **112**, 115, 118, 135, 141, 159, 174–75, 180, 188; Albert, 48, 109–13, 117, 124, 153, 188–89
Albums Jabot series, 74, 98, 143–45, 153
"Albums Töpffer," 5
Algeria, 101, 104–7, 146, 155
Ali Khodja, 104
Ally Sloper, 165
Alps, 3, 28, 62, 128, 130, 132–35, 137, 141, 155
Aosta, 63, 141
Arminius, 63
Arndt, Walter, 183
Association du Trois Mars, 111
astronomy, 41–47, 54
Atlantic Monthly, 176
Aubert, Gabriel, 68, 73, 74, 84, 98, 118, 126, 143, 153, 169
Augustus, Emperor, 63
Austria, 15, 16

balloon travel, 48
Balzac, Honoré de, 5–6, 28, 67, 75, 82, 84, 115, 142; *Le Père Goriot*, 28; Vautrin, 28
Basel, 37
Baudelaire, Charles, 4, 7, 84, 113–14, 126, 132, 134
Bautte (jeweler), 28–29
Bautte, Jean François, 10–11
Beast of Gévaudan, 24, 34, 47
Beccaria, Cesare, *Crimes and Punishments*, 26

Belgium, 74, 83, 121
Bell's Life in London and Sporting Guide, 162
Béranger, Pierre-Jean de, 40, 75
Berne, 12, 37, 64
Bertuch, F. J. J., 49
Bessel, F. W., 44
Beyle, Marie-Henri. *See* Stendhal
Bibliothèque Britannique, 64
Bibliothèque de mon Oncle, La, 26, 39, 52–53, 62, 114, 132; Ratin, 132
Bibliothèque Universelle de Genève, 43–44, 57, 60–61
Biskra, 105
Blake, William, 45, 59, 126
Blondel, Auguste, x, 75
Bogue, David, 99, 162
Bornstedt, Baron Adelbert von, 57; *Basreliefs*, 57
botany, 44, 47, 54
Branagh, Kenneth, 47
Brine, John Grant, 167
Brittany, 156–57
Bryson, Bill, 130
Bugeaud, Thomas-Robert, 105
Buonarrotti, Filippo, 113
bureaucracy, 24
Burney, Edward, 48
Busch, Wilhelm, x, 54, 66, 77, 119, 126, 150, 156, 159, 176, 178, 180–81, 183; *Max and Moritz*, 91
Byron, Lord, 5, 6, 32, 40, 128

Calame, Alexandre, 7, 134
California Gold Rush, 175–76
Callot, Jacques, 9; *Miseries and Misfortunes of War*, 158
Calvinism, 3, 31–32, 116
Candolle, Augustin-Pyramus de, 44
captions, 118–19
Capucins, 37
Carbonari, 28, 55, 110–13
caricature, English Golden Age of, 84, 159, 171

Caricature, La, 23, 84, 162

Caricature provisoire, La, 152

Carlyle, Thomas, 53

Carrel, Armand, 39

Carroll, Lewis, xi, 45, 66, 126–27, 138–39, 162, 165; Alice, 127, 138; Humpty Dumpty, 139; Mad Hatter, 138

Catholicism, 31–37, 55, 99

Cavour, Count Camillo, 109

"Cécile, daughter of Fitz-Henry . . . ," 76

Cervantes, Miguel de, xi

Cham, 4, 48, 74, 97–101, 108, 120, 140, 143–52, 155, 157, 161, 169; *Aventures de Télémaque*, 154; *Barnabé Gogo*, 143; *Boniface*, 145, 152; Crac, Baron de, 147; *Episodes from the History of a Savage Nation*, 146, **147**; *Foreign Gentleman in London*, 163; *Jobard*, 144–45; *Journey from Paris to America*, **148**, 149; *Lajaunisse*, 143, **144–46**; *Lamélasse*, 143; *Lithographic Impressions of a Journey*, 146–47

Chamonix, 136

Champollion, Jean-François, 22

Chaplin, Charles, *A King in New York*, 36

Charivari, Le, 28, 74, 84, 97, 147–48, 162

Charivari genevois, 84

Charles X, king of France, 54

Charles-Albert, king of Sardinia-Piemont, 44

Charpentier (publisher), 74

Chateaubriand, François-René de, 23

Chatterton, Thomas, 40

Chaucer, Geoffrey, *The Canterbury Tales*, 183

Cherbuliez, Abraham, 74, 100

Chodowiecki, Daniel, 158

cholera, 9, 21–24, **21**, 30, 47, 83

Cicerones, 136

Claudius Berlu (scenario), 48, 101, 138

Collet, John, 159

Combe, William, 81; *Tour of Dr. Syntax*, 159–61, **160**

Comical Adventures of Beau Ogleby, The, 162

Como, 29

Condé, Prince of, 41

Congress of Vienna, 29

Conseil d'État, Geneva, 32

Cook, Thomas, 128

Coquemolle, Aventures de, 104

Corneille, Pierre, 7

Corot, Jean-Baptiste-Camille, 150

Counis-Bautte, Adam, 11, 12

Courbet, Gustave, 150

Courrier de Genève, 77, 95, 111

Crépin, Monsieur, 9, 12, 26, 28–29, 39, **42**, 60, 61–68, **63**, **65–66**, 74, 100, 108, 110, 117–18, 121–22, 132, **137**, 143, 159, 167, **180–81**, 181, 188–89; Bonichon, 28, 64, 189; Bonnefoi, 66, 119; Craniose, 68, 124, 189; Crépin, Madame, 64, 66, 189; Crépin, Monsieur, 37, 62, 64, 66; Fadet, 26, 41, 63, 188–89; Farcet, 64, 136; Institut Parpaillozzi, 64; smuggler, 26

cretinism, 134

Crockett, Davy, 175

Crowe, Eyre Evans, 167

Cruikshank, George, 4, 47, 53, 59–60, **60**, 147, 159, 161–62, 164, 169, 172; *The Bottle*, 169; *The Drunkard's Children*, 169; *Phrenological Illustrations*, 67; *The Progress of Mr. Lambkin*, 169; "Scraps and Sketches," 161; *The Tooth-Ache*, 169

Cruikshank, Robert, 161–62, 169

Cryptogame, Monsieur, 36, **50–51**, 52, **55**, 77, 95–108, **96, 97**, **102–3**, **105–6**, 114, 117, **119**, 122, 146–48, 152, 162, 165, 169, 176–78; Abbé, 36, 54, 56, 68, 99–100, 103, 106, 155; Belle Provençale, 103, 106, 176; Cryptogame, 36, 40, 48, 54, 56, 97, 103–4, 106, 132, 164; Dey, 98, 101, 103–4, 106; Elvire, 40, 54, 56, 97, 100–1, 103–7, 108; Missionaries, 99–100; whale, 104

Cuba, 176

customs officers, 28

Cuvier, Georges, 22, 54

Cyrano de Bergerac, 48

Darwin, Charles, 54, 163

Daumier, Honoré, 4, 9, **27**, 28, **29**, **38**, 58, **65**, 66–68, **67**, **69**, 83–84, 88–89, 99, 143, 148–50, 152, 156–57, 187; *Gogo*, 152; *Histoire Ancienne*, 154; *Teachers and Kids*, 62

David, Jacques-Louis, 7

Deism, 32

Delacroix, Eugène, 53, 84

Delord, Taxile, 125

Demosthenes, 57

Derby, Earl of, 174

Detmold, Johann, *Deputy Piepmeyer*, 88, 165, **178**, 180

Dick and Fitzgerald, 176

Dickens, Charles, ix, 6, 28, 58, 87, 126, 159, 169, 175; *Nicholas Nickleby*, 41; *The Pickwick Papers*, 161–62; *Sketches by Boz and Cuts by Cruikshank*, 161

Diday, François, 7

Divett, Edward, 12

doctors, 23, 47–48, 101

Dodgson, Charles. *See* Carroll, Lewis

Doré, Gustave, 74, 150, 153–55, 157, 164; *Adventures of Baron Munchausen*, **155**; *Dis-Pleasures of a Pleasure Trip*, **154**, 155; *History of Holy Russia*, 119, 155, 164–65; *Travaux d'Hercule*, 153–54, **153**

Doyle, Richard, 153, 165; *The Foreign Tour*, 164, **164**, 169; *Manners and Customs of the Englyshe*, 149, 150; *The Pleasure Trip of Messrs. Brown*, 164–65

Droin, Jacques, x
Drummond, Henry, 31
Du Maurier, George, 163
Dubochet, Jacques-Julien, 6, 48, 95, 97, 99–101, 108, 111–13, 117, 122–23, 139, 162
Duché de Vancy, Gaspard, **114**
dueling, 39–40
Dufour, G.-H., 30
Dumas, Alexandre, 29; *Count of Monte Cristo*, 20, 91
Duval, Marie, 165
Duval-Töpffer, François, 7

Easter Island, 115
Eckermann, Johann Peter, 49, 52–54; *Conversations with Goethe*, 53
Edgworth, Maria, *Practical Education*, 64
education, 61–68, 126
Egan, Pierce, 165; *Life in London*, 161
Einstein, Albert, 45
Eliot, George, 6, 174–75
Encyclopédie, 74
England, 31, 158–65
Enlightenment, 111
Essai d'Autographie, 77–78, 116
Essai de Physiognomie, 61, 78, 98, 108, 113, 115–17, **116–17**
Exmouth, Lord, 104

fart, 52
Fazy, James, 12, 14, 16, 111–13; *Les Lévriers*, 14
Fellenberg, Philipp Emmanuel, 64
Feltre, Duc de, 143
Fénelon, François, *Adventures of Télémaque*, 64
Ferney-Voltaire, 30
Festus, Dr., 9, 12–17, **13, 17**, 24–25, **25**, 31, 34–38, **35, 39, 42–43**, 45, **46**, 48, 52–54, 57, 64, 74, 79–82, **80**, 108, 122, 133, **160**, 161, 165, 188; Apogée, 41, 79; Armed Force, 16–17, 24–25, 37, 46, 55, 79; astronomers, 40, 46–47, 188–89; Balabran, 13; Baune, Jean, 36; botanist, 47; Coudraz, 34; Festus, 17, 34, 36–38, 79, 82, 91, 127–28, 130, 161; Frelay, Louis, 24–25; Gamaliel, 36; garde champêtre, 25; Ginvernais, 13–14, 31, 37, 82; Lantara, Pierre, 13; Luçon, George, 36, 37, 82; Mayor, 13–14, 16–17, 24–25, 31, 41–43, 55, 66–67, 79, 140, 178, 188; Milady, 13, 17, 24, 31, 55, 79, 82; Milord (Dobleyou), 13, 17, 55, 79, 82, 145; Micisispi nut, 47; Police Lieutenant, 15; Porelières, 34, 82; Porret, Samuel, 36; prose version, 12–13, 15, 36–37, 81–82, 108, 121, 140; Roset, Claude, 25, 36; Taillandier, 82; Thiolier, Claude, 38; Vireloup, 12–15, 31; whale, 36
Fliegende Blätter, 77, 178, 180–81, **180**
food in Alps, 134–35

Foolscap Library, 167
Fortunes of Ferdinand Flipper, 176
Fourierists, 111
Fragonard, Alexandre Evariste, **103**
frame lines, 117–19
France, 14, 16, 28–29, 31–32
Frankfurt parliament, 88
French Revolution, 10, 23, 49, 54, 83, 89, 111
Freydig (printer), 59
Fröbel, Friedrich, 64
frontiers, 29–31

Gaberel, Jean, 143
Gall, Franz Joseph, 67
Gallois, Imbert, 40
Galois, Evariste, 39
garde champêtre, 21, 38–39
Garnier (publisher), 118, 156
Gautier, Théophile, 4, 29, 113–14; *Mademoiselle de Maupin*, 114
Gavarni, 4–5, 143, 148, 187–89
Genevan revolution, 16, 111–13
Geoffroy Saint-Hilaire, 54
Géricault, Theodore, 7, 84
Gex, 29–30
Gillray, James, 49, 53, 159
Girodet, Anne-Louis, 7
Goethe, Johann Wolfgang von, 23, 46, 49, 52–56, 57, 75, 79, 95, 114–15, 122, 130, 165, 174, 187; *Faust*, 53; *Metamorphosis of Plants*, 49; *Werther*, 40
Goethe, Ottilie von, 166
goitre, 12, 134
Gombrich, E. H., ix, 114–15; *Art and Illusion*, 115–17
Gothicism, 6, 32, 68
Gourary, Marianne, x
Goya, Francisco de: *Caprichos*, 32; *Pilgrimage to San Isidro*, 32; *Pinturas Negras*, 32; *Saturn Devouring His Son*, 32
Grand St Bernard, Le, 6
Grand-Carteret, John, 4
Grandville, 67, 84–85, 89, 124, 126, 159, 161; *Un Autre Monde*, **123–24, 129**
Greuze, Jean-Baptiste, 158
Grimm, Jacob, xi
Groensteen, Thierry, ix
Gros, Baron Antoine Jean, 40
guides, 136

Haldane, Robert, 31
Hannibal, 136
Haye, Martin de la, **76**

Hébert, Henri, **151**

Heritage, L', 26, 142

Herschel family, 45

Hetzel, Jules, 108

Hine, H. G.: *How My Rich Uncle Came to Dine at Our Villa*, 164; *Mr. Crindle's Rapid Career upon Town*, 163–64, **163**; *The Surprising Adventures of Mr. Touchango Jones, an Emigrant*, 164

Histoire d'Alger, 104

Hodler, Ferdinand, 7

Hoffmann, E. T. A., xi

Hofwyl, 64

Hogarth, William, ix, 4, 47–49, 57, 59, 75–76, 84, 98, 115, 121, 123, 158–59, 162, 167, 169, 188; *Characters and Caricaturas*, **116**; *Harlot's Progress*, 162; *Idle Apprentice*, 167; *Marriage A-la-mode*, 116, 167

Holofernes, 103

Holy Alliance, 111

Hôtelin, Best, Leloir, 96

Huestin and Cozans, 175

Hugo, Victor, 5–6, 28, 75, 84, 110; *Les Misérables*, 155–56

Hungary, Budapest, 22

Illustrated London News, 162

Illustration, L', 4, 36, 95, **96**, 97–101, 107–8, 146–48, 150, 152, 158

Imagerie d'Epinal, 75–77

Indians, American, 146

Ingres, Jean Auguste Dominique, 103

Inquisition, 32, 34

Italy, 15, 32, 83, 136, 141

Jabot, 29, 52–53, 58–61, **59, 60**, 73–74, 99–101, 108, 121–22, 143, 162, 167; Jabot, 40, 55, 59–60, 81, 91, 169, 180, 188–89; Marquise, 60, 91

Jacotot, Joseph, 64

Jahrbücher der Gegenwart, 187

Jesuits, in Lucerne, 32

John Bull, 139

Jonah, 104

Journal Amusant, Le, 156

Journal de Genève, 22, 121

Journal pour Rire, 153, 164

Journée d'un célibataire, 152

Jubilee celebration (1835), 32

Judith, 103

"Jules Marié," 6

Julien, B. R., **103**

Jussieu, Laurent de, 108

Justinian, *Pandects*, 40

Kaenel, Philippe, x, xi, 126

Kaufmann, Angelica, 167

Kessmann edition, 100, 120, 181, 187

Koch, Robert, 23

Kunst und Alterthum, 53–54, 57, 59, 165

Lac de Gers, 133

Lafayette, Marquis de, 110–11

Lamarque, General, 22

Lamartine, Alphonse de, 75, 110

Lampione, Il, 111

lamplighters, 111

languages, 140–41

laughter, 131–32, 135

Lausanne, 74, 83

Lavater, Johann Kaspar, 140; *Physiognomic Fragments*, 117

Lavey, 48, 122

Lear, Edward, xi, 126, 138, 162, 165, 172–74; "Adventures of Daniel O'Rourke," 174; "Adventures of Mick," 174; *Book of Nonsense*, 78, 167, 172–74; "Visit to Capt. Hornby," **173**, 174

Lebras, Auguste, 40

Leech, John, 163, 174

Leighton, John, *London Out of Town*, 164

Lescousse, Victor, 40

Leuchtkugeln, 111

Lewes, George Henry, 174–75

Lewis, Matthew, *The Monk*, 32

Lichtenberg, G. C., 49

Liddell, Alice, 127

Life and Death of Don Guzzles of Carrara, 163

limericks, 174

Limner, Luke. *See* Leighton, John

Linné, Carl von (Linnaeus), 128

logic, 138–41

Lombroso, Cesare, 67

London, 47, 159

London und Paris, 49

Lord Turneps, 101

Louis-Napoleon, Emperor, 16, 147–48, 155

Louis-Philippe, king of France, 9, 84, 111

Lyons, 89

Macaire, Robert, 66, 88, 111

Magasin pittoresque, 75

Maistre, Xavier de, 19–20, 39, 74–75, 122; *Voyage autour de ma chambre*, 39, 74

Man in the Moon, 163–64

Mangini, 15, 111

Manual of Lithography, A, 78

Massacre of the Innocents, 9
Maunoir, Dr., 48
Mayhew, Henry, 165
Mazzini, Giuseppe, 15, 111–13
McClellan, John, *Chevalier Slyfox-Wikof*, 176
McConnell, William, *The Adventures of Mr. Wilderspin*, 165
Methodism, 31
Meyer, Helène, x
Milan, 137, 140
military, police, war, 9, 12–21
Mogador, 105
Molière, ix, xi
Mont Blanc, 44, 128
Montaigne, Michel de, 114
Montgolfier, Etienne, 48
Morland, George, 76, 159
Mortimer, John, 159
Mozart, Wolfgang Amadeus, *Don Giovanni*, 105
Munchausen, Baron, 104, 147, 154–55, **155**, 163
Museé Rath, 7
Muslims, 104, 106
Musset, Alfred de, 75, **150**

Nadar, 48; *Réac*, 152–53, **152**
Napoleon Bonaparte, 11, 40, 49, 89, 152
Napoleonic wars, 128
National Guard, 83, 89, 91
nature, 19, 134
Nef edition, 181
neologisms, 139–40
Neuchâtel, 83
Newton, Richard, 159
Nile River, 47, 93–94
Nodier, Charles, 75
Noé, Charles Amédée de. *See* Cham
nonsense, 138–41, 172
Normandy, 156–57
Northcote, John, 159
Nourrit, Adolphe, 40
Nouvelles Genevoises, 74, 129
Novara, 137

Oeuvres Complètes, 131, **137**
Omar-Pacha, 104
Orsay, Count Alfred de, 169
Osborne, Cynthia, x

Paris, 15, 22–23, 47, 84, 166
parliamentary debate, 82

passports, 29
peasants, 37–38, 157
Pencil, 9, 16–24, **18–19, 22**, 30, 34, 38, 44–45, 48, 55, 74, 78, 84–90, **85–89**, 121–22, 180, **183**; army, 17–19, 21; Burgher, 90; cholera, 21, 23–24, 30, 86, 90; Jolibois, Mr., 21, 23–24, 30, 34, 40, 85–86, 90–91, 138, 188–89; Jolibois, Mrs., 30, 47, 85, 90; Luçon, George, 16, 19; Pencil, 30, 47, 86, 90, 188–89; Professor, 23–24, 47, 85–86, 90–91, 188; Psyche, 47; Psychiot, 47, 85; Ricard, Captain, 19; Rotschild, 88–89; Servant, 24, 30, 86, 90; telegraph, 83, 86, 90
Penny Magazine, 75
Pension Heyer, 129
Pension Töpffer, 128
Périer, Casimir, 22
Pestalozzi, Heinrich, 64
Petit, Léonce, 37, 40, 156–57; *Bonnes Gens de Province*, 157; *Histoires Campagnardes*, 156–57; *M. Tringle*, 156; *Misadventures of M. Bêton*, 156, **156**; *The Usurer*, **157**
Peur, La, 6
Philipon, Charles, 66, 74, 84, 88, 152–53; *Gogo*, 152; *Robert Macaire*, 88, 111
phrenology, 26, 67–68, 117
physics, 44
Pictet, Adolphe, 16, 67
Pictet, Marc-Auguste, 44
Pictet de Rochemont, Charles, 140
Picture Magazine, The, 167
Pierce Egan's Life in London, 161
plagiaries, 74, 124, 143, 162, 169, 175
Pleasure Trip of Herr Blaumeier and his Wife Nanni, 180
Pocci, Franz von, 178; *Der Staatshämorrhoidarius*, 24, **177**, 178, 180
Poland, 15, 83, 121
politics, 142
postage stamps, x
potato riots (1817), 15
Presbytère, Le, 74
Progress and its relations to the petty bourgeois and schoolmasters, 142
Prussia, 180
Punch, 150, 162–63, 165, 167, 169
Pushkin, Alexander, 39; *Eugene Onegin*, 39

Rabelais, François, ix, xi, 81, 139–40
Racine, Jean, 7
Radcliff, Ann, 6
railways, 149–50
Ramberg, J. H., 49
rats, 107

Read, J. A. and D. F., *Journey to the Gold Diggins*, 175, **175**
Réflexions et menus-propos d'un peintre genevois, 113–15
Reform Bill (1832), 23
Reinhardt, Carl, *Tailor Lapp*, **179**, 180
Relave, Pierre-Maxime, x, 75
Restoration, 32, 49, 59
Revue Comique, 152
Revue de Genève, 121
Revue des deux mondes, 74, 113
Ries, Hans, x
Ripoll, Cayetano, 32
Rive, August de la, 5, 58
Robinson Crusoe, 76
Romanticism, 6–7, 68, 84, 110, 114–15, 128, 134, 161
Rosa and Gertrude, 6, 95
Rosenkranz, Karl, 5
Ross, Charles, 165
Rossini, Gioacchino, *L'Italiana in Algeri*, 105
Rothschild, 88
Roubaud, Benjamin, *Les Aventures de Scipion l'Africain*, 147
Rousseau, Jean-Jacques, 4, 74, 128
Rowlandson, Thomas, *Tour of Dr. Syntax*, 159–61, **160**
Royal Academy, London, 11, 85
Ruskin, John, 6, 128, 174; *Art of England*, 174
Russia, 155

Saint Gervais, 83, 113
Saint Martin, 141
Saint-Cricq, comte de, 28–29
Sainte-Beuve, Charles-Augustin, 4, 74–75, 91, 95, 113, 120–22, 127, 152
Saitout, Dr., 48, 101
Sand, George, 6, 67, 115, 142
Saussure, Horace Bénédict de, 44, 128
Saussure, Nicolas-Théodore de, 44
Savoy, 14–16, 28–29, 31–32, 37, 136; Vintimiglia, 15
Schiller, Friedrich, 7
schools, 126–28
Schrödter, Adolf, *Deputy Piepmeyer*, 88, 165, **178**, 180
Scipio, 63
Scott, Walter, 59; Waverley novels, 59
Sébastien Brodbec, xi, 6, 108, 138, 185–86
Seymour, Robert, 23
Shakespeare, William, ix, 7
Shelley, Harriet, 40
Shelley, Mary, 40, 128; *Frankenstein*, 40, 47, 128
Shelley, Percy Bysshe, 5, 32, 40
Smith, Albert: *How My Rich Uncle Came to Dine at Our*

Villa, 164; *Mr. Crindle's Rapid Career upon Town*, 163–64, **163**; *The Surprising Adventures of Mr. Touchango Jones, an Emigrant*, 164
Société des Arts, 7, 10, 44–45
Soret, Frédéric, 49, 52–54, 79, 81
Spain, 32
St. Petersburg, 22, 24
Staël, Anne Louise Germaine de, 75
Stauber, Carl, *Baron Blitz-Blitz-Hasenstein and Rittwitz*, 180
Stendhal, 28, 48, 84
Sterne, Laurence, ix, xi, 53; *Tristam Shandy*, 53, 90
Strange Adventures of Bachelor Butterfly, The, 162
Sue, Eugène, 6, 75, 84, 115; *The Wandering Jew*, 98
suicide, 85

Tartuffe, 109
Tenniel, John, 127, 150, 163, 174; "Adventures of Mr. Peter Piper," 169
Thackeray, Anne Isabelle, 171
Thackeray, William Makepeace, xi, 49, 162, 165–72; *The Adventures of Dionysius Diddler*, 167–69, **168**; "Bandit's Revenge," **166**, 167; "The Count's Adventures," 167; *Fitzboodle's Confessions*, 169; *Henry Esmond*, 165; "The Heroic Adventures of M. Boudin," 169, **170–72**; *Letters and Private Papers*, 167; *Pendennis*, 169; "Specimen-Extracts from the New Novel," 169, 170; *Vanity Fair*, 165, 166, 169
Thurgau, 16
Tilt and Bogue, 162, 175
time, 45
Tisseron, Serge, 118
Töpffer, Adèle, 139
Töpffer, François, 118–19, 156, 158
Töpffer, Wolfgang-Adam, 10–12, 14–15, 31, 57, 64, 74, 84, 158, 162; *Café Public*, 10; *Caricature des troupes d'artillerie suisse*, 12; *Foire de Village*, 11–12, **11**; *The happy Reformation against the Catholic Faith*, 31; *Les Conscrits*, 10, **10**; *Machine à hacher les écritures*, 31; *The Young Conscript*, 11
Toulouse-Lautrec, Henri de, **151**
tourism, 126, 129, 135–38, 140–41, 180
Town Talk, 165
Traviès de Villers, Charles Joseph, 4
Trictrac, 9, **14**, 15, 20–21, **20**, 25–26, 28, 79, 90–94, **92–93**, 101, 108, 127; doctor, 48; Police Lieutenant, 15, 20–21, 26, 93; Thief, 20–21, 91, 93; Trictrac, 47, 91, 93–94
Turner, Joseph Mallord William, 6
Twyman, Michael, x

United States, 175–76

Valais, 142

Valencia, 32

Vaucher, Jean-Pierre, 44

Venice, 142

verbal invention, 139–40

Vernet, Horace, 23, 105

Vichy, 48, 100–1

Victorian novels, 159

Vidocq, Eugene, 28

Vienna, 22

Vieux Bois, Monsieur, 6, 26–28, **27**, 32–34, **33**, 36, **41**, 60, 68–74, **69–72**, 76, 99, 101, 108, 118, 121–22, **125**, 126, 137, 143, 156, 162, 165, 167, 169, 175; Beloved Object, 32, 34, 45, 68, 72–73, 126, 155; brigands, 34; dog, 118; monks, 34, 36, 126; Rival, 45, 68, 72, 117; Vieux Bois, 26–27, 31–32, 34, 40–41, 45, 68, 72, 117, 132, 144–45, 155, 189

Vigny, Alfred de, 40, 75

Villa Diodati, 32

Vischer, Friedrich T., xi, 4–5, 56, 122, 181, 187–89

Voyages en Zigzag, xi, 29–30, 36–37, **36**, 52, 60–62, **61**, 64, **82**, 101, 111, 121–22, 127, 128–40, **130**, **132–33**, **136**, 155, 174;

beds, 135–36; flânerie, 134; food, 134–35; guides, 136–37, 141; hunger, 135; "Jabots," 136–37; languages and dialects, 140–41

Vuarin, abbé, 32

watchmaking, 44–45

weather, 134

Weber, Eugene, 157

Weimar, 49, 52, 59, 79, 166, 174; duke of, 49

West, Benjamin, 167

Wilkie, David, 12; *Chelsea Pensioners*, 12

Wollstonecraft, Mary, 40

Wonderful and Amusing Doings . . . of Oscar Shanghai, 175–76

wordplay, 138–41

Wordsworth, William, 5

workers, 83, 89, 113, 141–42

"Young Switzerland," 37, 111

Zschokke, Heinrich, 6, 140